Robert F. Mulligan

Entrepreneurship
and the
Human
Experience

AMERICAN INSTITUTE FOR ECONOMIC RESEARCH

Entrepreneurship and the Human Experience
By Robert F. Mulligan

ISBN 978-1-63-069183-7

Cover design: Vanessa Mendozzi

Robert F. Mulligan

Entrepreneurship
and the
Human
Experience

AIER | AMERICAN INSTITUTE
for ECONOMIC RESEARCH

For my mother,
who has loved, nurtured, and inspired.

Contents

Introduction

What do economists mean by market process theory? Although market process was well established early on in the economics literature, significantly predating Adam Smith, over time the process of how markets work became increasingly overlooked, deemphasized, and ignored. In many ways market process is implicit in the mainstream economics of the last quarter millennium—it has come to be taken for granted. Eventually this most fundamental economic theory of market exchange being driven and directed by entrepreneurial innovation came to be explicitly supplanted in the mainstream economics literature by more mundane and deterministic comparative statics and general equilibrium approaches. How, why, and to what extent, did this occur? Over what period did this happen? What are the advantages of market process theory over general equilibrium? Does market process have shortcomings compared with general equilibrium and comparative statics? This book will address these questions.

The actions of the entrepreneur are central to market process, which is driven by entrepreneurial alertness, innovation, and experimentation. Entrepreneurial innovation is always forward-looking, always experimental, and always speculative—and has to be applied in the face of the unknown, uncertain, and unfolding future, where any entrepreneurial innovation or decision is inherently risky and potentially subject to failure. However, entrepreneurs would not have too much to gain from merely examining past market conditions with a view to speculating on how they might have been better implemented, or otherwise have been more fully exploited. Such an analysis can inform entrepreneurs about how they can improve on past production decisions and better market the introduction of alternative and new goods and services. Nevertheless, the more pressing problem facing entrepreneurial planners is to successfully introduce new products and techniques in the face of prevailing or emerging market conditions in order to improve on the satisfaction of consumer wants today and in the near future. Entrepreneurs can accomplish this, for example, through introducing new goods and services, suggesting new uses for old goods and services, or employing new ways of marketing or combining goods and services.

Entrepreneurial planning is central to the definition of market competition, going far beyond the conventional and familiar static equilibrium models. Standard approaches to modeling and describing competitive markets emphasize a final market outcome satisfying arbitrary formal requirements. In sharp contrast, market process economics examines the actual workings of real world markets in preference to the idealized mathematical formalism of constrained optimization exercises. The focus of market process economics is on the entrepreneurial management of business enterprises in the face of market dis-equilibria which change and evolve over time. This approach represents a major conceptual departure away from mainstream neoclassical formalism and toward greater realism.

Perhaps the central feature of market competition that is often lost is that in a competitive market, entrepreneurs compete with one another to offer better ways to coordinate the forward-looking plans of consumers and other producers. Successful entrepreneurial innovations may create short run disruptions, but always lead to a higher level of cooperation among producers and consumers, and a greater degree of mutual coordination among the entrepreneurial plans of others. This book will introduce the reader to market process, and apply market process theory to explaining how entrepreneurs contribute to and arrive at market outcomes, such as the prices goods and services are sold for, the quantities of output produced, and how market organization emerges. Markets are driven by competitive entrepreneurs to self-organize as perfectly-competitive, monopolistic-competitive, oligopoly, or monopoly markets, and it is the interaction among competing entrepreneurs which determines which kind of market develops. Market process theory can also help explain the progress of an economic expansion through the interdependent mutual coordination of entrepreneurial plans. The degree of complexity and mutual dependency among these entrepreneurial plans can become unsustainable, which leads to recessions. Finally, market process theory will be used to illuminate various shortcomings of socialist economic planning.

Market Process

The first four chapters of Part One introduce market process and discuss how the expanding understanding of market process contributed to the progress of the history of economic thought. Part One will explain how market process ideas and approaches came to be largely displaced and superseded by general equilibrium and comparative statics models of a competitive market equilibrium, and argue in favor of some of the explanatory advantages of market process.

Chapter 1, What is Market Process: How do Markets Work & What do they Do?, provides a general introduction to what is meant by market process. Chapter 2, The Market Process View v. the Equilibrium or Market Outcome View, explores and develops some of the differences between viewing market interaction as a process and viewing it as an equilibrium outcome. Chapter 3, How Market Process Theory Came to be set Aside in Favor of Equilibrium Views, presents some of the relevant history of economic thought and provides a discussion of how the formal equilibrium view came to dominate the economics profession and literature. Some implications and limitations imposed by the profession's inability to address market process phenomena, particularly entrepreneurial innovation, are also developed and discussed. Chapter 4, The Future of Market Process Economics, speculates on how market process concepts may regain the primacy they once held in microeconomics and price theory, and suggests some areas for future analysis and research. The role of entrepreneurs is central to market process and is emphasized throughout the book. Entrepreneurship is not so much the mysterious activity of a special class of market innovators, as much as it is a routine and omnipresent process of innovation and risk taking.

CHAPTER 1

What is Market Process: How do Markets Work & What do they Do?

The theory of market process views entrepreneurship as an essential part of every market interaction, and at a minimum, all economic actors always apply some small but particularly vital amount of entrepreneurial talent, and assume some element of entrepreneurial risk-taking in everything that we do. Consumers are acting as entrepreneurs whenever we try a new product, or an alternative brand, in order to discover whether something new and different, and so far untried by us, can still satisfy our wants, or perhaps satisfy them better than the familiar products we were already used to, or perhaps at lower cost. Not to be open to trying new things and experiences represents true stagnation, and is the opposite of entrepreneurship. We more commonly think of producers as being entrepreneurs, but to be an entrepreneur, a producer must also experiment with new products and combinations of goods and services, new production methods, alternative inputs and marketing methods, etc. (Kirzner 1973: 7-9). Their efforts to produce and market new goods and services incorporating these innovative methods and approaches uncover new information regarding the technical feasibility of what entrepreneurs are attempting, as well as new information about what customers want. When producers fail to innovate and experiment, they always leave that aspect of market process potentially open to their competitors.

The central role of the entrepreneur had been recognized by Richard Cantillon (1680-1734) and Anne Robert Jacques Turgot (1727-1781) writing before Adam Smith (1723-1790). Smith was an important proponent of viewing the market as a process through which buyers and sellers cooperated to arrive at mutually beneficial exchanges, although Smith preferred to think of markets being driven by an invisible hand rather than by entrepreneurial planners. The primacy of the entrepreneur was reintroduced into the economic mainstream, at least briefly, by Jean-Baptiste Say (1767-1832). David Ricardo (1772-1823) retreated back to Smith by disregarding and ignoring entrepreneurs, and attempted to explain how income is divided among landlords, workers, and owners of capital. Although entrepreneurs may own capital, they do not necessarily own any, and not all capital owners or capitalists are entrepreneurs—it depends on what they do with their capital, or with the capital owned by someone else, that makes someone an entrepreneur. Ricardo's model was even more simplified than Smith's, and also left out the entrepreneur. John Stuart Mill (1806-1873) held that the only source of profit was labor, and that entrepreneurs merely directed workers and provided a special kind of supervisory labor.

Léon Walras' (1834-1910) *Elements of Pure Economics* (1874) introduced the general equilibrium model, where all product markets for all goods and services are simultaneously in equilibrium throughout the economy, but there was no role for the entrepreneur in his construc-tion of the market. Alfred Marshall (1842-1924), in his *Principles of Economics* (1890) presented the partial equilibrium model of perfect competition which is reiterated in some form in every modern micro-economics textbook. This model describes a competitive equilibrium in the market for a single well-defined good or service.

1.1 Market Process & Equilibrium

The standard supply-and-demand model of a competitive market is familiar, but it is important to realize how badly it fails to capture the most essential features of how markets work and how buyers and sellers interact in markets. Specifically, it would be more helpful for an economic model to explain how the theoretical market equilibrium is initially arrived at in a competitive market, how it is maintained and what makes it evolve over time, how and why markets are moved into unstable and transient dis-equilibria, and how a new equilibrium state might be reached or reestablished. Market process economics provides this understanding. In the standard model, the downward-slop-ing demand curve is used to illustrate the behavior of consumers, and slopes downward to show the consumers' preference for paying lower prices. Similarly, the upward-sloping supply curve illustrates the behavior of producers and suppliers, and slopes upward to show the suppliers' preference for receiving higher prices, as well as the greater unit cost of producing a larger volume of goods necessitated by having to buy larger amounts of inputs. The geometry of the two curves ensures they always cross in an x, demonstrating how the market jointly determines the price and quantity for each good and service.

The equilibrium or market-clearing price ensures that the amount produced and the amount purchased are equal, and clear the market with no waste or shortage (Figure 1.1).

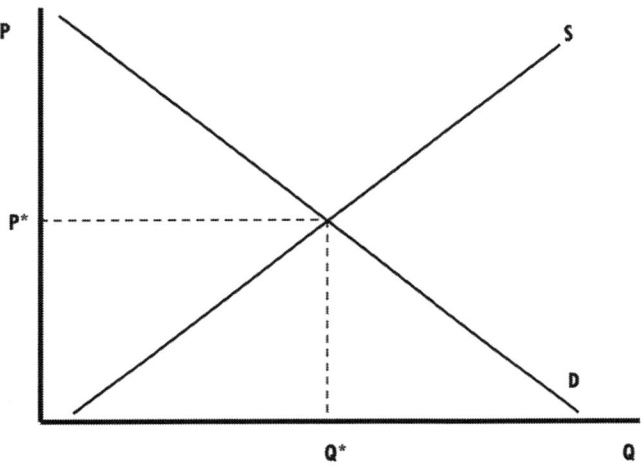

Figure 1.1 Supply & Demand

Further exercises with the basic model demonstrate that if the price were ever to be set above the equilibrium at PH, that higher price would create a surplus of the product where the quantity supplied by sellers is greater than the quantity demanded by buyers (Figure 1.2). Once producers become aware a surplus of this good is present, they can dispose of the surplus output by lowering the price and producing less. At this point, we must already note the subtle interjection of a generally overlooked role for entrepreneurial awareness. If the producers remain unaware there is a surplus of the product, they are in no position to bring about any adjustment toward the market-clearing equilibrium. Furthermore, if less alert producers remain unaware of the surplus, anyone else who is alert to the entrepreneurial opportunity can undercut these less alert producers who are unconsciously dreaming of the status quo being preserved indefinitely, unaware that the market is already failing to clear in reality. Entrepreneurial alertness rewards alert entrepreneurs directly, penalizes unalert producers and sellers directly, and rewards everyone else indirectly by making the product available at a lower price. Entrepreneurial planners exercise entrepreneurial alertness to potential profit opportunities as much because they want to avoid being surprised unnecessarily by other competing innovators, and because they want to profit by introducing innovations of their own (Kirzner 1963: 44-46).

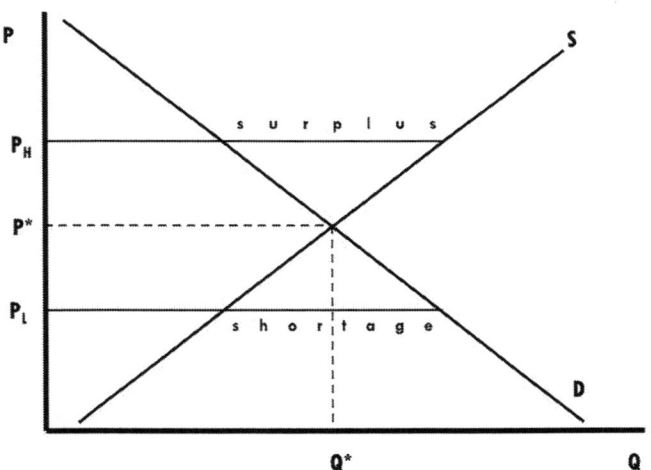

Figure 1.2 Non-market-clearing prices create
Shortages or Surpluses

Conversely, if the price were ever mistakenly set below the market-clearing equilibrium at PL, that would cause a shortage where the quantity demanded is greater than the quantity supplied. Now alert producers would remedy the shortage by raising the price and producing more. Once more, if entrepreneurs fail to exercise alertness, they will not be in a position to initiate or benefit from any subsequent adjustment toward market-clearing equilibrium. However, their failure leaves the door open for any other market participant who can exercise the necessary entrepreneurial alertness. Normally the producer who mistakenly set the price too high or too low for the market to clear is the one who first notices their mistake and first makes the adjustments toward market-clearing equilibrium. The opportunity is always there, but for anyone to move the market toward the market-clearing equilibrium, they must be aware of the shortage or surplus, and must be in a position to act to take advantage of the situation to better benefit consumers.

The entrepreneur whose experiments with innovation created the shortage or surplus condition in the first place is generally in the best position to first observe that the market is not clearing for the good they are trying to sell, that there is a shortage or surplus of their product. Furthermore, they are normally in the best position to immediately adjust the price and level of output. However, if these producers are not sufficiently alert to shortages or surpluses of their own product, and do not notice that the market for their output has failed to clear, their inability to recognize their error creates an entrepreneurial opportunity for anyone else who is alert to it. Any alert potential competitor is free to enter the market, as long as they are willing to try to undercut sellers who overcharge for the product, or try to buy up underpriced output to be sold at a markup. If a given seller-producer overlooks these opportunities or the general need to adjust prices, anyone else can enter the market and potentially benefit from the market conditions, provided they are the first to notice and act on them.

Mainstream economics has long understood that there are numerous limitations to the standard model of market equilibrium (Henderson &

Quandt 1980: 157-165). There is no question that market forces work to move the market toward the equilibrium price which clears the market. Unfortunately our economics largely takes for granted this essential process of recognizing, reaching, and maintaining this equilibrium. Market process economics focuses on how entrepreneurial planners discover, overcome, and profit from previously unknown opportunities, and benefit others through doing so. In order for producers to recognize shortages and surpluses, they have to be alert to and become aware of these conditions, or else they cannot respond to adjust the market toward equilibrium. Without an awareness of a shortage or surplus of the product, there will never be any basis or justification for them in making any changes or price adjustments. Recognizing this role for entrepreneurial alertness is one of the basic starting points for the theory of market process.

1.2 Market Efficiency: Arbitrage & the Law of One Price

Even more fundamentally, conventional price theory assumes that a single price prevails in any given market—the law of one price. In reality, only alert entrepreneurs who engage in a process of arbitrage can enable the market to reach this hypothesized market clearing equilibrium price. Kenneth Arrow (1921-2017) pointed out that if people buying and selling in markets are price takers, and accept the market clearing price of the competitive market, there would still remain the question of explaining how prices arrived at or adjusted to this idealized equilibrium (Arrow 1959, 1994). This is not something which happens on its own. Instead it calls for a process of alert entrepreneurs experimentally adjusting prices and carefully observing the results

(Kirzner 1973: 11-12).

Market process theory answers the question of how a single price emerges in any given market by examining how entrepreneurial planners adjust prices, what motivates them to experimentally adjust prices, why prices leave equilibria, and how the process of adjusting to a new equilibrium works. This one market price can only be maintained as a uniform one-price equilibrium through the continuous alertness on the part of entrepreneurs to potential arbitrage opportunities which emerge all the time, but can only be acted on after an alert entrepreneur has noticed them (Kirzner 1963: 44-46). These arbitrage opportunities are created by the presence of any variation in the prices for a single good or service, combined with an awareness and a willingness on the part of the entrepreneurs to engage in arbitrage if and when price variations occur, and alert entrepreneurs observe this variation.

When people offer a product for sale, there is not necessarily any clear mechanism for them to instantaneously set the same equilibrium price throughout the market, which simultaneously clears the quantities supplied and demanded by setting them equal. Unless the entrepreneurial planner acting as a price setter has extrasensory perception, they cannot know what prices are being asked or offered elsewhere by other buyers and sellers, or at other places at any point in time. Prospective buyers may accept the search cost of shopping around to find the best price in terms of the time and effort required. Or instead they may decide that their time is more valuable than any savings they believe they are likely to achieve through searching for a lower price, based on their own subjective appraisals or expectations of what savings are most likely or possible, and how much shopping effort is likely to be required. Or, alternatively, they may trust that prices are probably the same at any other prospective sellers.

The buyers' past experience may have been that prices have generally always been very close with little variation within a narrow range of different prices over a variety of prospective sellers. If prospective buyers can conclude that the time cost of shopping around for the best price has generally not been necessary or justified, these prospective buyers are likely to conclude that the market is relatively efficient. They will either not shop around at all for a better price, or will do so only infrequently and to a relatively more limited extent. The prospective buyers' appraisal of market efficiency and price dispersion focuses especially on the most recently experienced past, because that is most likely to be more informative about current and near future market conditions.

If instead, the experience of prospective buyers has been that prices have always varied widely, they will be more likely to continue their practice of shopping around extensively for the best price. The need in an inefficient market to shop around for the best price is an instance of search cost, a special case of transactions cost. These are extra, non-monetary costs which make a market exchange more costly and less beneficial, and therefore, less likely to take place. If markets are efficient, and search costs are relatively high, there will be little need to search for the best price. If markets are inefficient, search costs are still high, but now it is more likely to be worth it to invest substantial time to find the lowest price, since prices vary greatly in an inefficient market. Both behaviors are instances of entrepreneurial awareness exercised by the consumer.

If a consumer finds the markets they seek to buy in, to be constantly inefficient with a wide variety of high and low prices for the same product, they will generally find that shopping around will be justified to get the best price. However, in such an inefficient market with a wide variety of different prices for the same good or service, eventually it will occur to at least one consumer that they can take advantage of the specialized local market knowledge which they gain from shopping around solely for their own benefit. Without necessarily intending to, they have discovered conditions where they can buy low and sell high. This enables them, in effect, to sell their shopping around time and labor, to other consumers who will purchase the product from these new entrepreneurs at a smaller but uniform markup, saving on search costs. The consumer-seller in this case is increasing the efficiency of this market by incurring the search cost once, and then allowing other consumers to compensate the consumer-seller for their search efforts. In addition, the other consumers benefit because they save on the high search costs they would have had to suffer, and will willingly pay to avoid the need to shop around. Market efficiency and consumer welfare are both improved because one consumer-seller incurs the search cost on behalf of all the other consumers. Otherwise each consumer would have to incur the search cost separately, over and over again.

Shopping around or searching for the lowest price is not an inherently productive activity, and is only necessary and rewarded when we find that markets are inefficient and that prices vary extensively across the same market. The consumers who take advantage of the knowledge of price variations they gain from shopping around, which is very specific knowledge which otherwise has very limited value, will eventually realize they can use this knowledge gained through search activities to help benefit other consumers, and profit themselves. The consumer-seller who incurs the original search cost must be compensated with an amount equal to or exceeding the search cost they incur,[1] but not to exceed the sum of the search cost avoided by all the buyers who benefit. When these consumer-sellers are buying product X at the lowest price they can find, their demand adds to the demand already faced by those who sell low, which contributes to raising the price charged by the lowest-priced sellers of the product. Similarly, when the same arbitraging consumer-sellers sell the product to others at a higher price, either to other sellers or directly to consumers with a markup to provide a profit, this addition to the supply of product X already facing those who willingly buy at a high price, contributes to lowering the price paid by the highest-paying buyers. Together, the two sides of any arbitrage play contribute to the convergence of multiple prices for the same good, toward a single equilibrium price which clears the market (Kirzner 1963: 44-46).

Such acts of arbitrage are often criticized as unproductive and exploitative (Marx 1894, vol. 1: 477, vol. 3, chs. 29, 33, 36, Wolf & Resnick 1987: 165-166), but arbitrage can only take place success-fully when markets are initially inefficient and goods trade at a variety of different prices. Arbitrage rewards alert entrepreneurs who make markets more efficient, and clearly benefits all the low-price sellers and high-price buyers. Arbitrage also benefits everyone else by lowering transactions costs and search costs, because it lessens or eliminates the need to shop around for the lowest price. The threat or possibility of arbitrage keeps most markets at least relatively efficient most of

---

1 Search costs can include objective accounting costs which a buyer must pay for, such as gasoline or shoe leather, subjective appraisals of the value of the buyer's time engaged in search activities, and the opportunity costs, which may be subjective or objective, of foregoing the opportunity for the buyer to engage in the next less pleasurable or desired activity, etc.

the time. Arbitrage cannot occur, however, unless some individuals are initially alert to and searching for any potential arbitrage opportunities, seek them out, and are then willing and able to act on them (Kirzner 1963: 44-46). This is true whether the alert entrepreneurs are the original producer-sellers of a good or pure arbitrageurs who only engage in arbitrage.

From the foregoing it should be clear that markets do not clear automatically, and that they need the self-interested alertness of entrepreneurs along with their willingness to act. Entrepreneurs improve the efficiency of existing, real-world markets, and their activity and alertness are essential for a single price to emerge in any market. The alertness of entrepreneurs is also necessary for markets to clear, as entrepreneurs need to take notice of the shortage and surplus conditions indicating that supply and demand are not fully in adjustment with one another. As entrepreneurs act to benefit from the temporary dis-equilibrium by arbitraging the product, the arbitrageurs help to reduce and remove the dis-equilibrium (Kirzner 1963: 271).

1.3 Equilibria & Dis-equilibria in Market Process: the Demand Side

Next we will examine the role of entrepreneurial planners in changing and restoring market equilibria. Economists identify five determinants each of demand and supply. The determinants of demand are (1) consumer income, (2) consumer tastes, (3) prices of related goods and services, specifically the prices of substitute and complementary goods, (4) consumer expectations, and (5) the number of consumers. The determinants of supply are (1) technology, (2) prices of related goods and services, here the prices of alternative or switching outputs—substitutes in production, and byproducts or complements in production, (3) resource prices, that is, the prices of inputs used to produce the good being supplied, (4) producer expectations, and (5) the number of producers.

If any of the determinants of supply change, that changes the supply curve, destroying the old equilibrium, or at least leaving it behind, and triggering a transition toward a new equilibrium. If any of the determinants of demand change, that changes or shifts the demand curve, also triggering a transition to a new equilibrium. Although the comparative statics approach to supply-and-demand analysis largely ignores the process of transition from one equilibrium to the next, all these changes can be largely considered to be included in the general equilibrium model. The comparative statics approach is to ignore the process of change, and assume that changes in equilibrium are automatic and generally instantaneous or nearly instantaneous (Silberberg 1978: 209).

The key insight of market process is that the market is not so much an equilibrium, but a process of transition from equilibrium to dis-equilibrium and back again. Market process examines the sequence of events and the forces of change, especially entrepreneurial innovation which is omnipresent, which result in market exchanges at particular prices and in particular quantities, which move the market through dis-equilibrium, and from one equilibrium to the next. Market process examines the entrepreneurial acts of arbitrage, experimental price setting, and innovation in production, marketing, distribution, and supply chain management. It also looks at cost-saving innovations in production or underlying essential services such as office overhead, as well as the introduction of innovative new or modified products, and efforts to market existing products to new markets and identify new market niches, and identify ways to sell established products to new demographic groups or otherwise untapped markets.

Market process can always be seen as working through the awareness of some alert entrepreneur who first notices the initial state of any of the determinants of supply, and then also notices any change in any of the supply determinants. Suppose, for example, that consumer incomes increase. An alert entrepreneur has to become aware of this somehow. They may not be able to react at all until they have observed the resulting dis-equilibrium which higher incomes introduce in the markets for certain goods. Alert entrepreneurs can respond to restore the market to an equilibrium condition of clearing equal quantities of goods supplied and demanded. Some entrepreneurs may, however, be even more alert and more proactive, first hearing of the intelligence of an anticipated coming increase in consumer incomes, through news media or perhaps from an informally cultivated network or grapevine. They will likely further refine and flesh out this intelligence to determine in greater detail how well it will apply to the consumer demographic they already serve, and perhaps to potential future consumers, and evaluate this intelligence against their understanding of whether their good is a normal or inferior good for these current and potential future consumer demographics.

It is easy to conclude that the more proactive entrepreneurs are the more alert ones, who anticipate future market conditions before they occur, and to some extent, actually play a role in shaping market conditions in the process of their emergence. Normal goods face increased demand when consumer income rises. Inferior goods, in contrast, face *decreased* demand when consumer income rises. This relevant market knowledge and awareness to its significance enables an alert entrepreneur to adjust their plans to address the change in incomes and potentially profit from it. This is how entrepreneurs keep markets close to equilibrium, even as they introduce innovations that disrupt the market and move it out of equilibrium.

Or imagine consumer tastes have changed, also a determinant of demand. The most alert and proactive entrepreneurs who are aware of this before it noticeably affects the market for their product can benefit more by bringing to market completely new goods addressing the emerging consumer preferences which they were the first to notice and have had the most time to plan how best to cater to. The most alert entrepreneurs can do this before the markets for their established product lines even begin to stop clearing and they can observe shortages and surpluses. Or they can adapt their established product line more subtly if consumer tastes change less dramatically. Less alert entrepreneurs will have to wait until they can actually observe shortages or surpluses in their product markets before they will react. The most moribund and slothful producers will not react at all, and later, will not be in a position to compete for a share of the market for the emerging product.

Entrepreneurs also need to be aware of the prices of goods and services which might substitute for whatever they produce, because if the prices of potential substitutes fall, since these goods can serve the same uses more cheaply, the entrepreneur's product will now face lowered demand, reducing the equilibrium price and quantity in the market they sell in. If the entrepreneur anticipates this market transition correctly, they can minimize the damage and resource waste by lowering their output level and selling price, though this will necessarily lower the firm's profits and revenue compared to what they had been before the price of the substitute fell. If the entrepreneur is less alert and waits for a surplus condition to occur, the negative impact on the firm's profits and revenue is even greater. On the other hand, if instead the prices of substitute goods and services rise, this is a favorable development for the firm which will now face increased demand as consumers substitute away from the newly more costly alternative and toward the firm's product. Now the firm can charge a higher price for a larger amount of output, and if entrepreneurs anticipate this, they will ramp up production and raise prices accordingly. If they wait until they observe the resulting shortages of their product, they will still benefit, but not as quickly and initially not by as much.

Complementary products are used together, and changes in the price of either affects the demand for the other. If the price falls of a good or service which is a complement to the firm's output, that is beneficial for the firm, because demand for the firm's product will rise, enabling the firm to charge a higher price for a larger amount of output. Some marketing strategies are built on enhancing more complementary uses for a firm's products, such as food advertisements with recipes calling for the use of other products, which are thus rendered complements. Alert entrepreneurs who anticipate this before it actually happens can benefit the most. Less alert entrepreneurs who fail to act until they observe the shortage condition benefit once they respond appropriately, but the benefit is delayed and more limited for these less alert firms. Conversely, when the price of a complementary good or service rises, this lowers the demand for the entrepreneur's product, lowering both price and quantity which will now clear the market after the change. Alert entrepreneurs who see what is coming and know what this means for their product market immediately cut back on production or acquisition and lower the price, resulting in lower profits and revenues to the firm. Less alert entrepreneurs who fail to respond until they observe surpluses in their product markets make adjustments after the fact, incurring greater resource wastage, and reaching the lower sustainable output and price levels with a delay, resulting in greater cost and expense to the firm, and thus even lower profits in the short run.

Entrepreneurs also need to be alert to consumer expectations. When consumers come to expect that the price of some good or service is going to rise in the future, this becomes a self-fulfilling prophecy as they start to purchase larger quantities at the current low price to acquire a stockpile against the expected price increase, increasing demand and eventually driving the price up. The price increase causes a phenomenon called price rationing, where at the higher price, the product will only be provided to, and used by, those who are willing to pay the higher price. These are the people who value the product the most, and this group is nearly always a strict subset of those who would have purchased it at a lower price. Alert entrepreneurs can also raise prices preemptively, to capture more of the consumer surplus, and they can expand production or acquire more of the product in antic-ipation of the higher future demand. To the extent producers expand production, the price increase will be alleviated, and to the extent the price increase is implemented by alert entrepreneurs anticipating higher demand, some part of the original supply will be reserved for the future, when, based on consumer expectations, it will be more urgently needed. Less aware entrepreneurs wait for the shortage condition to occur before raising prices. The least aware entrepreneurs, barely worthy of the title, allow consumers to buy out their inventories at the original low, unadjusted prices, forgoing some profits and preventing their inventory to serve the coming greater demand when it appears, assuming it actually does appear as consumers expected.

When consumers expect the price of some good or service will fall in the future, this also becomes a self-fulfilling prophecy as they start to purchase lower quantities at the original price. To the extent they can, consumers will reduce their current demand as they wait for the anticipated future low price. This drives the price down and results in surpluses of the product. Alert entrepreneurs will have already lowered prices preemptively, to capture as large a share as possible of the shrinking market, and reduced their production. To the extent producers reduce their output, the fall in prices will be alleviated, and to the extent the price decrease is implemented by alert entrepreneurs anticipating the reduced demand, resources which would have been used producing this product can be allocated to other output more desired by consumers, given the consumer expectations. Less aware entrepreneurs wait to observe the surplus condition before lowering prices and reducing production levels. The least aware entrepreneurs allow unsold inventories to languish on their shelves. This is always a much greater and more expensive problem for perishable than for non-perishable goods.

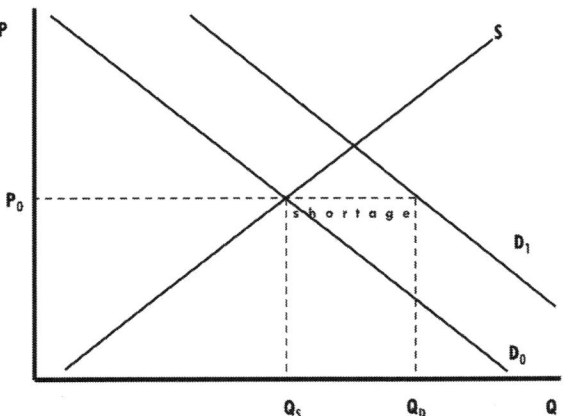

Figure 1.3 An increase in Demand results in a
shortage at the original price

When the number of consumers increases, alert entrepreneurs know they can now sell more output at a higher price, in response to the increase in consumer demand. The most alert entrepreneurs will be proactive in producing more and marking up the price accordingly. Less aware entrepreneurs will follow suit eventually, but not until they observe the shortage condition occurring which signals to them the need for and feasibility of increasing both price and output. When the number of consumers decreases, the most alert entrepreneurs know they can only sell a smaller quantity of output at a lower price in response to the decrease in consumer demand. These entrepreneurs will be proactive in producing less and marking the price down. Less aware entrepreneurs will also follow suit eventually, but not until they observe directly the surplus condition which signals to them the need and feasibility of decreasing both price and output.

When any of the determinants of demand change so that the demand curve shifts to the right; that is, there is an increase in demand, this creates a dis-equilibrium until the first and most alert entrepreneurs correctly perceive the situation and begin the process of adjusting the price upward (Figure 1.3). Initially there will be a shortage of the good in question, but this condition signals to alert entrepreneurs the need to allocate more resources to producing this product, and simultaneously to raise the price. Similarly, when any of the determinants of demand change so that the demand curve shifts to the left; that is, there is a decrease in demand, this creates a dis-equilibrium until entrepreneurs correctly perceive the situation and begin the process of adjusting the price downward (Figure 1.4). Initially there will be a surplus, but this condition signals to alert entrepreneurs the need to allocate resources away from producing this product, and simultaneously to lower the price.

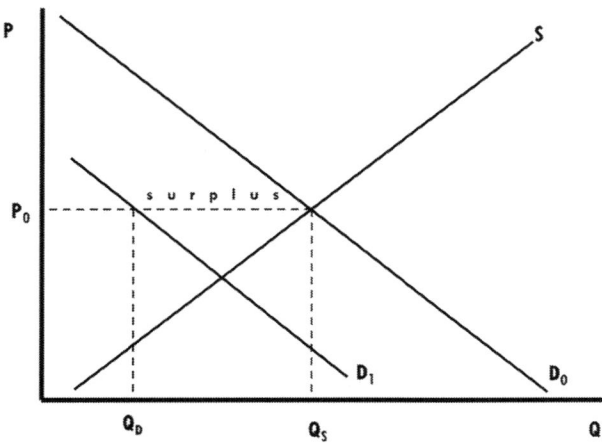

*Figure 1.4 A decrease in Demand results in
a surplus at the original price*

In every case, the most alert entrepreneurs respond first, and either benefit more from alleviating the dis-equilibrium (Kirzner 1963: 271), or the market penalizes them less. Reactive, less-aware entrepreneurs who wait to observe a shortage or surplus condition before adjusting prices and output levels respond with more of a lag, and incur greater costs to capture benefits which are at least initially lower for them. Planners who never bother to respond at all pay the highest price in the face of changing market conditions.

1.4 Equilibria & Dis-equilibria in Market Process: the Supply Side

Next we will examine how entrepreneurs respond to changes in the determinants of supply, and how this side of market process causes supply to change. Technology is unique as a determinant of supply in that it only changes in one direction, always improving, always creating new markets, and reducing the costs of production. Firms and entrepreneurs can expend untold effort in trying to uncover and create new scientific knowledge which advances the state of technology. In many situations, however, an entrepreneurial planner merely applies knowledge which is already readily available, in that it has already been discovered by others, and is ready and waiting to be taken off the shelf to be applied to a problem faced by the planner's firm, or to benefit a new group of consumers. Thus, technological progress can be applied without the firm ever having to expend resources to make the relevant scientific discovery on which the new technology or technical application relies—the firm's entrepreneurial planners need only be alert to relevant technological advances.

The most common motivation for the firm in financing and carrying out technical research and development is principally to apply scientific knowledge which has already been discovered and has perhaps already been applied in other areas. To a far lesser extent firms actively seek to uncover original new knowledge of basic science, which they hope will be directly relevant to problems the firm seeks to address with new goods and services to meet new or established consumer needs. Alert entrepreneurs are always seeking to discover or learn about new technological approaches which might reduce costs in their established production plans, but the most alert and innovative entrepreneurs also seek to use and apply new and emerging technologies. This can enable their enterprises to leapfrog over their competitors into developing fields and capture the greatest, first-to-market benefits.

Entrepreneurs must also be alert to changes in the prices of alternative or switching outputs, otherwise known as substitutes in production. When the price of a substitute in production goes up, alert entrepreneurs know they can now sell that alternative output at a higher price in response to the increase in consumer demand or greater scarcity. The entrepreneurial planner faces the situation that the firm's current production will now provide lower profits than could be earned from an alternative output the firm can switch to producing. Alert entrepreneurs will be proactive in switching their production to the output most desired by the market at the highest price, and marking up the price accordingly. This increases the supply of the alternative good or service which commands the higher market price because it is more desired by users, while simultaneously reducing supply of the original good or service which the firm switched out of producing. Some less aware entrepreneurs will follow suit eventually, but not until they observe the higher profits earned by the pioneering firms which led the charge in switching their output to the higher-priced, more desired product.

As the supply of the higher-priced alternative product increases, its price falls, reducing the benefit to the first firms to switch. The pioneering firms which switch output first can potentially capture greater market share, which can transform a short-term benefit into a longer-term one. Other less aware entrepreneurs will initially refrain from switching output and may benefit more from continuing to produce the original product. They benefit from not switching output because the supply of the original output falls as the more innovative, more entrepreneurially alert firms switch to producing the higher priced alternative output. At some point the interplay between alert firms which switch outputs from lower priced products to higher priced products tends to equalize the price differential between the two alternative products.

Entrepreneurs must also be alert to changes in the prices of byproducts or complements in production. A byproduct or complement in production is something which is produced as part of the process of producing the firm's primary product. In the most extreme case these byproducts or complements in production can be waste products which either have no known economic value at present, or even worse, the firm may have to pay to dispose of the byproducts of their production process. If the economic value of the byproduct rises, this is a direct benefit to the firm which is initially producing the byproduct at zero marginal cost. It can mean the difference between producing the primary product at an accounting loss, and producing two economically valuable products together at a profit.

As an example, natural gas (methane) and helium are two byproducts of petroleum production. At one time natural gas was a dangerous and economically useless byproduct of drilling for oil, and the natural gas had to be burned off because of its dangerous explosive properties. The presence of natural gas in a petroleum deposit still greatly complicates the process and risk of extraction. When alert entrepreneurs devised a way to make the natural gas economically valuable, that automatically boosted the profitability of every oil well in proportion to the amount of gas it could also produce. Now that natural gas is an economically valuable resource, when the price of natural gas rises, that makes marginal oil wells profitable, and they are put back in production. If the price of natural gas falls, marginal wells become unprofitable, and they are taken out of production. Changes in the price of petroleum have the same effect on natural gas production, because if one good is a complement in production for the other, the other is necessarily a complement in production for the first.

The most alert entrepreneurs will know what their byproducts are, and appreciate the additional profits they can earn if they can find or create new markets for these byproducts. There are basically three entrepreneurial strategies which can be applied when a production process generates waste products—(1) reduce the amount of waste which has to be disposed of, (2) reduce the cost of disposal, or (3) find new uses and markets for the waste products. Less alert, more imitative entrepreneurs will merely wait for some primary innovator to create a market for the byproducts. Once this is done, the primary innovator has already assumed and successfully overcome all the risks of introducing the innovative use for the byproduct, and the secondary innovators can simply imitate them by selling their byproduct to the same groups of buyers.

Entrepreneurs must also be alert to changes in the prices of resources; that is, the prices of inputs used to produce the good that the entrepreneur supplies. If relevant resource prices rise, this shifts the product supply curve to the left, reducing supply, raising the equilibrium selling price, and reducing the market-clearing quantity of the product to be bought and sold. Entrepreneurial alertness is necessary to process the implications of the added production costs, and adjust the firm's asking price and output level accordingly. Supply only decreases as one firm adjusts its output and asking price, and imitative firms follow suit. If relevant resource prices fall, this shifts the supply curve to the right, increasing supply, lowering the selling price and increasing the quantity of goods or services which will clear the market. Market supply increases as one firm's entrepreneurial planner notices the reduced production costs and takes advantage of this new situation to adjust the asking price and quantity of output accordingly. Competitive pressures contribute to the entrepreneurial decision which increases supply. The first entrepreneur to lower their price to pass on the cost savings or some share of it to their customers is now underselling their competitors, until the competing firms follow suit.

Entrepreneurial planners can take advantage of lower input prices to earn higher profits without lowering the output price, but more alert entrepreneurs will attempt to capture higher profits and expand their market share by passing along most of the cost savings to their customers (Kirzner 1963: 44-46). Less alert, more imitative entrepreneurs and firms simply follow strategies they observe the industry leaders pursuing. Their imitative behavior helps shift the supply curve, but if the industry leader gains market share, it will be at the expense of the more imitative firms. The lower output price, which clears the market after an increase in supply, expands the extent of the market. The most alert and innovative entrepreneurs capture most of the benefit and additional profits of the expanded market, at the expense of the more imitative firms.

Entrepreneurs form their own expectations of future market conditions, but they must also be especially aware of the expectations of competing producers. Especially rare, unique, or idiosyncratic expectations and beliefs held by any one entrepreneur can be a tremendous competitive advantage provided the unique expectation is subsequently born out in reality. Entrepreneurial planners who first anticipate an increase in demand for their product will expand their production capacity first, and will be in a position to benefit from the expected changed conditions, provided that it actually materializes in reality. Planners who anticipate changes which never come to pass generally only contribute to wasting resources and suffer lower profits as a result. Entrepreneurs who correctly anticipate the course of techno-logical change can contribute to implementing and exploiting it as the new advance is implemented. If correct expectations are widely held throughout an industry, the firms in the industry will most likely act in concert to address changed conditions together.

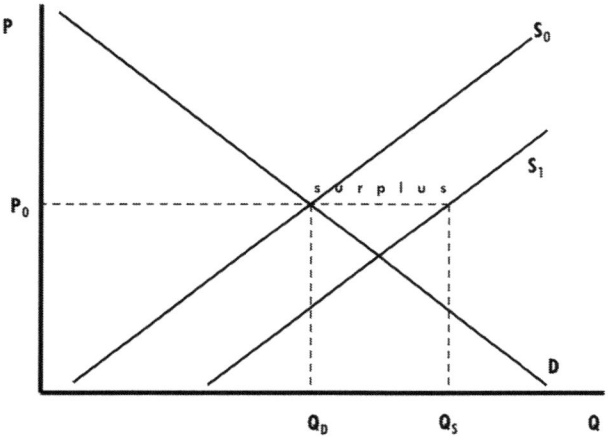

Figure 1.5 An increase in Supply results i
a surplus at the original price

Entrepreneurs must also be alert to changes in the number of competing producers. If new competitors enter the market, the most entrepreneurial among the established firms will be alert to the fact that they will now be facing higher competitive pressures. The established firms may seek regulatory relief to discourage new entrants. They may seek to build market power through product differentiation and monopolistic-competitive behavior (Kirzner 1963: 308-309). They may seek to expand to capture the market share which would otherwise be captured by the new entrants.

When any of the determinants of supply change so that the supply curve shifts to the right; that is, there is an increase in supply, this creates a dis-equilibrium until the first and most alert entrepreneurs correctly perceive the changed situation and begin the process of adjusting the price downward (Figure 1.5). Initially there will be a surplus of the good in question, but this condition signals to alert entrepreneurs the need to reallocate resources away from this product, freeing them up for the production of other, more urgently desired products, and simultaneously to lower the price. Similarly, when any of the determinants of supply change so that the supply curve shifts to the left; that is, there is a decrease in supply, this creates a dis-equilibrium until entrepreneurs correctly perceive the situation and begin the process of adjusting the price upward (Figure 1.6). Initially there will be a shortage, but this condition signals to alert entrepreneurs the need to allocate more resources to producing this product, and simultaneously to raise the price.

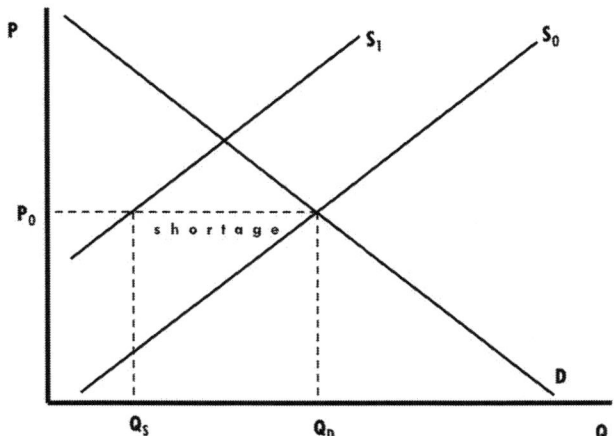

Figure 1.6 A decrease in Supply results in
a shortage at the original price

From the foregoing it should be clear that the market response to any change in any of the determinants of supply and demand identified by economists is not an automatic transition to a new equilibrium. For the transition to occur in reality once an established equilibrium is lost, this requires first entrepreneurial awareness of the changed market conditions, and second, the willingness on the part of the most alert entrepreneurial planners, the industry leaders, to assume the risk and make changes in their ongoing production plans to address the changed market conditions. Other firms, with less alert entrepreneurial planners, will become aware of changed market conditions only after they see shortages or surpluses arise, and will respond later. Entrepreneurial awareness of, and willingness to act on, opportunities to profit from pure arbitrage makes markets as efficient as they are, but knowledge limitations, transactions costs, and search costs can never be eliminated entirely and will always prevent markets from being perfectly efficient (Kirzner 1973: 35, Horwitz 2000: 29-30).

Economists claim competitive markets are highly efficient, not perfectly efficient. Everything economists attribute to this fictionally effortless and automatic market equilibrium is actually accomplished through the laborious work performed by risk-taking entrepreneurial planners. But entrepreneurial planners do even more—they also move markets out of equilibrium by introducing new products and different activities which were not anticipated by the entrepreneurial plans of others. In fact there are two aspects of market process which are perpetually in play; the equilibrating forces of arbitrage, profit seeking, and cost reduction, and the dis-equilibrating forces of change, innovation, and experimentation.[2] Both aspects depend critically on entrepreneurial alertness.

---

2 Joseph A. Schumpeter (1883-1950) and Israel M. Kirzner (1930-) present competing or alternative visions of the role of entrepreneurial planners. According to Schumpeter, entrepreneurs disrupt established market equilibria and reduce the level of mutual coordination among competing entrepreneurial plans, at least in the short run. These disruptive innovations may reduce mutual coordination of entrepreneurial plans in the short run, but increase it in the long run, once other entrepreneurial planners have an opportunity to adjust to and take advantage of the new market conditions brought about by the disruptive innovation. Kirzner's view is that entrepreneurs profit from introducing innovations which enable higher levels of mutual coordination among the plans of others, benefiting everyone, and profiting with a share of the subjective benefit they provide and allow everyone else to enjoy. Both kinds of phenomena appear to occur in the real world and any theory of entrepreneurially driven market process needs to acknowledge and accommodate both kinds of entrepreneurship. Schumpeterian entrepreneurs destroy equilibria (Schumpeter 1934: 64, 1962: 104-105, 132), whereas Kirznerian entrepreneurs effect adjustment toward new equilibria (Kirzner 1973: 72-73, 1984b: 160). "Entrepreneurship for me is not so much the introduction of new products or of new techniques of production as the ability to see where new products have become unexpectedly valuable to consumers and where new methods of production have, unknown to others, become feasible (Kirzner 1973: 81)."

CHAPTER 2

The Market Process View v. the Equilibrium or Market Outcome View

The entrepreneurial planning of individual producers and consumers plays a central role in allocating resources and producing goods and services. Entrepreneurs form plans which are exploratory, tentative, and speculative, being designed to be implemented in an unknowable future which unfolds before us in the fullness of time. As these plans are carried out, the entrepreneurial planner has to rely on the plans and actions of others, and has to take into account any changes made by other entrepreneurial planners whenever those changes affect how the plan in question needs to be carried out. This interplay among numerous interdependent entrepreneurial plans which evolve over time is what creates and responds to changing market conditions, determines market prices, and adjusts them over time. Thus, the theory of market process both complements and extends Arrow-Debreu (1954) equilibrium theory.[3] General equilibrium is best understood as an abstract formal condition which need not mirror reality too closely to add to our understanding of how markets work. Market process is "a systematic process in which market participants acquire more and more accurate and complete *mutual knowledge* of potential demand and supply conditions (Kirzner 1997: 325, emphasis in original)."

Fundamentally, market participants acquire knowledge of each others' wants and capabilities, which better positions them to construct and adapt new entrepreneurial plans to fulfill the wants of others while taking best advantage of others' available capabilities which can either be hired on the market, or create goods and services which are also offered on the market. Entrepreneurial plans succeed and earn profits only to the extent they enable the planners to contribute to better satisfying the wants of others. Successful entrepreneurial plans add value to the plans of others, whether producers, consumers, or both. Knowledge is mutual in this sense because the actions of each entrepreneurial innovator occur in the open and thus are visible to others. Innovations invite an appropriate and complementary response, which other market participants reward to the extent it improves the satisfaction of their wants, and contributes to providing a higher level of coordination among the entrepreneurial plans of others (Kirzner 1996: 39-41).

---

3 Arrow-Debreu equilibrium theory presents the most sophisticated model of general equilibrium, treating markets which are separated geographically and separated in time as being distinct markets. One requirement for an Arrow-Debreu general equilibrium is that there be well-developed and fully-functional futures markets for all products across all time periods. It is not clear that this is entirely realistic.

2.1 Kirzner's Two Knowledge Problems

Israel M. Kirzner (1990) defined two Knowledge Problems, A and B, which entrepreneurial planners compete to overcome. Successful entrepreneurship always acts to remove one or both Knowledge Problems, or lessen their extent. Both Knowledge Problems arise due to asymmetric information deficiencies on the part of one group of potential market participants, either potential buyers or potential sellers, and results in the group with the deficient information forming a mistakenly optimistic or mistakenly pessimistic set of expectations about the behavior of the other group of market participants. This circumstance results in a systematic inability to improve mutual coordination of entrepreneurial plans throughout the market, at least until the knowledge problem is removed.

Kirzner's Knowledge Problem A occurs whenever some beneficial market exchanges fail to take place due to a mistaken over-optimism on the part of some economic agents, who may be either buyers or sellers. Knowledge Problem A can occur, for example, due to sellers' over-optimism in their appraisal of the price they believe buyers are willing to pay them for a product, which the sellers mistakenly believe is higher than it actually is. In other words, the sellers mistakenly believe the market demand they face is greater than it actually turns out to be. Alternatively, Knowledge Problem A can also occur due to buyers' over-optimism in their appraisal of the price they believe sellers are willing to accept for the product, which buyers mistakenly believe is lower than the higher minimum reservation price which sellers are actually prepared to accept. In this case, over-optimistic buyers mistakenly believe the supply of the product is greater than it actually is. Thus, Knowledge Problem A can originate with mistaken over-optimism on the part of buyers or on the part of sellers. Regardless of which group the over-optimism originates with, Knowledge Problem A can only apply to those hypothetical exchanges which would be voluntarily entered into by both parties and actually be mutually beneficial if they were to take place. Knowledge Problem A is a problem which market process must overcome, because whenever it occurs, it results in preventing mutually beneficial exchanges from taking place.

Knowledge Problem A results from buyers or sellers acting on beliefs which turn out to be mistaken—in this case these beliefs or expectations are mistakenly over-optimistic, either from the perspective of the buyers or from the perspective of the sellers. Either the prospective buyers want the product, but are not willing to pay as high a price as that asked by the prospective sellers, or the prospective sellers want to sell the product and would willingly do so at a lower price, but they mistakenly believe the buyers are willing to pay more than the buyers actually are. Knowledge Problem A is always a problem of over-optimism, regardless of whether it originates with the buyers or the sellers.

However, Knowledge Problem A has the benefit that it is also self-correcting—over-optimistic sellers eventually lower their asking price to dispose of their unsold inventories, or else over-optimistic buyers ultimately realize they cannot obtain the product they want at the lowest price they initially anticipated. Eventually the over-optimistic prospective buyers accept the need to either pay more or do without the product entirely. To some extent, these conditions and the process of resolving Knowledge Problem A are captured reasonably well in the conventional equilibrium account of adjusting to the market-clearing price in a perfectly competitive market. What is missing from this conventional account is the intentional actions of entrepreneurial

planners that ultimately allow for the conversion of prospective buyers
and sellers into actual buyers and sellers.

Market process works to correct Knowledge Problem A in two
different ways. First, suppose over-optimistic sellers mistakenly believe
buyers are willing to pay more than the buyers actually are, and produce
a good or service and bring it to market based on this mistaken belief.
The next step is that the sellers find that their product will not sell at
the price asked, and eventually the sellers will perceive this. When
this happens, the sellers do not have to be extraordinarily alert entrepreneurs to see that their product is not selling as anticipated. At this
point the sellers can write off the whole production run as a loss, but
more frequently they should try to minimize their losses by offering
their product for sale at a lower price, and keep reducing the price,
until they successfully dispose of their whole initial product run. They
should also take advantage of this disappointing initial experience
because it should provide valuable market research intelligence about
the price and quantity that will ultimately clear the market given the
actual market conditions faced by the firm. The entrepreneurial planner
should learn through this how much to reduce the anticipated price,
and whether the production run should be increased or decreased. It
may be that the initial run cannot be disposed of, except at such a low
price that the product cannot be profitably produced, but this only
signals to the entrepreneur to use their talents and financial resources
elsewhere and in producing a different product.

Alternatively, suppose over-optimistic buyers mistakenly believe
sellers will accept a lower price than the minimum reservation price
at which they will willingly sell the product. The potential buyers
search for the product and find it to be more expensive than they
had anticipated. They may shop around further based on their initial,

over-optimistic, and mistaken expectation. Eventually, they may decide to do without the product, or buy less of it, or pay the higher asking price. If over-optimistic consumers refrain from buying the product at all, or reduce their purchases due to the unexpectedly high price, these behavioral choices on their part contribute to reducing the quantity demand, moving the market closer to clearing. Once the most entre-preneurially alert buyers recognize they face a lower market supply than what they had originally anticipated, this begins the process of adjusting the buyers' perception of, and response to, the lower level of market supply. Actual market supply is lower than what the buyers over-optimistically assumed when they formulated their initial buying and consumption plans and initially attempted to put them into action. Once the buyers accept the need to pay the higher price, that merely validates the sellers' expectations regarding the market demand they face.

In contrast, Kirzner's Knowledge Problem B is more interesting, though equally ubiquitous—in contrast with Knowledge Problem A, Knowledge Problem B is a problem of over-pessimism. Here, voluntary market exchanges which would be mutually beneficial whenever they take place never occur at all. This can happen either because of sellers' over-pessimistic and mistaken belief that buyers are not willing to pay as much as they actually are, leading sellers to produce or acquire less of the product, or because of buyers' over-pessimistic but equally mistaken belief that the sellers' asking price will be higher than what sellers will actually accept. When Knowledge Problem B originates in misperceptions by sellers, the prospective sellers' appraisal of the prospective buyers' perception or expectation of the likely benefits of the product is mistakenly low, and sellers respond to this condition by refraining from bringing the product to market. This error in judgement or perception leads sellers to the apparently justified yet wholly incorrect conclusion that prospective buyers will not be willing to pay a high enough price to justify the seller in producing or otherwise acquiring for sale the product in question. In this case, prospective sellers mistakenly appraise the asking price they would have to set, as exceeding any potential benefits they think the buyers could be persuaded they could obtain from the product, and furthermore that the sellers' reservation price is also strictly higher than what they believe prospective buyers are willing to pay for the product.

Alternatively, buyers can be the over-pessimistic group who cause Knowledge Problem B. If buyers mistakenly believe the sellers' asking price is higher than it actually is. Here, the prospective buyers' appraisal of the prospective sellers' production or acquisition costs, their desired minimum profit margin, etc.is mistakenly high, and buyers respond to their misconceptions by refraining from shopping or searching for the product. This error in judgement or perception leads buyers to the apparently justified yet wholly incorrect conclusion that prospective sellers will not be willing to accept a sufficiently low price to justify the buyer in purchasing the product in question. In this case, prospective buyers mistakenly appraise the asking price they would have to pay, as exceeding any potential benefits they believe and expect they will obtain from the product, and furthermore buyers mistakenly believe that the sellers' reservation price is also strictly higher than what pro-spective buyers are actually willing to pay for the product.

In either case of over-pessimism, unlike with Knowledge Problem A, there will be no unsold inventory to be marked down for disposal—because it was mistakenly never produced or acquired. It does not matter whether it is the buyers or sellers who mistakenly misjudge market conditions as being less favorable to their entrepreneurial plans than it actually is; the error of over-pessimism prevents a market for this product from ever developing. Kirzner's Knowledge Problem B presents a greater challenge to entrepreneurial planners and to market process theory, because it is not automatically self-correcting. Knowledge Problem B is never visible to either the producers or consumers. Thus, Knowledge Problem B calls for, and rewards, deeper entrepreneurial awareness to identify these hidden—though omnipresent—missed opportunities for beneficial exchange. Here the necessary entrepreneurial awareness is less a matter of cut-and-dried identification of a shortage or surplus condition which can be remedied through simply adjusting the price, than one of deep conjectural speculations that some such unseen entrepreneurial opportunity may be present. It is primarily the presumed ubiquity of such unobserved instances of Knowledge Problem B which entrepreneurs compete to uncover and remedy.

This is what drives alert entrepreneurs to produce and offer new products. They are trying to satisfy latent demand no competitor had imagined. Knowledge Problem B can only be overcome by introducing innovations no one else would undertake, and which other potential producers or competitors have thus far failed to perceive, anticipate, or suspect. In sharp contrast with Knowledge Problem A, attempts to remedy Knowledge Problem B are not automatic or routine, and these attempts are far riskier. Basically, an entrepreneur acts on their gut hunch or suspicion that Knowledge Problem B may be present in some form. The entrepreneur formulates and acts on a plan to produce or acquire and market a prospective product which is not presently being marketed, and might not even exist yet. The risk-taking entrepreneur's hope is that this product might actually meet with a better reception from the market than what is believed by virtually everyone else who is making decisions for a particular industry.

For example, suppose the established firms in a particular industry have done their due diligence and concluded that a certain product which will cost them $4 per unit to produce, can only be sold, at most, for $3.75. Their informed appraisal is that the maximum benefit they believe consumers will ascribe to this product will not justify a selling price greater than $3.75. In other words, their informed appraisal of the state of demand is that it is not sufficient to justify producing this product given the cost of production. Accordingly, they decide not to produce it, and this is certainly the correct decision based on their knowledge and belief. But suppose an alert entrepreneur either identifies an innovative and cheaper production method, which, when implemented, allows for production of the same product or a close and satisfactory substitute at the lower cost of $3.25 per unit. Now this product can be produced and sold at a profit. This is one example of how an alert entrepreneur can profit from overcoming Knowledge Problem B. Or perhaps the entrepreneur is able to correctly identify or at least suspect the likely existence of a specialized niche market of consumers who are willing to pay $4.50 for this product. This would also be an instance of overcoming Knowledge Problem B. In this case it is the willingness of an alert entrepreneur to take risks, which no one else in the industry was willing to incur, allowing the wants of some consumers which the market was previously unable to satisfy, to be satisfied.

Some relationships between Kirzner's Two Knowledge Problems are illustrated in Table 2.1.

Table 2.1 Kirzner's Two Knowledge Problems

	Knowledge Problem A		**Knowledge Problem B**	
Cause	Over-optimism		Over-pessimism	
Group problem originates from	Buyers	Sellers	Buyers	Sellers
Mistaken belief	Buyers' over-optimistic appraisal of market supply from sellers leads them to mistakenly believe asking price from sellers will be lower—actual asking price too high	Sellers' over-optimistic appraisal of market demand by buyers leads them to mistakenly believe offer price from buyers will be higher—actual offer price too low	Buyers' over-pessimistic appraisal of market supply from sellers leads them to mistakenly believe asking price from sellers will be higher—actual asking price too low	Sellers' over-pessimistic appraisal of market demand leads them to mistakenly believe the offer price from buyers will be lower—actual offer price too high
Manifests as	Price below market-clearing price	Price above market-clearing price	Buyers refrain from entering market & withhold demand	Sellers refrain from entering market & withhold supply
Dis-equilibrium condition	Shortage $(Q_D > Q_S)$	Surplus $(Q_S > Q_D)$	No market emerges $(Q_D = Q_S = 0)$	No market emerges $(Q_D = Q_S = 0)$
Diagram				
Market-clearing price	Above dis-equilibrium P	Below dis-equilibrium P	Below hypothetical dis-equilibrium P	Above hypothetical dis-equilibrium P
Equilibrium account of resolution	P & Q adjust upward to clear market	P & Q adjust downward to clear market	Market fails to develop; "clears" at $(Q_D = Q_S = 0)$	Market fails to develop; "clears" at $(Q_D = Q_S = 0)$
Market process account of how resolved	Alert entrepreneur perceives buyer over-optimism or shortage condition and acts to exploit profit opportunity to alleviate market & information failures	Alert entrepreneur perceives seller over-optimism or surplus condition and acts to exploit profit opportunity to alleviate market & information failures	Alert entrepreneur perceives buyer over-pessimism and acts to exploit profit opportunity to alleviate market & information failures, earning temporary monopoly profits	Alert entrepreneur perceives seller over-pessimism & acts to exploit profit opportunity to alleviate market & information failures, earning temporary monopoly profits

Note—The black dots in the diagrams indicate whether the buyer's offer price or the seller's asking price is the source of the initial dis-equilibrium which is created by Knowledge Problem A or B. The dashed lines indicate the misperceived Supply

(S) and Demand (D) curves. Misperceived Supply and Demand are indicated as (S_o) for Supply over-optimistically misperceived by buyers, (D_o) for Demand over-optimistically misperceived by sellers, (S_p) for Supply over-pessimistically misperceived by buyers, and (D_p) for Demand over-pessimistically misperceived by sellers (Kirzner 1984b, 1990).

When entrepreneurs encounter the self-correcting over-optimism of Knowledge Problem A, they simply adjust prices to remove the surplus or shortage condition (Kirzner 1997). This automatic entrepreneurial response is simply a form of the autonomous housekeeping of the market order. However, the unobservable and potentially persistent over-pessimism of Knowledge Problem B calls for deeper and less routine, more extraordinary entrepreneurial alertness to opportunities to improve market outcomes, exploit incentives which are invisible and generally overlooked by everyone else, and earn profits by introducing new products, methods, and techniques. In other words, the latent incentives to overcome Knowledge Problem B, to which alert entrepreneurs respond, are not yet actualized in the market until an alert entrepreneur sees the potential opportunity for innovation, accepts the risk of failure, and acts on their vision. Entrepreneurial plans which remove or alleviate Knowledge Problem B actualize these latent incentives, which cannot be seen or anticipated beforehand except by alert entrepreneurs, and unambiguously improve plan coordination and resource allocation throughout the economy, establish new dis-equilibria, improve the satisfaction of consumer wants, etc. When entrepreneurs are unsuccessful in their planned efforts to overcome Knowledge Problem B, they incur losses from implementing their unsuccessful attempts. The unsuccessful plan implementation may better inform entrepreneurial planners in making decisions in the future, formulating and carrying out more effective or better motivated plans, or leave entrepreneurship to those with better talents for it, or merely deeper pockets!

2.2 Overcoming Knowledge Problems: Equilibrium v. Market Process Accounts

Kirzner's Two Knowledge Problems provide a clear illustration of the superior explanatory power of the market process approach to examining microeconomic behavior over the equilibrium, comparative static approach. First, suppose the knowledge problems originate with misinformation on the part of sellers rather than buyers. For Knowledge Problem A, this means we will assume it is the seller who is over-optimistic. The seller mistakenly believes or expects the price buyers are willing to pay is higher than it actually is. A lower price, which the buyers will willingly pay, would hypothetically clear the market, but the sellers' over-optimism leads them to set the price too high. As a result of seller over-optimism, the market will not clear. This mistaken expectation regarding buyer behavior on the part of the sellers creates a surplus of the product. From the view of conventional microeconomics, resolving the initial dis-equilibrium is simply a matter of adjusting the price downward until the surplus condition is removed and the market clears.

However, from the perspective of market process, entrepreneurial alertness is required before the sellers can initially even notice that there is a surplus of their product. This may simply be a matter of sufficient and appropriate diligence in monitoring the firm's own inventory levels, or it may involve further effort in gathering extensive information from an extensive and spread out network of geographically dispersed retail outlets. Once entrepreneurial planners do finally realize they have created a surplus of the product, only then can they respond by lowering the price and rate of production. If any current sellers fail to exercise sufficient alertness to the surplus condition, or if they notice the surplus but refrain from acting on it by making these appropriate and obvious adjustments to price and production levels, they leave the door open for the more alert entrepreneurs among their competitors to competitively preempt them by lowering their prices first.

If no firm producing this product is the first to lower their price, the industry's firms create a condition where any new entrant could come in, undersell the established firms, and capture significant market share away from the not highly vigilant established firms. Often the threat of any competitor's or potential competitor's lowering of their prices will be more than sufficient to motivate and preempt the firm's decision and swiftly compel them to lower the price. In this situation, in many cases each firm will lower the price preemptively to forestall the mere possibility of being undersold, either by current competitors or new entrants. However, these strategies to preserve the firm's market share require the firm's alert entrepreneurial planners to become aware in the first place that they are trying to sell their product at a price above what will clear the market.

Entrepreneurial planners have to be alert to surplus and shortage conditions before they arise, and must be constantly engaged in monitoring the extent that every market for their product clears, or fails to clear, simultaneously in every market they sell in. Although the market process account of Knowledge Problem A is more satisfactory and adds some valuable detail over and above what was contributed by the equilibrium account, it is difficult to conclude that market process offers any overwhelmingly decisive explanatory advantages. For the most part, market process only offers a more detailed and realistic account of the same process as the comparative static account of adjustment to equilibrium market clearing from an initial dis-equilibrium or disturbed equilibrium.

Next, consider Knowledge Problem B, a problem of over-pessimism, by assumption still originating in misinformation on the part of sellers rather than buyers. Here the seller mistakenly believes or expects the price buyers are willing to pay is lower than it actually is. Some higher price, which the buyers will willingly pay in reality, will actually clear the market, but the sellers are unaware of this and their over-pessimism leads them not to set the price lower than will clear the market, which would create a shortage, but to refrain from producing the good or offering it for sale in the first place. This mistake on the part of the sellers creates an absolute shortage of the product. From the perspective of conventional microeconomics, resolving the dis-equilibrium is no longer simply a matter of adjusting the price upward until the shortage condition is removed and the market clears. No market is ever created for this product which is thus never offered for sale in the first place. This product would readily sell at a market-clearing equilibrium price which would be mutually advantageous for many buyers and sellers, but this market outcome is not perceived or anticipated before the fact. The overly-pessimistic misinformation and mistaken beliefs the sellers act on prevent any possibility of resolving the potential shortfall in output through a mere adjustment to equilibrium.

However, from the perspective of market process, entrepreneurial alertness is required for the sellers to notice or imagine the possibility that the product in question might potentially satisfy certain consumer wants. The alert entrepreneurial planner has to correctly identify and anticipate consumer wants to conclude that the prospective product is or will be actually desired by consumers, either by consumers in general or by some demographic niche, and that at least some consumers in the target demographic will pay a higher price than what the seller previously anticipated. The task facing alert entrepreneurial planners may fairly be described as one of anticipating latent, emerging, or future consumer wants, which are currently not satisfied with substitute goods, and which consumers often will be unable to articulate explicitly. Entrepreneurs assume the risk of bringing the good to market in hopes consumer wants will be satisfied and fulfilled to the extent consumers reward the entrepreneur, not merely with sales, but with profits. Although often taken as prima facie evidence of capitalist exploitation of consumers and labor, the existence of entrepreneurial profits actually demonstrates that the value of a product to the consumer exceeds what the consumer pays for it, which in turn exceeds the cost of production. It is actually a partial measure of the benefit of the product captured by the consumer.

Obviously the entrepreneurial alertness necessary to overcome the over-pessimistic mistaken beliefs and misinformation of Knowledge Problem B calls for and requires a far deeper and more uncommon form of awareness and risk management than is provided by simply monitoring inventory levels. Once entrepreneurial planners realize the product is more desired by consumers than other, less alert entrepreneurs previously believed or anticipated, the most alert entrepreneurs can now respond appropriately by bringing the good to market at a higher asking price than what they previously believed the market would bear. The sellers who do this create the initial market for the good, and initially enjoy a monopoly until and unless they are followed by imitative new entrants (Kirzner 1963: 310). There is no question that the conventional equilibrium account of Knowledge Problem B is far less complete and satisfactory than the market process account.

For completeness, next suppose the same two knowledge problems occur, but now assume they originate with misinformation on the part of the buyers rather than sellers. For Knowledge Problem A, this means the buyer is overly optimistic and mistakenly believes or expects the price sellers are willing to accept is lower than it actually is. Some higher price, which the sellers will willingly accept, will clear the market in equilibrium, but the buyers' over-optimism leads them to offer and search for a price which is lower than what is necessary to clear the market. This mistake on the part of the buyers creates a shortage of the product. Once again, from the view of conventional microeconomics, resolving the dis-equilibrium is simply a matter of adjusting the buyer's offer price upward until the shortage condition is alleviated and the market finally clears. However, from the perspective of market process, some degree of entrepreneurial alertness, even awareness of a fairly low order, is required for the sellers to notice that there is a shortage of the product. This may simply be a matter of monitoring inventory levels at the factory or warehouse and observing that they are falling below normal or desired levels, or it may involve gathering extensive information from a network of many geographically spread out retail outlets.

Once entrepreneurial planners realize that there is a shortage of their product, they can now respond by raising the price and the rate of production. If the current sellers do not make this adjustment, they leave the door open for the more alert entrepreneurs among their competitors to preempt this opportunity, and capture market share at the expense of the laggards who fail to notice changes in their own inventory levels, or who fail to make appropriate adjustments to price and output. Adjustment to equilibrium market clearing can also come from buyer behavior, as buyers who desire the product will eventually recognize that there is a shortage of the product and start bidding up the price, which ensures producers will eventually supply a larger quantity.

The market process account of overcoming Knowledge Problem A starts with entrepreneurial alertness on the part of those individuals among the consumer-buyers who are initially most alert to the shortage condition. This will generally be most keenly felt, and be manifested first, among those consumers who desire the product the most and are willing to pay the highest price for it. So it seems quite natural for them to be the first to notice and address the shortage's immediate local impact on their welfare and consumption plans. They are most likely to start offering higher prices to ensure some access to the limited supply. As the price is bid up, the shortage condition is alleviated. As before, when Knowledge Problem A originated from misinformation or mistaken beliefs among the buyers, the market process account is basically a more detailed way of describing exactly the same adjustment toward equilibrium as is provided by the market equilibrium account.

Finally, consider the case of Knowledge Problem B still rooted in over-pessimistic misinformation on the part of buyers rather than sellers. Here the buyer mistakenly believes or expects the price sellers will require is higher than it actually is. Some lower price, which the sellers will willingly accept in reality, would potentially clear the market. Here however, the buyers' over-pessimism leads them, not to set their offer price higher than what would clear the market, which would create a surplus, but to refrain from shopping for the good or including it in their purchase and consumption plans in the first place. This mistake on the part of the buyers creates what can be theoretically be described as an absolute surplus of the product—if any is brought to market, no one buys it. From the perspective of conventional comparative-static microeconomics, resolving the dis-equilibrium and getting the market to clear is once again no longer simply a matter of adjusting the price downward until the surplus condition is removed and the market clears. There is no market for this product available to clear. Although sellers may be trying to sell this product, there are no buyers willing to purchase or bid for it. The mistaken anticipation of too high a price has resulted in the product being excluded from buyers' planned consumption. Though the product might potentially satisfy consumer wants, it is not on their radar. In some cases unsold inventories will have to be disposed of at a loss, but in other cases no inventories of this product were produced in the first place.

The misinformation and mistaken beliefs the buyers act on now prevent any possibility of resolving the shortfall in output through a mere adjustment to equilibrium. However, from the perspective of market process, entrepreneurial alertness is required for the sellers to notice that the product might potentially satisfy consumer wants. Alert entrepreneurs will now have to map out a plan which takes advantage of the fact that the product is actually more desired by consumers, that appropriate marketing and advertising might inform and persuade consumers of the product's potential benefits, and that consumers may willingly buy it at a price at which sellers will willingly offer it for sale. Once again, this realization always calls for a deeper form of entrepreneurial awareness and risk taking than simply monitoring inventory levels and observing the surplus condition. Once entrepreneurial planners realize the product can actually or might potentially be sold at a profit at a price consumers will willingly pay, they can now respond appropriately by bringing the good to market at an asking price which clears the market because it is equal to the offer price sellers would have actually set in the first place. The sellers who do this create the initial market for the good, and initially enjoy a monopoly until and unless they are followed by imitative new entrants (Ellig 1994).

From an equilibrium perspective, Knowledge Problem A, where the over-optimistic buyer mistakenly expects the seller's asking price will be lower than it actually is, or the over-optimistic seller mistakenly expects the buyer's offer price will be higher than it actually is, creates situations of dis-equilibrium which are generally temporary and self-correcting. When dis-equilibrium prices result from Knowledge Problem A, these dis-equilibria can be removed, usually rather easily and transparently, by the normal response of buyers and sellers to conditions of shortage and surplus. For example, whenever over-optimistic buyers mistakenly expect the seller's asking price will be lower than it actually is, there is a temporary mismatch between the seller's higher asking price and the buyer's lower offer price. The seller's higher asking price will clear the market, but the fact that the buyer's offer price is lower results in a shortage. The shortage is temporary until some buyers bid up the price and the market clears. The buyers who bid up their offer price are the alert entrepreneurial planners in this case, and they are rewarded with the benefit of obtaining the product first and initially at a lower price, than will be available later to other consumers.

Similarly, whenever over-optimistic sellers mistakenly expect the buyer's offer price will be higher than it actually turns out to be, the temporary mismatch is still between the seller's higher asking price and the buyer's lower offer price, but now it is the buyer's lower offer price which will clear the market. This mismatch causes a temporary surplus, which will only be resolved when some sellers—who are the most alert entrepreneurs in this group—lower their asking price until the market clears. The most alert entrepreneurs who reduce prices first are rewarded with the first sales, perhaps at lower profits that they had once hoped for and anticipated. In contrast, the less alert entrepreneurs, who do not lower their asking prices initially, will face the condition that the longer they delay lowering their asking price, the more they will have to reduce the price when they finally do so, and until or unless they do so, they will be unable to sell their product at all.

In instances of Knowledge Problem B, problems of over-pessimism, sellers' over-pessimistic but mistaken belief that buyers are not willing to pay as much for a certain good or service as buyers actually are, leads potential sellers not to even enter the market. Since buyers will actually pay a higher price which would actually clear the market, this condition also creates a shortage, but in an even more extreme outcome, the market for this product never develops. Or buyers' over-pessimistic but equally mistaken belief that the sellers' asking price will be higher than what sellers will actually accept causes the potential buyers to never search for the product. In the face of Knowledge Problem B, markets never clear, not even eventually, because under these circumstances, the goods are either never brought to market in the first place, or potential consumers never shop or search for them.

The competitive equilibrium account is more satisfactory in explaining how Knowledge Problem A can be overcome than in addressing Knowledge Problem B. It is actually the market process deficiencies in the underlying information and beliefs of potential buyers and sellers which creates both Knowledge Problems. From a market process perspective, Knowledge Problem A, where the over-optimistic buyer mistakenly expects the seller's asking price will be lower than it actually is, or the over-optimistic seller mistakenly expects the buyer's offer price will be higher than it actually is, both result from information deficiencies. It is insufficient and insufficiently shared

information which permits one group, buyers or sellers, to form systematically over-optimistic beliefs. It may actually be more precise
to refer to an information asymmetry than mere deficiencies, because
the information available to buyers and sellers permits one group to
form over-optimistic beliefs and expectations, but does not permit a
symmetrical over-optimism to take root in the other group.

Recall that from the equilibrium perspective, the temporary dis-equilibrium brought about by Knowledge Problem A is naturally removed
by the normal response of buyers and sellers to conditions of shortage
and surplus. The temporary mismatch between the seller's higher asking
price and the buyer's lower offer price creates a shortage condition,
because the seller's higher asking price will clear the market, but the
fact that the buyer's offer price is lower results in a shortage. The
shortage is temporary until some buyers bid up the price and the market
clears. From a market process perspective, the buyers have to be led
by the most alert entrepreneurs among them in recognizing first that
their over-optimistic expectations have not been realized, and second
that the seller's asking price is not as low as they had initially hoped.
The buyers are the group who have to adjust their price expectations
upward, because they are the group that initially suffered from the
over-optimism.

Or the sellers have to recognize that their price expectations were
wrong and overly optimistic, and that buyers will not actually pay a
price as high as the buyers had mistakenly hoped. In this instance of
Knowledge Problem A, the sellers have to adjust their price expectations downward and lower their asking price. They have to adjust
their expectations and behavior because they are the group which
had initially suffered from the over-optimism. These market process
and equilibrium accounts of how Knowledge Problem A is overcome

are best understood as two complementary descriptions of the same process, which results in the same outcome.

In the case of Knowledge Problem B, problems of over-pessimism, sellers' over-pessimistic but mistaken belief that buyers are not willing to pay as much for a certain good or service as buyers actually are, leads potential sellers not to even enter the market. Because the sellers never offer the product for sale, there is really no equilibrium or dis-equilibrium to discuss. Only market process can observe or explain the information asymmetry which leads the over-pessimistic sellers to refrain initially from offering the good for sale at all, since they mistakenly believe it cannot be sold at a profit. When Knowledge Problem B originates from the buyers' mistakenly over-pessimistic beliefs or expectations about seller behavior, this leads the over-pessimistic buyers to never desire or shop for the product in the first place, since they mistakenly believe the asking price will exceed the potential benefits they would potentially hope to receive from the product. Knowledge Problem B describes the situation of all unknown, not yet devised or marketed products, because for products of which potential buyers are ignorant, for them the potential benefits are zero. For an unknown or not-yet-existing product, buyers are ignorant of potential benefits, as they are ignorant of the potential existence of the product in the first place, since it does not yet exist. When such new products are introduced, their benefits typically have to be extolled through advertising to introduce the product and its purported benefits to potential consumers.

Equilibrium theories of competitive markets, whether partial or general equilibria, suffer from numerous and familiar limitations and departures from reality. In reality, the most successful entrepreneurs are alert to the market dis-equilibria the neoclassical model assumes away, and alert entrepreneurs profit from removing these through arbitrage and the introduction of new products. Entrepreneurs are always alert to the potential existence of multiple dis-equilibrium prices and quantities which may prevail in any real world market, and only the alertness of these entrepreneurs to potential profit opportunities, combined with their willingness to act on that knowledge through assuming risk, can bring a real market toward a single competitive equilibrium (Kirzner 1963: 271). Furthermore, real market equilibria are not only multiple targets, but always moving targets, as the market conditions underlying any market clearing equilibrium are constantly in flux. These moving targets are probably never actually reached, and if they ever are, are neither sustainable nor persistent. Changing market conditions move markets out of equilibrium, as profit-seeking entrepreneurs first exercise awareness of the changed conditions, and second, experiment with new business plans aiming at greater allocative efficiency and greater coordination with the plans of others.

A key feature of a successful entrepreneurial plan is that it succeeds only to the extent it improves the mutual coordination among the entrepreneurial plans of others (Kirzner 1996: 38-42). Every other individual in society constructs implicit plans for the production and consumption they intend to engage in. These are all instances of entrepreneurial plans, and all can only succeed if they can be mutually coordinated and simultaneously brought to fulfillment or completion. The entrepreneurial act of modifying a plan on which other plans have been designed to coordinate creates new dis-equilibria and initially spreads discoordination throughout the economy, also creating new opportunities for temporary arbitrage profits—but only for entrepreneurs who are alert to the new and temporary opportunity. Nevertheless, any successful change in an entrepreneurial plan, though it initially disrupts the coordination which existed beforehand with the interdependent entrepreneurial plans of others, in the near-long run, always makes possible a higher level of overall coordination and want satisfaction throughout the economy.

CHAPTER 3

How Market Process Theory Came to be set Aside in Favor of Equilibrium Views

In one form or another, market process was the original focus of economics, and was particularly well-developed among economists who preceded Adam Smith, particularly Richard Cantillon and Anne Robert Jacques Turgot. Smith did not downplay market process so much as take it for granted by assuming the operations of the entrepreneur occurred in a more-or-less automatic fashion. Smith's relative neglect of the entrepreneur led many subsequent economists to systematically undervalue the entrepreneur and their contributions to constructing and maintaining the market order. Smith's most important popularizer in France, Jean-Baptiste Say, reintroduced the entrepreneur and extended the analysis of market process by building on the work of Cantillon and Turgot. If Say had remained more influential over a longer period of time, it seems likely that market process concepts would never have been eclipsed.

The next landmark works of economics, which held sway for decades, especially in the English-speaking world, were by David

Ricardo and John Stuart Mill. Following Smith, they both downplayed the role of the entrepreneur or entrepreneurial planner. Though their analyses of the incentives faced by economic agents, principally workers, landlords, capitalists, and consumers, were penetrating and largely accurate, by leaving out the entrepreneur, they left major gaps in their accounts of how markets work and what they do.

Alfred Marshall, one of the co-inventors of marginal analysis along with Carl Menger and Léon Walras, followed the tradition of Smith, Ricardo, and Mill in disregarding the role of the entrepreneurial planner. Marshall's *Principles of Economics* (1890) originated the kind of modern static equilibrium analysis which focuses on market outcomes, but does so largely to the exclusion of market process. As the discipline of economics developed further throughout the twentieth century, it became increasingly formalized, increasingly mathematical, and in many ways divorced from reality. This chapter will outline that process and discuss some of its consequences.

3.1 Cantillon: the Entrepreneur as Risk Bearer

Writing almost a full generation before Adam Smith, the Irish-French banker and statesman Richard Cantillon (1680-1734)[4] relied extensively on his own practical business experience in framing a sophisticated theory of the entrepreneur in his *Essai sur la Nature du Commerce en Général*. For political reasons, this path-breaking work remained unpublished at Cantillon's death in 1734, though many manuscript copies circulated privately among the economic cognoscenti. The *Essai* was finally published in 1755. Cantillon's (1755: 73-77) account of entrepreneurship is founded on a very stylized model of agricultural production, and employs a plausible though somewhat arbitrary rule of thumb about how the proceeds of agriculture should be divided among the providers of the productive resources which contributed to the process of production. According to Cantillon, farmers rent agricultural land at a cost to them of approximately one-third the expected value of the agricultural yield. Based on this rule of thumb, Cantillon develops his theory of the three rents for agriculture (1755: 66, 124). Out of the expected value of the final output, one third is either paid up front or promised on credit to the landlord, or to the lender if the

---

4 The Cantillon effect in monetary economics is named for him. If the supply of money increases, the real impact is focused on whatever the people who receive the new money spend it on, increasing demand for that output, thus increasing the amount produced and the price of those products. As the added new money becomes further dispersed throughout the economy, other prices are driven up, though to a lesser extent the farther one looks from the point and time of the original injection of new money. The industries which produce products bought by the original recipients of the new money expand, and all the other industries contract because the general increase in prices results in consumers being unable to buy as much real output as they could before. Cantillon was the first to identify the real effects of inflation and understand why they would be focused on particular sectors of the economy.

crop is planted on credit. One third is paid to the agricultural workers who plant, cultivate, and harvest the crop for their labor, and this amount generally has to be advanced to them up front by the farmer. The remaining third is retained by the farmer as profits, but keep in mind the farmer's prospective profits are only one third of the expected yield. If the crop fails or cannot be sold for the anticipated price, the farmer may incur a loss.

In Cantillon's account, the farmer-entrepreneur is exposed to significant risk because the costs of production are always fixed in advance, and in most cases must be advanced prior to reaping and selling the harvest. The sales value of the crop cannot be known in advance, and could turn out to be significantly lower than what the farmer might hope for, due to either a bad growing season or to suddenly unfavorable market conditions. If the farmer's yield turns out to be lower than expected, the shortfall comes first out of the farmer's profits. Wealthier gentlemen farmers who own their own land and do not have to rent from a landlord face the decisive advantage that they can retain two thirds of the expected future value of their output. If the farmer needed funds to be advanced in order to plant the crop, then one third of the expected value will be paid after the harvest to lenders in the form of interest and principal, provided the revenue from the sale of the harvest is sufficient to repay the interest and principal on the loan. Thus, people who lend or otherwise advance funds to the farmer-entrepreneur assume a share of the risk, and should require compensation in the form of interest. If a landlord were to refrain from requiring payment from the farmer up front at the start of the planting season, and would be willing to wait until after the harvest was brought in and sold to receive payment, they would share this risk with the farmer and any lenders. Notice particularly that the farmer's expenses are always fixed in advance, though in the case of interest and in some cases rent, they may not come due until after the harvest.

Cantillon views the farmer as an entrepreneurial risk taker, because the farmer assumes the principal burden of uncertainty—there may be a drought or pestilence which destroys the crop, making it more difficult, and perhaps impossible, to pay what is owed to the lenders and landlord after the harvest. If this happens, a smaller residual profit will be left over for the farmer, if anything. The farmer also faces uncertainty in his choice of which combination of crops to plant. He should try to choose the combination that will sell for the highest price once it is delivered for sale in the market in the future, but this also cannot be known in advance. The farmer faces the burden of selecting the right crops to plant in the face of climate and market conditions which are variable, uncertain, and unknowable in advance.

Even if the farmer is blessed with a perfect growing season which guarantees a physically abundant yield, the relative glut of output which results after such a bountiful harvest may prove equally ruinous, as the increase in supply will tend to depress the selling price of the agricultural output. Therefore, the farmer is further exposed to risk because the market conditions in which the output is sold may vary substantially, and this cannot be known in advance any better than the weather conditions. Regardless of how sound or conscientious the farmer's entrepreneurial planning and decisions about the choice of output, composition of output, production methods, amount, kind, and quality of labor, employment of complementary resources, etc., the farmer is still exposed to risk. There is always the risk that the market conditions will be less favorable than anticipated or hoped for when it is time to sell the harvest.

Cantillon goes on to sketch the contributions of other entrepreneurs who occupy different niches later in the production process; for example, arbitrageurs who purchase agricultural goods in the country after harvest at a definite price, thus unburdening the farmers from some of the uncertainty they would still subsequently face as long as they held on to this output. These arbitrageurs assume some of the risk for the farmers. This is due to the fact that, although the price the arbitrageurs pay for the product is known and fixed at the time they buy it from the farmers, the arbitrageurs cannot know in advance what price they will be able to sell their goods in the city, or how rapidly they will be able to sell these goods.

The arbitrageurs' contribution is that they enable the farmers to lock in a certain profit—or loss—at some time prior to the sale of the output to the consumer. The arbitrageurs shield the farmers they buy from, from subsequent market risk that the price may fall, or risk of subsequent loss, theft, or spoilage. This benefits the farmers because they can avoid both some of the risk that they would otherwise be exposed to, and the transportation costs necessary to bring their product to the city. The arbitrageurs may sell the produce directly to consumers in the city, but Cantillon notes that other arbitraging merchants are also set up in the cities to purchase the country produce from the first set of arbitraging middlemen, to relieve these middlemen in turn of some of *their* burden of uncertainty. This next layer of enterprising, risk-bearing entrepreneurs will offer the produce for sale at retail or wholesale over a longer period of time. Although the benefit of the second set of middlemen being located permanently in the city as shopkeepers is somewhat limited for perishable agricultural produce, it is more substantial for less perishable products such as wine, dried grain, milled flour, sheared wool, butchered meat, etc.

As before with the farmers and the original arbitrageurs, it is always the current possessors of the output who assume all the uncertainty going forward of what the market conditions will be when they are able to sell the product to the next purchaser. The entrepreneur who owns and possesses commodities for sale also incurs all risks of theft, loss, spoilage, changing market conditions, etc., as long they own the product and keep it in their possession. When an entrepreneur sells output to others, at that point in time the sale locks in a certain realized profit or loss, which removes further uncertainty at that point, but also removes any beneficial possibility of realizing greater profits or losses on the same units of output. The profit on the entrepreneurs' sale of commodities is the selling price minus the original purchase price paid by the entrepreneur, minus any carrying, transport, storage, processing, interest, or overhead costs.

Cantillon sees the essence of entrepreneurship as facing and accepting the certain fixed and sunk cost that the entrepreneur pays up front for the goods they purchase, or in the case of farmers the cost of planting for cultivation, in the face of the uncertain future sales. This uncertainty is introduced by the unknown and unknowable future sales price, as well as by the precise timing of the future sales, which only become apparent in the fullness of time. This is equally true whether the entrepreneur purchases or produces the goods for pure arbitrage or further processing to add additional value. Further uncertainty is introduced by the generally unknown timing of the final sale—goods that sell quickly do not carry as much uncertainty for the entrepreneur as goods which languish on the shelves. If perishable, these goods may ultimately spoil and have to be written off as a total loss.

To the extent the entrepreneurial planner succeeds in their enterprise and earns a profit, they have successfully overcome these various obstacles, not the least of which are uncertainty and risk. An entrepreneur-arbitrageur who buys goods and is able to sell them later the same day at a ten percent markup should congratulate themselves on doing spectacularly well. Their annualized return on this transaction is astronomical, and if they can repeat the process many times they will rapidly amass tremendous wealth. A further benefit comes from the brief holding time between the entrepreneur's initial purchase and the sale, which results in exposing them to minimal risk. The same entrepreneur who sells the same goods with a hundred percent markup, but only after a year, is not getting anywhere near the same return. The longer an entrepreneur-arbitrageur has to hold the goods they deal in, the lower the actual return. A ten percent return after a day or even a month is generally outstanding, but a ten percent return after one year may not cover overhead, rent, taxes, interest, etc., to provide either a profit or a return which matches the most conservative financial instruments.

3.2 Turgot: Savings and the Capitalist-Entrepreneur

Anne Robert Jacques Turgot (1727-1781) extended Cantillon's theory of entrepreneurship (Turgot 1766, 2011). He noted that the managers of productive activities, which might include both farmers and manufacturers, were what Turgot called capitalist-entrepreneurs. Turgot pointed out the importance of saving out of past output. In his view, this class of entrepreneurial planners have to first accumulate savings in order to advance wages to the laborers they employ, prior to the final output being produced or harvested, and before it can be sold to generate additional revenue. Without the capitalist-entrepreneur's own savings or capital,[5] or without their being able to borrow the savings of others, constraints on cash flow would prevent most productive activities from ever taking place. The only exception would be the very unusual kind of production which could produce immediate cash revenue. For example, agriculture could not be financed at all without the savings of the capitalist-entrepreneurs who lend to advance rents to the landlord, wages to the agricultural workers, and purchase seed corn and other supplies. As in Cantillon's account of agricultural production, the farmer has to pay workers at the beginning of the growing season to prepare the soil and plant the crop, perhaps perform some maintenance activities throughout the growing season, and at the end of the season, to bring in the harvest. These agricultural workers will not generally agree to work in the spring and through the summer, and still not be paid until after the crop is harvested in the autumn. Normally, the workers need to be paid up front as the work is done.

Similarly for a manufacturing activity, the output does not produce any revenue until it is sold. Turgot's capitalist-entrepreneur has to pay their factory workers up front for each hour of labor the workers

---

5 Today we distinguish carefully between financial capital and physical capital. Financial capital is money savings which has not yet been spent to purchase productive assets. Physical capital is productive assets such as buildings, tools, machines, and equipment which have been purchased with financial capital. Financial capital is not productive until it is used to purchase physical capital. Turgot describes entrepreneurial planners as capitalist-entrepreneurs because it is their accumulated saving, which directly constitutes financial capital, that enables them to purchase and acquire the productive physical capital which they use to carry out their entrepreneurial plans. Turgot's use of the term capital is primarily to refer to financial capital, thus he notes that the entrepreneur must have access to some saved wealth before they can acquire the physical capital required for their entrepreneurial plan. One exception is for farmers who grow grain, in the case that they might save some of last year's harvest as seed corn to plant the next year's crop. This is also a form of saving, but in this case consists of a physical rather than a financial asset.

provide over the whole course of the production process. Since, like agricultural workers, factory workers generally do not work on credit, their wages and the other upfront costs of manufacturing have to be financed by some form of saving. This circumstance that the producer incurs certain known costs up front, but does not necessarily know when the final sales of their product will take place or at what selling price, is one of the reasons entrepreneurs assume and are exposed to risk. They need to be rewarded for doing so, at least potentially rewarded if and only if they succeed, or they will never assume the risks of engaging in an entrepreneurial venture in the first place. Capitalist-entrepreneurs must have a plausible expectation that they will probably be able to sell their output in the future at a profit, but they can have no guarantee that market conditions will be as favorable as these entrepreneurial planners might have hoped when they formed their plans and entered into the production process.

In addition to saving funds in the past to meet future worker payroll, Turgot's capitalist-entrepreneurs also rely on saved funds to purchase input resources they need, such as supplies, buildings, tools, equipment, and any other physical assets or commodities; that is, the physical capital required to implement the production plan they have envisioned and designed. These saved funds must come either from the capitalist-entrepreneur's own accumulated savings, or they must be borrowed on credit out of someone else's savings. When the savings are borrowed, in this case the lender becomes an implicit participant in the capitalist-entrepreneur's venture, and assumes some share of the risk, though generally less than what is assumed by the capitalist-entrepreneur. If the entrepreneurial venture subsequently goes wrong, the capitalist-entrepreneur may not be able to repay the borrowed funds, and the lender can potentially lose everything they have advanced to the entrepreneur.[6] In either case, the capitalist-entrepreneur relies on the presence or existence of some accumulated savings set aside from past income, whether it is their own savings, or those of someone else who lends to them.

Turgot's capitalist-entrepreneurs, who accumulate savings over time, also seek the highest return on their savings. If they believe their own entrepreneurial plan will have the highest yield or at least is likely to have the highest yield, they will use their own savings to finance their own entrepreneurial plan, investing their own savings in their own vision. However, if they can be persuaded instead that the entrepreneurial plan of some other capitalist-entrepreneur will offer a higher return or perhaps even just a safer or more likely return, they will generally lend their own saved funds to this other capitalist-entrepreneur whose project is expected to yield a higher or more certain return. The key to this outcome that the capitalist-entrepreneur lends their savings to another is that the potential lender has to be persuaded of the higher likely return, not the prospective borrower.

Turgot (2011: 54-58) also proposes a hierarchy of interest rates and

---

6 Turgot discusses the process of lending to an entrepreneurial planner as an activity which is primarily done person-to-person from lender to borrower. In his account there are no banks or other financial intermediaries which take deposits from savers and lend them to entrepreneurs. Turgot was a banker himself and understood the process, but his account is more simplified. Today banks act to shield an individual depositor from most of the exposure to default risk that comes when the bank lends money to an entrepreneurial planner to finance a new venture. If the borrowing entrepreneur's new venture fails, the bank loses the principal on the loan plus any unpaid interest, minus what they can recover from the enterprise's liquidation. Here, the bank is assuming all the risk of the loan, not the depositors, and in most cases individual saver-depositors are entirely shielded from this entrepreneurial risk assumed by their banks. Venture capitalists who invest their own funds are more exposed to this risk of enterprise failure. Often, individual venture capitalists will try to spread this risk by enlisting additional investors.

market rates of return. The return on purchasing land is the lowest, though it is always expected to be positive, at least before the fact; the market loan interest rate to finance consumption spending and other unproductive activities should be higher; and because of the greater risk involved, the return on money advanced for agricultural, commercial, and manufacturing loans should be the greatest. Turgot's view here seems more embryonic than sophisticated or fully developed, but it seems to capture modern views that lenders should require, and borrowers be willing to pay, a higher return on riskier loans. This is the basis of the pure expectations theory of interest rates (Fisher 1896, Lutz 1940, Herbener 2011), which Turgot anticipated but did not develop further. Turgot also argues that these yields on different categories of loans cannot vary too greatly, because if they did, any large spread that might develop among different kinds of interest-bearing loans, deposits, or financial instruments would create arbitrage opportunities which alert entrepreneurs would eventually exploit to close the spread. This view of Turgot anticipated the more modern preferred habitat theory of interest rates (Modigliani & Sutch 1966).

3.3 Adam Smith & the Invisible Entrepreneur

The idea of a competitive equilibrium in the product market for a single well-defined good or service emerged in Adam Smith's *Wealth of Nations* (1776), and was developed further in David Ricardo's On the *Principles of Political Economy and Taxation* (1817), and John Stuart Mill's *Principles of Political Economy* (1848). Smith, Ricardo, and Mill further refined the description of the processes through which markets employed prices to guide entrepreneurial planners in allocating productive resources to satisfy consumer wants. The production, distribution, and final sale of the output is directed in pursuit of higher profits and more productive employment of available resources, all of which respond to the incentives for better fulfilling consumer wants. Through input and output prices, the competitive market develops, deploys, transmits, and processes information about resource availability and scarcity, production technology, and consumer wants. Alert entrepreneurs compete to read and interpret these signals, acting in accordance with them to earn the highest profits.

Adam Smith (1723-1790) introduces the division of labor, which is certainly one of the most important concepts in, and contributions to, economics. Specializing in those tasks in which we have a comparative advantage enables us to produce more for exchange with others than we would need for our own use, and the fact that no one produces all the goods they consume enables a greater quantity, quality, and variety of output to be produced for consumption, and in a more economical way. However, Smith neglects the entrepreneur, especially compared to the central role which Cantillon and Turgot had already identified for them.

The Wealth of Nations' Book 1, Chapter 9, Of the Profits of Stock, does not address how Turgot's capitalist-entrepreneurs employ their savings to take risks by introducing productive innovations. To Smith, stocks of agricultural produce or manufactured goods are clearly a form of physical savings, but if these stocks have accumulated as unplanned additions to inventory, they can only contribute to depressing prices and everyone's rate of profit, as a symptom of oversupply of a particular product. Smith acknowledges that the size of the capital stock, by which he means the amount of physical capital used by the workers; that is, machines, equipment, tools, etc. contributes to higher labor wages because it enables workers to be more productive. He recognizes that various countries become wealthier and more productive at different rates and to different extents, but he does not attribute any of these differences to the countries' offering better or worse environments for entrepreneurship.

In Smith's Book 1, Chapter 10, Of Wages and Profits in the Different Employments of Labour and Stock, he does recognize that business owners assume risks, engage in disagreeable activities on behalf of their customers, for which they should receive greater compensation, and provide convenient services to their customers. Smith sees the operation of a business as a more or less deterministic process, and though he understands business owners assume and are subject to risks, he does not discuss entrepreneurial innovation. Business owners assume the risks of operating their businesses and must be compensated for assuming market and physical risks. The rate of profit of a business is determined in part by the relative agreeableness or disagreeableness of the activity the business owner performs on behalf of, and for the benefit of, their customers, with more disagreeable activities calling for the highest profit. If the market does not somehow award a sufficient profit to the people who engage in disagreeable activities such as operating a butcher shop or coal mine, no one will undertake to enter this business, and the consuming public will either have to pay more for the product or learn to do without it. The convenience a business provides for their customers also contributes to determining the rate of profit, thus justifying higher rates of profit or markup for retailers than for wholesalers.

Smith returns to considerations of the productivity of capital in Book 2, Chapter 1, Of the Division of Stock, where he refers to capital stock as initially being financial capital or savings, which business owners convert to physical capital to be used for agriculture and manufacturing, and Chapter 3, Of the Accumulation of Capital, or of productive and unproductive Labour. Throughout his discussion, it is clear that business owners are subject to risk and uncertainty, some of which comes from uncertain future market conditions, and that business owners have to be compensated for their expertise and specialized knowledge. However, there is no real discussion of entrepreneurship or of the process of innovation in *The Wealth of Nations*. Smith adds tremendous detail to the treatment of many emerging economic concepts beyond what was understood or attempted by Cantillon or Turgot, but his treatment of entrepreneurship is a clear and unfortunate retreat from that developed by his predecessors.[7]

3.4 Say: Entrepreneurship as Production in the Face of Uncertainty

Jean-Baptiste Say (1767-1832) introduces the concept of the entrepreneur as the person who combines the factors of production, hitherto land, labor, and capital. Say (1803) is the individual who can be credited with recognizing a fourth factor of production, variously called management, entrepreneurship, entrepreneurial talent, entrepreneurial ability, or entrepreneurial planning. The term entrepreneurial planning is generally used throughout this book because it more accurately and completely describes and captures what the entrepreneur does, and

7 One reason why Smith is widely regarded as the father of economics is the extraordinary breadth of new concepts introduced in the *Wealth of Nations*, as well as his exhaustive treatment of numerous topics of continuing relevance. In comparison, Cantillon and Turgot's major works, though containing major contributions and which can still be read profitably today, are concise digests.

what they contribute to the firm and the production process. Say's contribution, though brief, is a major leap beyond even Cantillon and Turgot. Say was himself an entrepreneur, and sought to inject his own, real-world business experience into his reconstruction and presentation of the new Smithian system of economics. He is still considered the most important popularizer of Smith in the French language.

Say noted that some entrepreneurs own capital and some do not. All entrepreneurial planners must employ capital to manage the firm and implement an entrepreneurial plan to produce output. They may (a) use their own capital, or (b) lease equipment on credit from the actual owner, (c) borrow financial capital at interest from the actual owner, which they use to purchase or lease the physical capital they need, or (d) be hired by the owner of capital to manage the enterprise for the owner's benefit. When the entrepreneur is an employee of the capital owner, the profits generated by the entrepreneurial plan are shared between the entrepreneur and the capital owner. In this case it is the owner of capital who employs the entrepreneur who suffers any losses incurred due to failure of the entrepreneurial plan, but the entrepreneur's security as an employee would also be jeopardized.

As Turgot had noted, the entrepreneur hires the factors of production in advance at fixed cost, organizes production, and sells the output in the face of an uncertain future which only unfolds in the fullness of time. The entrepreneur incurs the risk of their planned production process not working out as anticipated or as called for in the entrepreneurial plan. They will normally respond to difficulties they encounter in carrying out an entrepreneurial plan by attempting to make technical adjustments as needed, or modifying the plan to respond to changing market conditions, especially changes in the market price of the output or inputs. The entrepreneur also incurs any risk of the future market conditions prevailing when the output is finally sold, which may have subsequently turned unfavorable. By the same token, if market conditions ultimately become more favorable at the right time, the entrepreneur will realize greater profits, basically through luck alone.

Entrepreneurial planners guard against the possibility of future market conditions turning unfavorable by monitoring them closely, and to the extent they are able, by responding appropriately. If market conditions affect the price of inputs into the production process, the entrepreneur should be alert to these changes, and respond by substituting relatively cheaper inputs for those that have become relatively more expensive, to the extent the substitution of inputs is technically feasible. If market conditions affect the price of the product, the entrepreneur can potentially substitute production of the newly more expensive product for units of an alternative output which has become relatively cheaper in the output markets. In extreme cases, an entrepreneur will shift production entirely and permanently from one product to another, because the new output will command a sustainably higher market price and provide the entrepreneur with higher profits. Say's view is that in this capacity the entrepreneur acts not merely as an arbitrageur, but also as a broker between buyers and sellers, and takes advantage of every opportunity to benefit from changes in market conditions to purchase the factors of production at the lowest prices, and sell the output most desired by final consumers or other intermediate buyers. This output which commands the highest price and provides the highest profits to the entrepreneur contributes the most to satisfying consumer wants. The entrepreneurs both profit from their actions as arbitrageurs and brokers, and share some of these benefits with the partners they transact with.

Although Say presumably had tremendous insight as a successful business practitioner, he is a bit vague on what makes a good entrepreneur or a successful one. Entrepreneurs must understand business and business processes well, and be alert to changing business conditions, but ideally they cannot be one dimensional, profit-seeking misers. The entrepreneur must have a knowledge of the world, patience, perseverance, sound judgement, etc. They must have the ability to calculate ever-changing costs as they hire employees and deal with their customers, and make decisions based on inchoate, inarticulable, implicit, forward-looking estimates or expectations of what future market demand for their product will be, or will be most likely to be. Say notes that the profit earned by an enterprise is an accounting quantity which cannot be known except after the fact. It consists of the return to capital, basically the market interest rate,[8] and an entrepreneurial profit. Say points out that entrepreneurs are always directed by consumer sovereignty and can only succeed to the extent they successfully anticipate future consumer demand. Thus alert entrepreneurs have to be vigilant to what consumers want and will buy. In Say's words, "The product most wanted is most in demand; and that which is most in demand yields the largest profit to industry, capital, and land, which are therefore employed in raising this particular product in preference; and vice versa, when a product becomes less in demand, there is less profit to be got by its production; it is therefore no longer produced (Say 1803: 394 [Book 3, ch. 1])."

---

8 The market interest rate is an opportunity cost for the entrepreneur who gives up the opportunity to earn interest on the funds he uses to finance an entrepreneurial venture, so it is subtracted from the accounting profit to arrive at the economic profit of the venture. The entrepreneur could earn the interest if he did not engage in the entrepreneurial activity, and has to give up or forego the opportunity to earn interest by lending the same amount to someone else or buying a bond.

3.5 Ricardo & Malthus: Production as a Deterministic Process

After Smith, David Ricardo's (1772-1823) *Principles of Political Economy and Taxation* (1821) became the leading English language economics text for a generation. Cantillon, Turgot, Smith, and Say all understood and addressed manufacturing enterprises; however, when they were writing, agriculture still accounted for a far larger proportion of most countries' national output, and England was the most advanced industrial economy in the world at this time. Ricardo also focuses on agriculture, especially noting that the limited availability of land imposes a hard limit on the amount of output that can be produced. Workers can produce more if they can be provided more capital equipment, which can only be financed out of the portion of past income earned on past production which is saved for that purpose rather than consumed. The amount that can be produced is strictly limited by the number of workers; that is, by a country's population, the amount of land available, and the amount of capital equipment. The operators of business enterprises can influence the amount of capital equipment through investing in its purchase, though the equipment wears out through depreciation as it is used.

Ricardo's treatment of production as a deterministic process which converts a fixed number and proportion of inputs into a precisely predetermined amount of output does not explicitly recognize any role for the entrepreneurial planner or for entrepreneurial innovation. His approach hearkens back to Cantillon's theory of the three rents in agricultural production, and it is important to realize that both are general observations or rules of thumb. Nevertheless, Ricardo's approach became the standard to be followed by subsequent theorists.[9] Holcombe (1998) argues that the Ricardian approach became the foundation for modern economic growth theory (Solow 1956).

In his first edition, Ricardo held that capital investment increased worker productivity and output. Investing in machines would lower the price of output, increase demand for resources, and raise worker wages, thus benefiting every strata of society. However, in his second and third editions, Ricardo added a Chapter 32, On Machinery, where he developed the argument that capital equipment could substitute for labor, and that it was possible for capital investment to both reduce the number of workers employed, and lower the wages paid to the remaining employed workers. He felt the competition from the newly unemployed workers would prevent those remaining employed from being able to capture any share of their increased productivity in the form of higher wages. Ricardo's view has been largely discredited.

The Reverend Thomas Robert Malthus (1766-1834), in his celebrated—or infamous—*Essay on the Principles of Population* (1798), had argued that population grows geometrically, while agricultural output can only grow arithmetically as more land is put under cultivation, and that this makes periodic famines and mass starvation

---

9 Eventually this would be formalized with the Cobb-Douglas aggregate production function, $Q = aL^bK^c$, where the amount of national output or GDP is a deterministic function of the amount of labor employed L and the amount of capital equipment K. The stock of physical capital K can be increased by consuming less of Q each year, and investing the amount saved in purchasing additional equipment. The amount of Q saved and not consumed each year is used to increase K for the following year. This enables a larger amount of Q to be produced year after year as long as K grows and L at least stays the same. The scale variable a can be used to represent the production technology, and this constant increases as technology improves. Ricardo described the process of production and economic growth in similar terms, but did not provide the algebraic formalism.

inevitable. Malthus also produced a *Principles of Political Economy* (1820). Improvements in agricultural technology were not included in his account of the production process. Perhaps more important than technological advances are the entrepreneurial innovations which spread technological improvements and discoveries throughout an economy, and provide additional efficiencies even in the absence of an improved technology. Malthus proved less influential than Ricardo, though he emphasized the importance of building the stock of capital equipment, investing in land improvement, and the persistence of market dis-equilibria (Sowell 1963). Malthus' belief that dis-equilibria could persist for some time anticipated Keynes' (1936) theory of general oversupply.

3.6 Mill: Entrepreneurs as Managers

Building on Smith and Ricardo, John Stuart Mill (1806-1873) constructed a more sophisticated version of the theory of the division of labor (Mill 1848). His Book 1, Chapter 8, Of Co-operation, or the Combination of Labor, seems as if it would have offered the perfect opportunity to reintroduce the theory of the entrepreneur. Instead, Mill was content here merely to express the advantages of the division of labor. He argues that an ever-expanding and more detailed level of specialization can bring about higher productivity, greater physical abundance, and a higher standard of living for a greater and ever growing number of workers and their families. The role of entrepreneurial planners in facilitating or directing cooperation among workers is overlooked. Mill writes here almost as if he believes that workers cooperate spontaneously under the incentive of earning potentially higher wages. Intentional choices on the part of workers which improve their productivity or enable them to earn higher wages would be examples of entrepreneurial alertness to these kinds of opportunities, but Mill overlooked this form of entrepreneurship. Workers spontaneously seek to improve their own productivity by further specialization and further expansion of the division of labor.[10] Mill did introduce the word entrepreneur from French into English. He acknowledges that entrepreneurs superintend, control, and direct firms and business enterprises (Schumpeter 1954: 556), but not that entrepreneurs innovate or even that they assume risk in the face of uncertainty. Mill sees entrepreneurs more as managers than innovators, and their work is only a specialized form of labor.

Adam Smith had advanced economics dramatically in many directions, but generally at the expense of any improved understanding of the entrepreneur. Ignoring the role of the entrepreneur, which had already been well acknowledged and developed by Cantillon, Turgot, and Say, seems to have begun with Smith, and continued by Ricardo and Mill. Although Mill did introduce the word entrepreneur into the English language, his view of entrepreneurship was largely restricted to passive management. Attempts to analyze what managers do tended to deemphasize their introduction of innovations. The question of the

---

10 Coase (1937) explains the existence of firms where the workers are employed as a mechanism to overcome transactions costs. Mill represents workers as if they are all independent contractors who negotiate directly with each other. Although entrepreneurial planners do not necessarily always work within firms, they often do. If the entrepreneur contracts directly with each worker without organizing a firm, this would not conflict with Coase unless the enterprise was sufficiently large to have high transactions costs so that the entrepreneur could gain significant efficiencies and lower transactions costs by organizing a firm. There is no entrepreneurial planner or even any firm in Mill's account of production in Book 1, Chapter 8.

source of innovation which results in the market and economy as it exists at any point in time was not really addressed.

3.7 The Rise of Static Equilibrium

By the middle of the 19th century, static equilibrium theories began to supplant the established, less formal descriptions of market process which had been developing in the literature. At this point the focus of microeconomics and price theory began to switch from the messier and less deterministic aspects of how people interact to best fulfill their subjective and diverse wants; that is, from market process, to increasingly formalized descriptions of what the final outcome should look like, and what mathematical conditions this outcome should satisfy. Gradually economics became a series of mathematical exercises detached from the observable reality of actual human behavior. The main reason for this evolution or retreat from reality is that any graphical or mathematical model is a simplified description of reality. In economic modeling, many confusing and complicating factors have to be assumed away, or in other words they are abstracted out of the model.

One of the most important things the static equilibrium model leaves out is the entrepreneur. This process of deemphasizing the entrepreneur might be seen to have been started by Adam Smith, who gives an account of market operation which is far less informed by the earlier and more entrepreneurially driven descriptions of market processes presented by Cantillon and Turgot. The comparative statics model assumes markets operate in equilibrium at all times—except we can see that in reality, markets are often out of equilibrium. For example, we can readily observe that gas stations frequently change prices in response to a change in the price charged by one of their nearby competitors, but not always, and often not instantaneously. Markets do not always obey the law of one price, and even where they do, they do not always do it right away. Sellers do not always change prices in lock-step with one another. Entrepreneurs are necessary to provide management, perform entrepreneurial planning, innovate, experiment, evaluate, assess, and take risks, etc., and are rewarded with profits—though if their innovations are unsuccessful and the firm suffers losses, the entrepreneur who is responsible may have to bear that burden as well.

Comparative statics, general equilibrium alternatives to viewing the market as a process of coordinating production, allocation, distribution began to dominate towards the end of the 1800s. William Stanley Jevons (1835-1882), Alfred Marshall (1842-1924), and others attempted to characterize market activity according to the formal characteristics of the theoretical outcome the market was supposed to arrive at and create, the competitive equilibrium, and the properties these scholars could identify and ascribe to these outcomes. This approach was more amenable to formal mathematical analysis and quantification, and initially the loss of realism was perhaps not terribly apparent in the excitement of an emerging new discipline. The process through which equilibrium prices and quantities are reached, approached, or approximated through market exchange came to be increasingly ignored in favor of the final destination of the market-clearing price and quantities—the equilibrium (Arrow 1994).

In the real world however, it is always the entrepreneurial planners who experiment with changing prices, sometimes moving the market out of equilibrium, sometimes moving it toward equilibrium. When entrepreneurs test a presumed or potential equilibrium by experimentally changing the price, they find out if shortage or surplus conditions are introduced, or if they are alleviated, completely remedied, or further aggravated. Markets would never be able to reach any reference equilibrium if entrepreneurs were not constantly experimenting with price adjustments to see if there might be any way for the firm to eke out some additional profit or provide some additional benefit to additional groups of consumers. Though this form of competitive behavior is often viewed as predatory and immoral (for example, St. Thomas Aquinas, *Summa Theologica*, 2-2, q. 77), the firm is only able to earn added profits to the extent some consumer wants are better satisfied.

Entrepreneurs also employ strategies such as modifying their products incrementally, bundling two or more products, and introducing completely new products. Their motivation is to extract additional profits, but they cannot succeed in this unless their innovation provides some added benefits for the buyer. In performing these functions, entrepreneurs make market process happen. They do not merely direct production within the firm, as Mill noted, but also facilitate and empower market process to improve human welfare. They disrupt existing equilibria, which the market may not yet even have successfully arrived at, moving the target for market equilibration to a new location. Other entrepreneurs, to the extent they are alert to emerging entrepreneurial opportunities, adjust their plans in response to their perceptions of the changed market conditions now being moved farther out of equilibrium, and they alter their entrepreneurial plans continuously to make possible greater mutual plan coordination, which they all profit from, and which further benefits consumers (Kirzner 1996: 39-41). The new equilibrium will be approached incrementally, but only as entrepreneurs adjust their plans, experimenting with price adjustments and new products. Consumers follow the lead of the entrepreneurs to better satisfy their wants, until a new disruptive innovation dislocates the market to a new center of gravity—the new target equilibrium (Lewin 1997).

Entrepreneurial action and innovation are everywhere in the real world, especially in real world competitive markets, but are nowhere to be found in the neoclassical model of competitive equilibrium. Entrepreneurship starts with information—this may be information which no one else has noticed or made use of, or information which supports beliefs and expectations held by no one else who is competing in this market. Or, it may be information combined with what is known uniquely by a particular entrepreneur to form an idiosyncratic information set unique to that entrepreneur, and on which they formulate their plans. Because each entrepreneur has distinct characteristics, perceptions, expectations, experience, etc., each entrepreneur will generally identify different speculative profit opportunities, and pursue unique and idiosyncratic courses of action. This results in markets evolving over time in non-deterministic ways, as the random circumstances of which items of information are applied by various competing entrepreneurs evolves randomly, though entrepreneurs always aim at earning higher profits by better satisfying consumer wants at lower cost. Entrepreneurs are disciplined by the profit and loss incentives which determine which entrepreneurial ventures succeed and dominate at any point in time (Ikeda 1994: 23-24).

3.8 Menger: Entrepreneurship in the Austrian School

Carl Menger (1840-1921), founder of the Austrian school of economics, included thorough discussions of the entrepreneur in his principal work, the *Grundesätze der Volkswirthschaftslehre* or *Principles of Economics* (1871). Menger distinguishes between goods of higher and lower order. Consumers use goods of the lowest order, first order goods, to satisfy their wants directly, for example, by plucking an apple directly from the tree to eat immediately. Entrepreneurs use various higher order goods to produce lower order goods with the ultimate goal of profiting by eventually satisfying consumer wants with some first order goods the consumer will pay for. The more additional services which still have to be added under entrepreneurial supervision before the final product can be used to satisfy consumer wants, the higher the order of the good (Menger 1871: 157, n. 18).

Menger dissects the role of the entrepreneur into four components: "(a) obtaining *information* about the economic situation; (b) economic *calculation*—all the various computations that must be made if a production process is to be efficient (provided that it is economic in other respects); (c) the *act of will* by which goods of higher order (or goods in general—under conditions of developed commerce, where any economic good can be exchanged for any other) are assigned to a particular production process;[11] and finally (d) *supervision* of the execution of the production play so that it may be carried through as economically as possible (1871: 160 emphasis in original)." Menger's entrepreneurial planners are alert to information, prevailing business conditions, and potential opportunities (Kirzner 1978). They employ input and output price data, some of which may be constituted by forward-looking expectations of future prices and market conditions. They

---

11 In Menger's terminology, goods of higher order are used to produce goods of lower order. First order goods are consumer goods like breakfast cereal or toothpaste which we use to satisfy our wants directly. The ultimate goal of all production is first order goods and the consumer satisfaction they deliver.

deploy this relevant information to construct their entrepreneurial plans.

The entrepreneurs' planning process fits their production plan, into a hierarchy of highest order goods, which are basically unprocessed natural resources, to which value will be added at each stage of the production process, through a series of successive lower order goods, less remote from the final consumer, to the first order goods which satisfy consumer wants directly. Menger also sees a role for the entrepreneur in adjusting the production process; that is, maintaining the entrepreneurial plan in response to new information or changed market conditions. However, in sharp contrast with Cantillon and Turgot, Menger downplays the entrepreneur's role as a risk bearer, perhaps still being under the influence of Mill. Menger argues that entrepreneurial services, whether planning or supervision, are essential to all production, and thus must be rewarded with profits.

The final retail sales price of any produced good must generally be exceeded by the value or benefit to the final consumer, or else the consumer would not freely exchange what they choose to give up for what they are buying. The values of all the factors of production, inputs, or resources used in producing the product are induced prices determined by the price paid by the final consumer and apportioned among the factors of production in accordance with the supply and demand conditions of the factor markets where these inputs were acquired. This includes the labor wage,[12] input resources or raw materials, the services of capital, and also entrepreneurial activity. Menger (1871: 172) considers entrepreneurial activity to be a special kind of labor service.

Ludwig von Mises (1881-1973) holds that "the market is a process, actuated by the interplay of the actions of the various individuals cooperating under the division of labor. The forces determining the—continually changing—state of the market are the value judgements of these individuals and their actions as directed by these value judgements. The state of the market at any instant is the price structure; that is, the totality of the exchange ratios as established by those eager to buy and those eager to sell. There is nothing inhuman or mystical with regard to the market. The market process is entirely the resultant of human actions. Every market phenomenon can be traced back to definite choices of the members of the market society. The market process is the adjustment of the individual actions of the various members of the market society to the requirements of mutual cooperation. The market prices tell the producers what to produce, how to produce, and in what quantity. The market is the focal point to which the activities of the individuals converge. It is the center from which the activities of the individuals radiate (Mises 1949: 257-258)."

---

12 Note that the labor wage is determined by the worker's contribution to producing a certain number of units of a particular output or combination of products. The prices consumers are willing to pay for these products determine what the seller can collect. Minimum wage legislation cannot do anything to increase the benefit of the product to the final buyer or compel them to pay more for the product, because it cannot increase the product's benefit to the consumer. Thus minimum wage legislation cannot increase the value of a worker's product or their productivity. In certain cases it can, however, have the wholly destructive effect of pricing workers out of the market by making it illegal for them to offer their services at a wage which matches their productivity.

Entrepreneurial action is necessarily always a multifaceted phenomenon which generally defies simple quantification or formalization. Blaug (1998: 227) cites several different historical views of entrepreneurship. Entrepreneurial action includes arbitrage (Cantillon 1755), coordination (Say 1803, Kirzner 1996, 1973), innovation (Schumpeter 1934), uncertainty-bearing (Knight 1921), and most recently (Casson 1982, 1985) increasing the range of available judgments regarding the most efficient distribution and allocation of resources.[13]

A more meaningful way to consider the influence of entrepreneurial planning, alertness, and innovation on market outcomes is to recognize that the work of the entrepreneur proceeds experimentally and so generates the information of the market through trial and error. This information can never be known in advance of a voluntary exchange, but only becomes apparent after an exchange takes place (Buchanan 1986), and once an exchange takes place it offers no necessary implications for subsequent potential exchanges. Once an individual has bought or sold a good or service at a certain price, which is always specific to the time, place, and parties to the transaction, unalterable historical information on the state of the market has been created. But this information does not necessarily have any significance for the future, and thus the objectively realized and unalterable knowledge of such past events cannot form the basis for the purportedly optimizing behavior of market participants, whether producers or consumers.

---

13 See more detailed accounts of the discussions of entrepreneurship given by Cantillon, Turgot, Say, and Menger presented earlier in Chapter 3. Blaug cited such a broad range of different definitions of entrepreneurship that he did not need to include Turgot or Menger.

3.9 The Function of the Entrepreneur

Joseph A. Schumpeter (1883-1950) identifies five types of entrepreneurial innovation: (1) introducing new outputs or improving the quality of existing outputs, (2) introducing new methods of production, (3) opening new output markets, especially new export markets, (4) finding new sources of supply for the raw materials or intermediate inputs used in the production process, and (5) creating new kinds of firms and industrial organizations (Schumpeter 1934). To Schumpeter, entrepreneurs are not so much inventors of new technologies, but decision makers who allocate resources to exploit inventions, which are typically the inventions of others; entrepreneurs are not Turgot's risk-bearing capitalists but borrow funds from the capitalists—the actual owners of land and capital equipment—to finance the innovations the entrepreneurial planners originate and seek to implement. Casson (1987: 151) notes that, as with Mill, Schumpeterian entrepreneurs are defined chiefly by their managerial or decision-making role.

Mises defines the entrepreneur as "acting man exclusively seen from the aspect of the uncertainty inherent in every action (Mises 1949: 253)." To Mises as to Cantillon, Turgot, and Knight, entrepreneurs are risk bearers. Entrepreneurship is not merely a particular personality type, but a category of economic behavior (Mises 1949: 251). To Mises uncertainty is everywhere and consequently, everyone is an entrepreneur. But the stylized mathematical optimization problems of standard neoclassical economics has been sterilized of all uncertainty, which has been assumed away along with the entrepreneur, simply by virtue of how the problem has been framed and set up in the first place. Uncertainty has been removed and there is also no role for entrepreneurial alertness.

Real world entrepreneurial planning always responds to and attempts to overcome the vagaries of an uncertain future, seeking to address and anticipate the uncertainties of future consumer demand and forthcoming changes in demand and supply in factor markets. Entrepreneurs also attempt to overcome the potential differences in each other's ability to exercise their own foresight with a compatible vision, which is the prerequisite for implementing mutually compatible entrepreneurial plans (Mises 1949: 212-214). The entrepreneur always faces uncertainty because production never occurs instantly but always takes place over a period of time, so any entrepreneurial planning necessarily has to involve some "speculation in anticipation of future events (Greaves 1974: 39)." Lachmann (1986: 65-70, 116-117) also emphasizes the extent that entrepreneurial planning responds to and seeks to address uncertainty about the future.

Much of Israel Kirzner's (1973, 1979, 1984a, 1997) work on entrepreneurship can be understood as a detailed critique of the standard view of economic decision making as a series of predetermined mathematical optimization problems to be solved by economic agents. Kirzner and Hayek stress the problem of dispersed knowledge that is never possessed by any one individual in its entirety (Hayek 1945: 520), a problem whose "extent and seriousness cannot be known in advance" by the entrepreneur, "arising out of unawareness of one's ignorance (Kirzner 1984b: 162)." Mises emphasizes the entrepreneurial response to, and exploitation of, market information: "Entrepreneur means acting man in regard to the changes occurring in the data of the market (Mises 1949: 254)." The Misesian entrepreneur is always alert to arbitrage opportunities which occur when prices in resource markets are not adjusted to prices in the product markets (Kirzner 1973: 85). This is a special case of Hayek's (1949) problem of dispersed knowledge which is never given to any one person in its entirety, but can only be deployed and exploited through a mutually cooperative market process.

In contrast, in some areas Hayek's understanding of the entrepreneur is less developed than that of Mises or Kirzner.[14] In Hayek's (1973: 27) view, business firms are designed artifacts like radios, toasters, or telescopes. Entrepreneurial planners take advantage of the laws of economics to design business organizations much the same way engineers employ the laws of natural science to construct machines. Hayek's account of firm organization proceeds according to a more or less military model, where the manager issues orders that are always fulfilled completely without question or exception by the firm's employees. Hayek recognizes that the entrepreneur works within and through the firm that they design, organize, and direct, but he fails to perceive that once a business enterprise starts to operate, its employees always enjoy some degree of autonomy. Employees in firms with a more entrepreneurial culture enjoy and are permitted more autonomy and a wider locus of control than in firms which are more authoritarian. Although the extent of employee autonomy can and does vary considerably, both across different firms and even for different employees within the same firm, once the firm starts to operate in the arena of the market, in effect the firm takes on a life of its own to some extent.

Given this bewildering variety of roles identified by different

---

14 Elias Khalil (1997: 302) offers an explanation of why Hayek's distinction between designed and spontaneous orders supports the interpretation that firms do not fit comfortably in either a design order or a spontaneous order. Firms are designed and directed by an entrepreneurial planner, but have to respond to and fit within the spontaneous order of the market. Also see Khalil (1995) and Dupuy (1996).

scholars of entrepreneurship, there would not appear to be any simple or straightforward way to model entrepreneurial behavior. However prices cannot be known with certainty until *after* an exchange occurs. In fact entrepreneurial planners are not ever able to optimize with respect to any objectively knowable information set. The real behavior of firms and consumers can be captured more accurately through more approximate and ad hoc heuristics or "rules of thumb," than through the supposedly rigorous solution of formal mathematical models. Because much human knowledge is tacit, and is thus inherently decentralized, subjective, and inarticulable, it becomes particularly difficult to justify blanket assumptions of perfect knowledge and foresight, and especially of perfect *mutual* knowledge and foresight, which underlie any attempt to view the behavior of producers and consumers as being accurately described by mathematical simplifications (Mises 1957: 13).

CHAPTER 4

The Future of Market Process Economics

Modern price theory, today's conventional microeconomics, is not too much of an evolving field. Most mainstream economists view basic microeconomics largely as settled science—in this view, price theory will continue to expand through applications to specialized niche areas, some of which might be exceptionally interesting. However, there is not much of a perceived need by the economics profession for a new frontier in microeconomics or price theory. From the perspective of market process theory, however, there is an endless frontier for better explaining the conditions which are necessary to bring together producers and consumers, and how markets can be allowed to become more efficient and effective as institutions directing production and satisfying human wants.

A further field of inquiry which will expand our understanding of and appreciation for market process is the design of institutional structures, law, legislation, and regulatory systems and environments

to further realize market efficiency and support and encourage entrepreneurial innovation. Market process theory should also inform
approaches to government regulation, both to address the content of
regulation over specific markets, and to critique and limit the application of what government regulation and planning attempts to constrain
or prevent. Market process can also offer additional insights into the
forces which influence democratic government, supplementing the
public choice theory which applies economic analysis to problems
of political science and democratic decision making. A deeper understanding of how self-interested actors choose to bypass and circumvent
market process to seek different outcomes through political coercion
will enable us to better appreciate the volatile combination, interplay,
and feedback between the economic and political spheres, which are
fraught with conflict and turbulence.

4.1 Entrepreneurs & the Market Price

There is a clear need for more encompassing and complete market
process accounts of the emergence and perhaps shifting evolution of
original supply and demand curves. The supply curve comes from the
firm's average cost curve, but the firm's real world behavior is more
dependent on its entrepreneurial planner's subjective perception and
belief of what the firm's average cost curve looks like. In addition, the
cost data used to construct cost curves can only be known after the
fact, once it has emerged as unalterable historical data of the market
(Mises 1957: 378-379). The entrepreneurial planner acts on subjective
expectations of what the firm's cost structure will be in the future as the
entrepreneurial production plan is implemented and carried out. The

more accurate and objective the entrepreneurial planner's information about the firm's cost structure the better. This will enable better and more accurate decisions, better informed by the actual costs faced by the firm. But the precise shape or algebraic form of these curves may not really be too amenable to precise measurement before the fact. Accurate accounting data may be available, but this can only be historical data which records, more-or-less accurately and objectively, what has transpired in the past. It purports to be a historical record. The future may unfold exactly the same way, but there will always some risk the firm's realized production costs may turn out to be different and the implementation of an entrepreneurial plan may unfold differently for a variety of reasons. The actual firm supply curve results from the efforts on the part of the entrepreneurial planner to uncover more forward-looking, *anticipatory*, information regarding what the firm's actual cost structure will be in the future, and apply this information to managing the firm's activities in maintaining and adapting the firm's entrepreneurial plan.

Entrepreneurs experimentally try out new prices. Sometimes this goes against the market, and the entrepreneur does not sell a sufficient amount of their product at a higher attempted asking price. Sometimes the entrepreneur sells out their stock in response to a lower attempted asking price, but this cannot be counted a success for the seller, only for the buyer. In this case the lower asking price does not become the new market price.

Underlying market conditions change from moment to moment, thus shifting supply and demand curves. We can think of this constant variation as the two curves engaging in a set of perpetual and mutual right-to-left, left-to-right vibrations. This means their intersection will never really be a single equilibrium point, but a probabilistic diamond shaped region in the price versus quantity space (Figure 4.1).

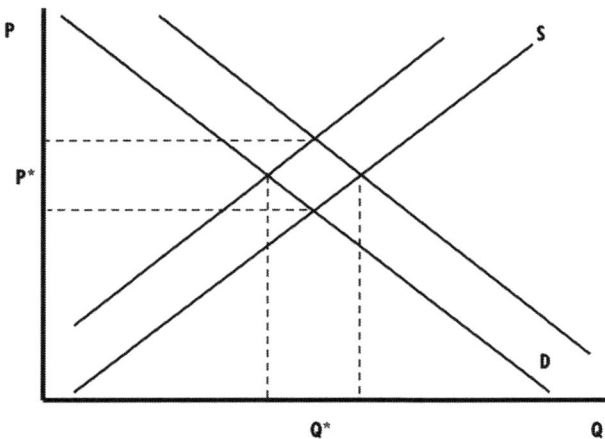

*Figure 4.1 Supply and demand curves
with no precisely defined location*

The comparative static equilibrium approach treats supply and demand curves as having fixed, knowable, and precisely known locations at any point in time. It would be a clear improvement in the realism of economic modeling if economists merely recognized that these curves move all the time, as in Figure 4.1, to represent or illustrate constantly changing market conditions. Furthermore, the same diagram would also be necessary to represent the wide diversity in subjective views and expectations regarding firms' cost structures underlying their supply curves. This calls for the true supply curve to be represented as existing in a range as shown in Figure 4.1.[15] The entrepreneurial planners who manage firm production do not directly

15 Firm behavior would imply a single cost curve for each firm, because each firm produces a certain amount, and when these are all added horizontally to get the total quantity supplied by all firms together at each price, the horizontal addition would arrive at a single supply curve. However, each buyer would have their own subjective perception of the market supply they face. The subjectivity of buyers contributes to making the supply curve a range.

or infallibly perceive the market demand they face for their product, and can only attempt to tease out information about buyer demand through experimentally adjusting the price. This range of uncertainty about the demand environment faced by firms can only be captured by representing the demand curve as a range. If the center of each range region of variation for each supply and demand curve is the most likely, highest probability location for each of the two curves, then the most likely location where the market will clear will still be where these probability contours intersect in the center of the diamond area. However, it will also be the case that there will often be a dis-equilibrium which occurs most frequently anywhere within the diamond shaped region.

The foregoing discussion relating to the real uncertainty which human action seeks to overcome has implicitly assumed a constant slope or known and constant elasticities of supply and demand.[16] Market outcomes can be observed after the fact, though never before the fact. It may also be the case that the slopes of the supply and demand curves vary over time, or are only realized in the market with significant uncertainty and practical variation, whether due to subjective variation in beliefs or expectations, ignorance, information dispersal, etc. In reality, the only information we can discover about supply and demand elasticities, slopes, and the shapes of the curves can only be in the very limited proximity to the actual market exchanges we can observe. This corresponds to the hypothesized

---

16 Supply and demand elasticities are quantities used to characterize the supply and demand curves. The demand elasticity (price elasticity of demand) is
$e_D = [dQ_D/Q_D]/[dP/P] = dQ_D P/dPQ_D = [(QD^1 - QD^0)/QD^0]/[(P^1 - P^0)/P^0] = d\log(Q_D)/d\log(P)$.
A large part of market research attempts to estimate the demand elasticity for various products. The supply elasticity (price elasticity of supply) is
$e_S = [dQ_S/Q_S]/[dP/P] = dQ_S P/dPQ_S = [(Q_S^1 - Q_S^0)/Q_S^0]/[(P^1 - P^0)/P^0] = d\log(Q_S)/d\log(P)$.

equilibrium price and quantity, or perhaps it may be more exact to say prices and quantities. The further away we get from this point, the greater the uncertainty regarding the location of the supply and demand curves, along with any of their other characteristics or properties (Figure 4.2).

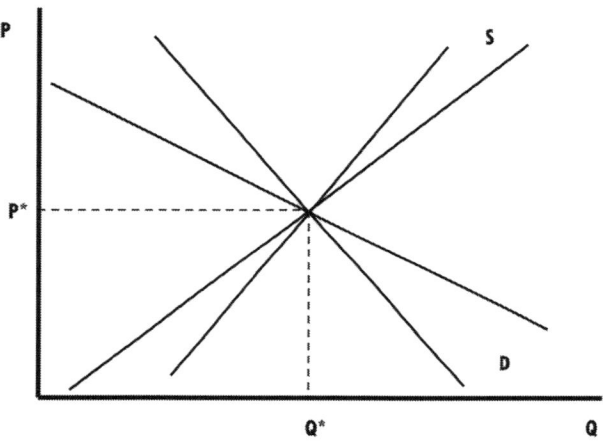

Figure 4.2 Supply and demand curves with a precisely defined intersection but no precisely defined or known slopes

The reality is likely to be even more complicated and less likely to lead to a well-defined solution. We are not likely to know either the slopes or the location of the supply or demand curves (Figure 4.3). This provides a region of likely potential market disequilbria corresponding to the star shaped region in the middle of the diagram.

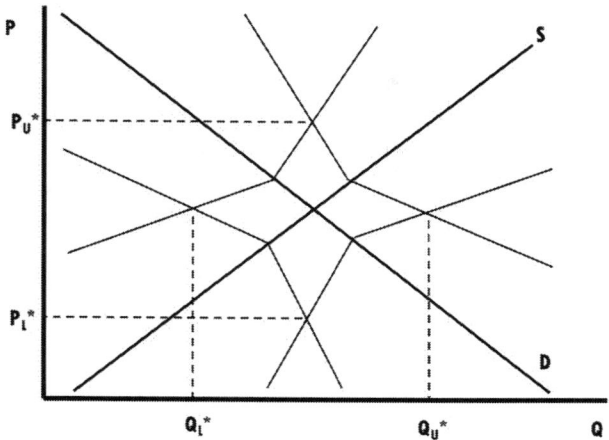

*Figure 4.3 Supply and Demand curves with
uncertainty of both slope and location*

Only considerations of market process can aim at addressing the
real complexity and richness of real world market outcomes. Some
of the examples presented in Chapter 14, showing how very limited
kinds of entrepreneurial innovation can be incorporated in optimization schemes, may be used for specialized modeling of limited cases.

4.2 Entrepreneurship & Monopoly

A further area which appears promising for future scholarship is
the analysis of monopoly through the lens of entrepreneurship and
market process, and the discussion of entrepreneurship as a competitive
process which may proceed from or give rise to monopoly behavior
and monopoly markets. Kirzner (1963: 288-289, 1973: 15-18) makes
the claim that there can be no monopoly producers, only monopoly

resource owners. Although the idea this suggests is of an owner who has successfully cornered the market for a particular resource, some resources may trade in markets which are easier to corner than others. A widely produced agricultural output might be very difficult, if not impossible, for one resource owner to control the supply. If the crop from one season actually was controlled by a single individual, that would lead imitators to plant that same lucrative crop, or plant close substitutes, progressively diminishing the original grower's monopoly power.

The threat and fear of such competitive pressures must often prevent someone from taking advantage of their monopoly position even if they have cornered the market, and may discourage them from the attempt to corner the market in the first place. Growing conditions, such as rich soil and climate, may be highly specific and highly beneficial for producing a particular crop and may endow the produce with particular qualities or desirable characteristics. These circumstances give the owner of the land where the desirable crop can be grown some degree of monopoly power. Nevertheless, the monopoly resource owner competes in the first place to make the best and most profitable use of their unique resource or land, and always faces existing and potential future competition from others.

Strong, light tropical hardwoods are especially sought after for producing furniture. It is entirely possible for the owner of a large plantation to be a monopoly resource owner, as the old growth of a particular variety or species of hardwood may be confined to a very narrow geographic region. New growth trees may take decades to grow to maturity, or at least to sufficient size before they can be harvested, but a particular variety or species may be desired as much for the aesthetic qualities of its wood as for the wood's strength and lightness.

Kirzner's particular point is that only resource owners can be monopolists, and that entrepreneurs always compete with one another, and are always potentially subject to future competition introduced by others' innovative entrepreneurial action. In fact, even for the owners of a certain supply of an otherwise generic and widely held resource, such as, for example, dried grain, the owner of each stock always has monopoly ownership of the specific stock they own. The quality and special characteristics may also be uniform over everyone's stocks, though that often will vary by lot, but the location of each stock is generally unique, giving each resource owner some monopoly power over the buyers nearest to each owner's stock.

Entrepreneurial innovators enjoy temporary monopolies, and can often extract temporary monopoly profits (Ellig 1994). There will be a natural tension between their desire to capture the highest profits possible, for as long as possible, even if not permanently—given their time preference—and the desire to preserve the monopoly. One way of preserving a monopoly is to avoid exploiting the position of being a monopoly producer, so as to avoid attracting new entrants as competitors. The other way is to bribe and lobby for government protection against potential competitors.

Future work on market process will likely examine the differences between beneficial and exploitative forms of monopoly. Many sources of monopoly, such as the acquisition or development of stocks of resources with unique characteristics which enable the stock to better serve consumer wants, differentiating products so they can better serve consumer wants, etc., clearly benefit the consumers who choose those varieties, thus justifying a price premium, which the consumers who benefit are willing to pay. Such benign and beneficial forms of monopoly need to be distinguished from those created by government regulation, regulatory restrictions which protect established producers, and other coercively enforced barriers to entry, which prevent potential entrants from contesting for market share and ever providing any potential benefit to consumers.

Market process theory, with its focus on entrepreneurial discovery that moves the market from one dis-equilibrium to the next, can be used to critique and inform, antitrust theory. Antitrust regulation prohibits charging a price which is too low, as that may constitute predatory pricing, or charging a price which is too high, as that is a monopoly price. Exceptions are made if the government wants the producer to charge a higher or lower price. Market process offers a sounder and more fundamental understanding of why there is never any one fair or correct price in the first place. A sounder understanding of market process should inform the theoretical basis for any rationale underlying legislation and regulation. Antitrust legislation is fundamentally misconceived (Armentano 1990: 26-27, 2007: 17-19).

Government intervention, in the form of central planning and regulation, constraints entrepreneurs from experimenting and innovating freely. Institutional structures which impair the exercise of property rights limit entrepreneurs' ability to contribute to raising consumer welfare and mutual plan coordination. This kind of regulation necessarily lowers welfare and consumer satisfaction. Regulations which lower the cost of asserting property rights and internalize external costs are beneficial and welfare improving. The stronger the environment for property rights, the better the institutional support for entrepreneurial discovery (Harper 1998: 265-266, Ikeda 1998: 43-45).

4.3 Social Justice & Welfare Economics

The concept of social justice rests on the implicit—though rarely articulated—assertion that social organizations can be ranked in a hierarchy
from least to most just or morally worthy. This is invariably a hierarchy
of predetermined outcomes rather than processes or institutional structure. It is an inherently Marxian concept that it is morally preferable
for wealth to be allocated to virtuously productive workers, rather than
to purportedly unproductive, exploitative capitalists or entrepreneurial
planners. This purportedly moral dimension has enabled social justice
to outlast such closely associated fallacies as the Marxian theory of
production and the labor theory of value.

Social justice is more than "justice in a social context." It purports
to offer a basis to perform a moral evaluation of various societies, as
well as progressively transform our society into a supposedly preferable
future (Popper 1962 II: 124-127). The ideal of social justice is for
wealth, income, power, privilege, and opportunity to be distributed
equally, whereas income and wealth inequality are to be condemned
and criticized. Social justice is frequently linked to positive obligations
on individuals, such as to join and support labor unions in order to
make their worker advocacy more effective, support enhanced rights
or programs for racial and cultural minorities or historically disadvan-
taged groups, reduce income inequality, etc. The term "social justice"
originated with the Jesuit priest Luigi Taparelli (1793-1862). Overt
positive obligations are implicitly, though not always explicitly, linked
to implied obligations to hold particular favored and progressive beliefs
and political positions. For example, workers are not merely required to
join and support labor unions, but would not be permitted to question
any leftist dogma, or hold dissenting views. Such dissenting views,

even if held secretly, would be demonstrative of moral failings. If an individual believed in private property or individual rights, that would make them enemies of social justice; in effect, a class-neutral form of class enemy.

Closely related to social justice would be the market process critique of welfare economics. Since market process arrives at competitive outcomes which would not be possible otherwise, market process economics offers a better understanding of the real world Pareto efficiency which is the goal of welfare economics. Engineer and economist Vilfredo Pareto (1848-1923) defined Pareto efficiency as a condition where no one can be made better off without making at least one person worse off. One practical difficulty which must be overcome to define or arrive at a Pareto efficient outcome is that the relationship of desired ends to available means is never known in advance but always becomes better known through market process. Issues of socialist central planning or government regulation under a mixed economy are also raised by the limitations of welfare economics and the market process critique of welfare economics. These are developed more fully in Part 4.

There is and can be no way to coherently compare the subjective welfare of two different persons; therefore there can be no meaningful social welfare function to maximize. If everyone in society shared precisely the same values with diminishing marginal returns to wealth, taking wealth or income away from the rich would only reduce their utility a relatively small amount, and redistributing that amount to the poor would increase their utility by a comparatively larger amount. This argument mistakenly suggests that redistribution of wealth or income can improve social welfare. Unfortunately, this argument fails because the ordinal utility of one individual cannot be compared with anyone else's.

It may seem fair, just, or more efficient to take from the rich and give to the poor, but there is no scientific basis to claim that the rich person whose wealth or income is being redistributed has a smaller loss of welfare than the subjective benefit gained by the poor who receive the redistributed wealth or income. This view that wealth redistribution could be welfare enhancing was held by many economists (Cannan 1888, 1932, Harrod 1938), but was definitively debunked (Robbins 1932, Hayek 1978a, Mulligan 2009), as well as violating Arrow's (1950) impossibility theorem.

Market Process & Market Organization

In Part Two the framework of market process theory is used to explain how different forms of market organization arise—perfect competition, monopolistic competition, oligopoly, or monopoly. Market organization is something which emerges spontaneously as a result of market process and the actions of entrepreneurial planners. How entrepreneurs respond to experimental changes and dis-equilibrating innovations introduced by other entrepreneurs will play a major role in determining which kind of market organization develops. Although some of the strategies entrepreneurs employ are determined by technological constraints and advances, the interplay and interaction among entrepreneurs' strategic responses results in the form of market organization which emerges.

Chapter 5, The Entrepreneur as Business Planner, explains how entrepreneurial planners exercise awareness to opportunities by introducing experimental innovations. This may include the introduction of new products, technologies, or even the creation of whole new industries, but may only involve the experimental adjustment to a higher or lower price for an existing product, or a minor modification of an existing product. In addition to introducing change in competitive markets, entrepreneurial planners also respond to the innovations of other entrepreneurs.

Chapter 6, Entrepreneurial Planning & Business Strategy, further explores the interplay and dependence among the entrepreneurial plans of the various entrepreneurs. Though entrepreneurs compete for profits and seek competitive advantages over each other, the introduction of many innovative products, practices, and techniques by entrepreneurial planners temporarily moves the market farther away from an idealized condition of mutual plan coordination. The chief task and most socially valuable function of the entrepreneur is to make possible a higher level of mutual coordination among the planned consumption and production activities of other people in the economy. Although disruptive innovation can reduce the level of mutual plan coordination in the short run, this always leads to higher long run welfare and greater coordination among the plans of others in the long run. Entrepreneurs profit to the extent they contribute to improving this mutual coordination among the plans of others over the long run.

Chapter 7, Strategy & the Emergence of Market Organization, discusses how entrepreneurial planners respond to innovation by others and how this determines the kind of market organization which emerges spontaneously as a result, namely perfect competition, monopolistic competition, oligopoly, or monopoly.

CHAPTER 5

The Entrepreneur as Business Planner

Economists generally think of entrepreneurship as a highly specialized, even somewhat exotic topic, which can somehow be divorced from the majority of economic theory and analysis. However, as we have seen, even at the most basic level of analysis, markets depend crucially on entrepreneurial planning, competition, innovation, experimentation, and profit-seeking speculation in the face of an unknown and uncertain future which unfolds before us in the fullness of time. Forward-looking entrepreneurial planning is the basis of market process. Without entrepreneurs, markets lack precisely the mechanism and characteristics which can account for their ability to coordinate production and further improve on any allocation of resources or productive activity, which may appear initially optimal, not to mention explain how markets arrive at this idealized optimum in the first place.

There may be no clear distinction between entrepreneurial planning and entrepreneurial strategy. At the margins, the two activities tend to blend into one another. An effective entrepreneurial plan needs to be highly adaptive and must be potentially subject to constant and ongoing modification as the entrepreneurial planner discovers relevant new information and as the market conditions of supply and demand evolve over time. This activity of entrepreneurial plan maintenance can be routine and automatic at some times, and highly innovative and extraordinary at others, depending on the opportunities and challenges perceived by the entrepreneurial planner, and which they decide to act on, or not.

The entrepreneurial plan emerges from and is formed by market process, and must be continually adapted as market conditions change over time. It can never be static if it is to succeed in the market. Even in the fictional and hypothetical condition of unchanging market conditions, entrepreneurs should always be alert to new opportunities which were always present in the environment, but which the alert entrepreneur is now the first to see. This chapter focuses on the more mundane and routine aspects of maintaining an entrepreneurial plan.

5.1 Entrepreneurial Planning & Market Process

Markets are cooperative information-processing activities where goods and services are bought and sold, resources are allocated, and prices are set and changed. Entrepreneurs make use of the signaling function of market prices to allocate resources, decide on the combinations of output to produce, and identify—if possible—profitable arbitrage opportunities (Kirzner 1963: 44-46). Ask and offer prices always signal relevant information to anyone who is alert to their implications and potential opportunities. Their ability to act on this information enables entrepreneurial planners to move markets into higher degrees of mutual coordination, coordinate their own plans with those of others, and make more informed expectations and decisions (Kirzner 1996: 39-41). Entrepreneurs constantly realign their activities with those of other entrepreneurs on an ongoing basis, whether competitors, suppliers, or consumers. They also rely on prices to communicate future wants from consumers to producers, etc. At the same time markets provide the appropriate financial incentives to reward participants who can improve any part of the process (Hayek 1946). Market exchange works through competition, with numerous entrepreneurial planners simultaneously engaged in experimentally adjusting prices to find and test the presumed market equilibrium. The actions of each person in a market economy generate and transmit information to other participants who are alert to the opportunities and challenges they represent, and rewards those with the greatest alertness to opportunities and willingness to act on them. This competition in experimentally adjusting market prices enables markets to find the equilibrium or market clearing price, but more importantly, it allows for higher levels of mutual coordination among the entrepreneurial plans of others (Kirzner 1996: 39-40). Given that social cooperation is always voluntary, higher levels of social cooperation are possible at certain prices than at others, and only experimental price searching allows entrepreneurs to contribute to achieving a higher level of cooperation and mutual coordination among entrepreneurial plans.

Entrepreneurial planners also compete to introduce new products and production techniques, make use of alternative inputs, implement innovative marketing and distribution practices, and bundle new combinations of goods and services that better meet consumer wants. In introducing these innovations, the entrepreneurs are always trying to provide greater satisfaction and value for the consumers they serve, whether directly or indirectly. Thus, market process is anything but static, and works through anything but a static equilibrium. In this regard, we would have to recognize the superior and dynamic exposition of market process presented by Cantillon, Turgot, and Say, in preference to the accounts of Smith, Ricardo, and Mill, which fail to emphasize the contribution of the entrepreneur. The market dis-equilibrium prevailing at any time and place is merely the raw material which market process acts on (Kirzner 1963: 271). The information processing aspect of market process is a form of autonomous and indirect communication—thus, it is not amenable to central planning or control—transmitting inarticulable knowledge which the market accommodates remarkable well, if not always flawlessly. Market process provides the backbone of a sophisticated system of social cooperation, from which we benefit but can take for granted most of the time.

The key to information transmission in a market economy is the alertness of entrepreneurial planners, who can be thought of as information relays that only work to the extent that each individual entrepreneur appreciates the significance of the information they discover or encounter. This only works to the extent that individual entrepreneurial planners are able to identify the opportunities or challenges contained in a particular item of information. By this we mean that entrepreneurial planners are alert to the latent profit opportunity contained in, or presented by, any specific item of information. Without entrepreneurial awareness on the part of someone, the information can never be recognized or acted on, and the latent opportunities can never be made to benefit or profit anyone. Entrepreneurs are rewarded with higher profits when they successfully offer innovative products and techniques which better satisfy the wants of others compared to what was previously available. When entrepreneurs fail, they bear the cost but potentially gain valuable information which may better inform their future decisions and support more successful revised strategies.

Entrepreneurial discovery depends on complex sequences of causal reasoning about the future likely or potential courses of evolution of the supply and demand conditions in these markets, which can only come from experience and intentional awareness (Menger 1871: 160). Once the entrepreneur discovers or envisions such a profit opportunity, or creates it through perception and their unique appreciation of its significance, they must then invest in whatever infrastructure and human capital are necessary to implement and take advantage of their unique vision. They must hire workers, and purchase or lease land, buildings, and equipment. Supposing this is the only opportunity the entrepreneur perceives, or merely the one they expect to be most profitable or least risky, they will attempt to implement it in reality. The entrepreneur who merely engages in simple arbitrage may need to transport goods to a geographically separate market, or store them for later sale in a temporally separate market, or both. Both kinds of processing are at least trivially productive activities, but they are the only kinds pure arbitrageurs perform (Kirzner 1973: 35, Horwitz 2000: 29-30).

Plan maintenance is a continuous process of evaluating and reevaluating the effectiveness of each part of an entrepreneurial plan, and adjusting each element to meet changed conditions or perform better in any way possible, making use of all relevant new information as it arises and is acquired by the alert entrepreneur. Entrepreneurial planners can improve their chances of ultimate success by accommodating various contingencies in a plan so constructed as to be as flexible as possible (Leijonhufvud 1981: 265-267). They must subsequently make any adjustments which become necessary to keep the plan as optimal as it can be made to be given the new information which entrepreneurs uncover through monitoring the progress and success of earlier stages of the plan.

From the consumer's perspective, we know in advance how well our past choices of products worked, how well they satisfied our wants in the past and at what cost, and any prospective new product must offer at least an apparently high likelihood of additional advantages before we will try it. The degree of mutual coordination or meshing between various interdependent entrepreneurial plans, as between the production and consumption plans of firms and consumers, is the degree the market succeeds in efficiently satisfying our wants (Kirzner 1996: 39-41). High prices signal to producers which resources are most scarce or in greatest need, and which are needed to produce the goods and services most desired by buyers. Prices of products are high either because the products enjoy high demand, or because the cost of production is high because the prices of inputs are high, perhaps because they are especially rare or are needed to produce other products as well. High consumer demand for the output results in greater producer demand for whatever inputs are needed to produce the output. Low prices present entrepreneurial opportunities if those resources can be substituted for more expensive ones. Alert entrepreneurs will take advantage of lower-priced alternative inputs to reduce the selling price to buyers, raise the firm's profit margin, or both.

5.2 Information Requirements for Entrepreneurial Planning

Because no market participant possesses complete information, real markets never reach the constrained optimum of neoclassical theory. The hypothetical competitive optimum assumes everyone shares the same information set, but the optimum is defined in terms of this common information set which may be incomplete. In reality, the information set available to each market participant is unique to the individual. The actual information set embodied in the process of the real market is fragmented across many individuals—we each possess and are free to act on a subset of the complete information. The very process of market exchange contributes to mutually reconciling much of this information and dispersing it more completely over many individuals. Much of the information set possessed by any one individual is subjective, incapable of being articulated or communicated, and cannot be shared or communicated explicitly with anyone else. Market process brings about real world market outcomes through competition to uncover potentially useful new information, set better prices, implement innovative production and marketing methods, satisfy new wants, consumers trying new products, etc.—and it should be little wonder that real world outcomes fail to conform to the dry formal descriptions of what a constrained optimum should look like.

Furthermore, what is the information set assumed by a general equilibrium model? In these models, firms seek to maximize profits, given the market selling price for the firms' output, subject to the technical constraints imposed by the firm's algebraic cost and production functions, and given the market prices of the necessary inputs. Equivalently, firms seek to minimize production costs, subject to the technical constraint imposed by the algebraic production function. In reality prices are never a given. Market prices are actually generated through market process, and although they are necessary inputs in any entrepreneurial appraisal of the state of the market or its likely future evolution, it is mistaken to think that prices can be considered in any way a given of economic decision making. It would be more valid and closer to the mark to observe that prices of specific past transactions which have already been completed can be observed. Entrepreneurial planners use this information (a) to make subjective probabilistic assessments regarding the most likely future trajectory of these prices, and (b) to trigger contingent decisions about how to respond if the price were to rise or fall by a certain amount.

From the consumer behavioral side of the market which determines demand for output—keep in mind that consumers are also entrepreneurs in the act of consumption—consumers seek to maximize their own utility subject to the constraint imposed by their budget. Basic models usually ignore the fact that consumers may save part of their income, but this can be addressed by assigning some part of the utility function as having saving (S) as an argument, which is a positive function of the interest rate earned on savings (r). This would explain people's motivation to save for the future; that is, to spend less, and to spend even less, the higher the return to saving.

Entrepreneurs construct a virtual reality of feasible or at least potentially feasible business opportunity sets. These business opportunity sets may be closely related, with only a single element changed to distinguish one possible business opportunity set from another. The entrepreneurial planner maps prospective entrepreneurial plans onto a subjective range of probable outcomes yielding ranges of expected profit-and-loss results (Ikeda 1994: 23). The entrepreneur bases their assessment of the range of probable outcomes on their past experience and available information. They evaluate the desirability of a given project in terms of the level of detail which is known in advance. This may be highly detailed information, and represent relatively low risk for projects which build on past successful endeavors, perhaps with only minor modifications, or which will be carried out across the more-or-less well-travelled landscape of a familiar business opportunity set.

Prospective entrepreneurial plans may also be extremely vague in the very earliest and most formative or speculative stages, where the entrepreneur may be contemplating a completely novel venture which does not build as much on the firm's established expertise, and is thus rendered much more highly risky and uncertain. Such a novel venture may be mapped out in high detail over certain stages which are more familiar, or about which more information is known or can be surmised, building on past experience and established expertise, but leaving major gaps in other areas. Either way, regardless of any vagueness, gaps, or missing steps in an entrepreneurial plan which is in the earliest and most speculative stages of formative development, the entrepreneur evaluates the likelihood of success to decide whether to further pursue a particular plan. This likelihood or probability of plan success can be considered the multiplicative product of the probabilities of success of each component of the entrepreneurial plan. If there is a gap in the plan at this stage, the entrepreneur may appraise that stage's probability of success as being very low, attempting to err on the side of conservatism. Or they may appraise it as more likely to succeed in that the particular unknown and undeveloped stage in the sequence of plan events will ultimately be better understood and become more completely realized once it becomes better articulated as an explicit part of the plan.

As more knowledge and detail is uncovered through experience or entrepreneurial alertness, that enables the entrepreneurial planner to assign a more precise appraisal of the probability of success for a particular stage of the prospective plan being considered. If the aggregate likelihood of success is not sufficiently high, the plan will be set aside at this point, though it may later be revisited when new information comes to light, enabling the entrepreneur to revise more favorably their appraisals of the likelihood of success of any stage, provided they come to appraise the probability of success more favorably. A plan may be otherwise perfect, but if a single stage in the production process cannot be successfully completed by the firm, and cannot be farmed out to another firm on contract who can complete it with a high probability of success, the plan has to be shelved because there is no way it can be completed in its entirety. The chain can only be as strong as its weakest link.

If the entrepreneur later discovers an innovative and superior way of completing that critical stage, the plan can be revisited and can now be evaluated more favorably. If the plan has gaps but is still appraised sufficiently favorably by the entrepreneur, the next stage for the entrepreneur is to remedy their information deficits and figure out how to fill in the gaps in the plan. This includes gaining a better understanding of the precise processes which will need to be followed to bridge the original deficiencies in the plan, as well as make more definitive and reliable estimates of the probability of the successful completion of the most critical stages of the plan. Generally a better understanding of the physical processes which will be implemented as part of an entrepreneurial plan and the likelihood of success go hand-in-hand.

5.3 Entrepreneurial Planning as Business Planning

A business plan is a formal written document and its purpose is primarily to raise venture capital to finance a new business, or expand an existing one. The audience for a business plan may be a bank's loan officers or lending advisory board, venture capitalists or other angel investors, or the document may be incorporated in the prospectus for an initial offering of stock shares. A business plan will typically consist of and include many or all of the following components:

1. An executive summary—presenting an introduction and summary of the business plan.
2. A description of the proposed company—describing the business's basic products, services, and activities.
3. Summary of market research—an analysis which establishes, or at least strongly suggests, that there will be a viable market for the firm's proposed product, along with an explanation of any particular features of the intended market, especially if these features need to be accommodated or can be exploited in distributing the product. This should include analyses of the established industry, if any, the new firm will compete against, competing firms, substitute products, etc., as well as industries the firm will serve or supply, and prospective consumers. The information in this section should inform the marketing plan.
4. Proposed firm organization and management—presents the proposed initial organizational structure. The initially proposed organizational structure will be subject to revision as the firm's needs and opportunities emerge, become clearer, change, or evolve over time, or as anticipated personnel requirements prove more difficult to fill than anticipated, or new opportunities are perceived, etc.
5. Analysis of the new firm's proposed services or product—this will describe the nature of the firm's proposed goods or services, highlighting the advantages the firm will introduce, how it will address targeted market niches, what unmet consumer needs will be met, or what established needs will be better satisfied by the new product, etc.

6. A marketing and sales plan—describes how the product will be promoted, advertised, distributed, and marketed, etc. Special advantages and distinctive approaches will be emphasized, but often a business plan can also achieve a higher perception of credibility by highlighting how its marketing approach is similar to, and perhaps builds on, those of established successful firms.

7. Funding request—consistent with the pro forma financial projections, this section will justify and quantify the amount of startup capital which the firm will need to begin operations. Normally this will be sufficient to finance the firm until its operations can become self-sustaining and the firm will start paying back its initial startup loans, repaying the venture capitalists, pay shareholder dividends, etc. As a rule of thumb, this should be based on the firm's sales revenues being projected to become sufficient to fund production and any other activities within the first three to five years of operations, or sooner. Potentially, in some cases the new firm can operate with reduced scale or scope if the full amount requested cannot be raised. In other cases, an inability to raise the minimum required funds means the proposal must be foregone.

8. Pro Forma financial projections—present hypothetical balance sheets or cash flow statements which project operations costs and revenues over the initial period. These should appear plausible and extend at least as far into the future as it will take for the enterprise to become self-sustaining.

9. Appendices—typically may include resumes of the top management team, including the entrepreneurial planner(s), specialists who will provide the necessary technical expertise, etc., copies of patents, licenses, legal permits, etc., as required given the business's proposed activities.

Each element of the business plan, which is always a formal written document—provided the firm actually has one, and regardless of whether the firm operates strictly under its business plan or not, is analogous to a corresponding element of the implicit entrepreneurial plan (Table 5.1). In contrast, a business's entrepreneurial plan is rarely a formal document, and if it were, it would potentially change from moment to moment as the underlying business conditions change and the entrepreneurial planner perceives these changes. As long as the entrepreneurial planner remains alert to constantly changing market conditions, any competently executed and maintained entrepreneurial plan would have to change to accommodate awareness to any changes in underlying business conditions, for example, to exploit new opportunities, respond to new challenges, take advantage of new production techniques, substitute cheaper inputs, etc. While a business plan is a formal written document used to raise venture capital to finance the firm, either as a startup, for expansion, or to fund ongoing operations, an entrepreneurial plan is used to guide the firm's routine operations, often along with some of its responses to foreseeable contingencies. These contingencies may include changes in technology, input prices, prices of substitute products, prices of complementary products, opportunities to explore new marketing strategies, opportunities to advertise in new media or other venues, reach new market niches, etc. Entrepreneurial plans may be exclusively mental constructs, as they are rarely written down or explicitly articulated, and the primary audience for an entrepreneurial plan is the entrepreneurial planner. Elements of an entrepreneurial plan might be made explicit and communicated to other members of the firm's top management team and even shared outside the firm.

Table 5.1 Business plan v. Entrepreneurial plan

	Business plan (explicit, written document)	Entrepreneurial plan (generally implicit—expresses entrepreneurial planner's tacit knowledge)
1. Executive summary	introduction & summary	generally not explicit
2. Description of proposed company	describes firm's product line, production methods, activities, etc.	addresses changes, i.e., potential new areas firm might expand into, subject to entrepreneurial awareness, conditions under which new activities would be advantageous, profitable, etc.
3. Market research	analyses of established industry, competing firms, substitute products, etc., industries the firm will serve or supply, & prospective consumers	examined to identify new areas where the firm's products can be marketed, potential new products, opportunities to capture additional market share, etc.
4. Table of firm organization	proposed initial organizational structure, which may be different once the firm begins operations	revised as firm's needs & opportunities emerge, become clearer, change, personnel requirements prove more difficult to fill, etc.
5. Service or product	nature of firm's proposed goods or services, highlighting advantages firm will introduce, how it will address defined market niches, etc.	adjusted to best deploy firm's resources to better satisfy the needs of others in society; that is, earn highest profits, subject to entrepreneurial awareness of new challenges & opportunities, changing market conditions, etc.

6. **Marketing and sales plans**	details how product will be promoted, advertised, distributed, marketed, etc. emphasizing special advantages, distinctive approaches, etc., but may also highlight how marketing approach is similar to that of other successful firms	evolves along with the firm's product line, production methods, technology, personnel, etc., but also changes to exploit, accommodate changes in underlying market conditions, changes in demand for the firm's product, changes in prices, etc.
7. **Funding request/ requirement**	initial request for startup funds, firm must become self sustaining after 3-5 years	analogous to initial funding request, firm needs sufficient ongoing revenues or cash flow to fund operations as an ongoing concern, ensuring firm's business model makes best use of resources, delivers highest rate of return, among all alternatives of which the entrepreneurial planner is aware
8. **Pro forma financial projections**	hypothetical financials which show the firm will be self sustaining after 3-5 years at a maximum	expected cash flows, within whatever margins of error apply, for prospective adjustments to the established plan, forming a basis for firm's future strategies & activities
9. **Appendices**	resumes, patents, licenses, permits, etc.	not explicit but may identify needed personnel requirements, talents, licenses, etc., associated with prospective adjustments to entrepreneurial plan

The entrepreneurial plan may include any of the components typically included in a standard business plan, because at each point in time the entrepreneurial plan has to address the same issues:

1. An executive summary—would generally not be included in an entrepreneurial plan. Entrepreneurial plans are not summarized because they are not written or explicitly articulated.

2. A description of the company—As with the initial business plan, this would describe the business's basic products, services, and activities. However, as part of an entrepreneurial plan this should also address potential new areas the firm might expand into, to the extent the entrepreneurial planner is aware of these opportunities, and the conditions under which these potential new activities would be advantageous and profitable. Only the entrepreneurial awareness of the planner limits what can be addressed in the entrepreneurial plan.

3. Market research—Generally, the firm will either internally generate its own market research or else contract with external consultants who specialize in collecting and analyzing it. Entrepreneurial planners should be alert to and examine this new data to identify new areas where the firm's products can be marketed, potential new products which might be marketed alongside the firm's established product line, opportunities to capture additional market share, etc.

4. Firm organization and management—The firm's initial organizational structure is always subject to revision as the firm's needs and opportunities emerge, become clearer, change, or evolve over time, or as anticipated personnel requirements prove more difficult to fill than anticipated, etc.

5. Description and analysis of the new firm's proposed services or product—As the entrepreneurial planner becomes aware of new challenges and opportunities, changing market conditions, etc., the firm's product line should evolve to best deploy the firm's resources to better satisfy the needs of society; that is, to earn the highest level of financial profits for the firm.

6. Marketing and sales plan—should evolve along with the firm's product line, production methods, technology, personnel, etc., but also must change to exploit and accommodate changes in underlying market conditions, for example, to address changes in demand for the firm's product, changes in prices, etc.

7. Funding requirement—Analogous to the firm's initial funding request, an operating firm requires sufficient revenues or cash flow to fund its operations as an ongoing concern. The entrepreneurial planner has to constantly monitor expected cash flows to ensure not merely adequacy, but that the firm's operations and current business model makes the best possible use of the firm's resources and delivers the highest rate of return, among all the alternatives of which the entrepreneurial planner is aware. The broadest entrepreneurial awareness, encompassing the most potential alternatives, contributes to maximizing the firm's opportunities for continued success.

8. Pro Forma financial projections—the entrepreneurial planner has access to the firm's historical financial data. Within a margin of uncertainty, these data can be projected into the future, generally with greater uncertainty the farther into the future they are projected. The entrepreneurial planner must also estimate expected cash flows, within whatever margins of error apply, for any contemplated adjustments to the established plan. These

projections or expectations form the basis for the firm's future strategies and activities.

9. Appendices—Since the entrepreneurial plan is an implicit rather than an explicit plan, it cannot have explicit appendices in the same sense as a business plan. However, the entrepreneurial planner may be able to identify needed personnel requirements, talents, licenses, etc., associated with prospective adjustments to the firm's entrepreneurial plan. These would enable the firm to know what kind of personnel it would need to hire, what qualifications they would be seeking, etc., if they subsequently chose to pursue such a path.

Each element of the entrepreneurial plan, which is generally never a formal written document, is not merely subject to potential revision, but must be constantly revised to respond to ever changing conditions, challenges, and opportunities perceived by the alert entrepreneurial planner. These actual and potential plan revisions are not generally observable because unlike a formal business plan, the entrepreneurial plan is only implicit. Only plans which map onto exclusively positive profit possibilities can be considered guaranteed to succeed, and to some extent this guarantee is illusory, since entrepreneurial expectations are always speculative, may be overoptimistic, and ultimately may not be completed in the real world as anticipated. Expectations formation is a perceptual strategy for dealing with uncertain future outcomes, but can never remove all uncertainty. Plans with very low ranges of probable losses may also be evaluated favorably. Any investment should have to yield a return at least as great as the prevailing market interest rate, implying that whenever an entrepreneur's own venture does not appear likely to yield as high a return as someone else's, the original entrepreneur should finance the higher expected yielding venture of the other entrepreneur. This enables the other entrepreneur to assume part of the risk in place of the investor. In exchange, the original entrepreneur receives a higher and more secure return for financing someone else's entrepreneurial plan, compared with the return they probably would have received on their own project.

The extent that the conduct of an entrepreneur differs conspicuously from that of their competitors'[17] determines the type of market organization, which emerges spontaneously through market process: perfect competition, monopolistic competition, oligopoly, or pure monopoly.[18] Thus, market organization results from the feedback between entrepreneurial innovations introduced by first-order innovators and the second-order response from competing or cooperating entrepreneurs. Entrepreneurs face network externalities in that their attempts to capture and maintain market power may fail due to the nature of the competitive response of other entrepreneurs. The market process account of entrepreneurial planning and business strategy focuses critically on pro-forma cost-benefit analyses, which entrepreneurial planners construct to guide and inform their own expectations, and use to help persuade financial intermediaries, potential investors, and other sources of venture capital to help finance the entrepreneurial plan. Just as the entrepreneurial plan is directed by the entrepreneur at an unknown and uncertain future which is continually unfolding before us, so pro-forma

---

17 Tarko (2013) refers to the diversity of entrepreneurial perceptions of market opportunities and challenges as epistemic heterogeneity. The greater the variety of different judgments and perceptions, the more will lead to successful entrepreneurial innovations, and the more different entrepreneurial decisions will result in temporary monopolies.

18 The role of entrepreneurial planners in driving market organization is developed in greater detail in Chapter 7.

cost-benefit analyses attempt to help us visualize the most likely or the most favorable version of the future in which an incipient entrepreneurial plan will have to operate. The entrepreneurial plan is subject to revision before the entrepreneur starts to carry it out. Furthermore, the plan will generally be subjected to frequent major and minor revisions in the process of its implementation, as the most relevant business conditions manifest over time in particularly concrete ways which were either not foreseen in the original plan, or were left unspecified, and have now emerged in a particular concrete form at a specific time.

Visualizing this future in as much and as clear detail as possible is an essential preliminary to creating it in reality. Actual costs and revenues will be carefully monitored as they unfold over time against the pro-forma statements, in order to assess how closely the plan in the process of being implemented fulfills the expectations under which the plan was predicated. Deviations from the pro-forma must also be monitored to assess whether and in what specific ways the plan needs to be adjusted to better conform to unforeseen contingencies. The entrepreneurial plan can take the form of a business plan; that is, of a formal document which could be presented to a bank or a venture capitalist in an effort to elicit a loan or other financing. It can be a written document, and will have many of the characteristics of a formal business plan, though it is rarely written down explicitly. Instead an entrepreneurial plan is more typically more-or-less implicit, or even entirely so. Although an entrepreneurial plan must contain all the information in a standard business plan, none of that information is ever necessarily written down by an entrepreneurial planner, and if any of it is, it may not be written down in any one place or document. Thus an entrepreneurial plan is neither static nor explicit. It represents a form of implicit, inarticulable knowledge. The essence

of successful entrepreneurial planning is the extent to which the entrepreneur can respond to and even direct the future unfolding of an
uncertain enterprise in an evolving market environment. Inevitably, the
entrepreneur must attempt to direct the course of that market evolution
to the extent they are able.

5.4 Changing Market Conditions & Plan Maintenance

The entrepreneurial planner can take for granted that a certain vector
of prices will evolve over the course of time in which their plan will be
designed to operate. Until the moment passes from instant to instant,
the actual future price vector is unknown and unknowable. In contrast,
the past price vector is always a fixed matter of the historical record
and cannot change. In many cases most prices will not vary greatly
from the values they had in the recent past. However, this is a general
not a universal rule, and the most interesting cases are where prices
change rapidly and without warning. The future price vector cannot be
taken for granted—it is only a given that prices will change over time.
The price vector includes all the prices of inputs and outputs that are
exchanged in the economy. The number of goods and services included
in the price vector; that is, its dimensionality, must vary over time as
new goods are introduced and obsolete ones are discontinued. The
total dimensionality also changes unpredictably, though perhaps not
too dramatically, at any point in time. It is the sudden, large changes
which have the most dramatic impact and the greatest potential for
disrupting entrepreneurial plans. Of the goods and services included
in the price vector, the entrepreneurial planners focus their attention
on their input and output prices. They must also be aware, though

less so, of the prices of substitute and complementary goods, whose prices can affect the price of the firm's output, and of the prices inputs used in producing the firm's product, along with any substitutes and complements for those inputs.

More generally, the supply of and demand for each output and every input in the economy will also evolve over time. These supply and demand configurations can be subsumed under the general rubric of business conditions. There will be a certain number of markets for the same number of goods and services. Their past evolution is always a fixed matter of the historical record. Their future evolution is always a matter of conjecture. The number of markets is the same as the dimensionality of the price vector, because each price for every input or output good or service is determined through market exchange and market process. New product introductions create new markets and increase the dimensionality of the price vector. The new product may displace an old one, removing the market as the good is no longer purchased, and before long will no longer be produced.

New ventures always introduce new products. These may be identical to products which are already available to the consumer but are now offered by the new firm at lower cost, or may be good substitutes for products already established in the market. The advantage the entrepreneur seeks to offer consumers in this case may be lower cost, better want-satisfaction, or a combination of the two. In deciding whether to offer a new product, the firm's decision makers must evaluate whether the potential benefits most likely to resonate with buyers will outweigh the most likely cost of producing and marketing the new product. In other words, the entrepreneurial planner has to make an appraisal of the most likely economic profit to the firm. Among their considerations will be the similarity of the new product under consideration with products the firm already produces—the greater this similarity, the less the additional production cost, involving relatively minor retooling and retraining, to produce a similar product with minor modifications from what the firm already produces. This may offer the benefit of using the firm's otherwise idle excess capacity, with no cost in terms of reducing production of the firm's other established output or the rest of its original product line. It also benefits from the established expertise and experience of the firm's personnel—if a product line is too new and different, the firm may have to look outside to find employees with the special expertise to produce it.

If it were necessary to reduce output of the old product line to free up capacity to produce the newly introduced, innovative product, that loss of output of the established product line and the associated profits would be part of the opportunity cost necessary to produce and market the new product. If the new product is more clearly distinct and more differentiated from the firm's established product line, this would generally suggest a greater cost barrier which would need to be overcome to justify moving production into the new product line. In this case, the firm's established expertise becomes increasingly less applicable. Generally speaking, it will be more uncertain that the firm's expertise, such as it is, can successfully support the new production activity and product line, the greater the divergence in the new product line from that in which the firm already has production advantages, and has built a reputation for quality in producing. More capital retooling or the equivalent will generally be required, perhaps including the cost of a completely new assembly line or factory. The greater these costs appear in advance, the less likely that the introduction of the new product can be made to seem feasible, unless other market benefits are truly spectacular.

If the firm's established product is highly sought after by consumers, in all likelihood minor variations on the original product, which require minimal additional costs to produce, will likely also find favor with the market. However, it will be important to avoid cannibalizing sales of the established product line. If sales of the new product will come at the expense of sales of the existing product line, or may potentially cannibalize them, then any lost sales are also part of the opportunity cost of selling the new substitute good or service—ideally, we want consumers to substitute our new product for our competitors' products, not our own.

Within an established firm, entrepreneurs should seek to make any possible improvements to the firm's established production technology, making use of emerging—including both proven and not yet proven—new technologies which can potentially enhance and improve any aspect of the production process. Technological improvement is generally understood in the context of a manufacturing enterprise, but consider that it applies equally to any innovative practices such as advertising through new media, online retail, marketing through smartphone apps, customer relationship management (CRM) systems, etc.

Entrepreneurs should also seek to experiment with the use of alternative, lower-cost inputs, and substituting among the resources they use as inputs in production. Entrepreneurial experimentation with substitute inputs is the only way the best or optimal resource combinations could have been discovered by alert entrepreneurs in the first place, and the only way combinations of inputs can be maintained in optimal balance as technology changes and advances, and the market conditions affecting input prices evolve over time. The optimal relationship among inputs is never an absolute, but is always subject to the state of technical knowledge available to society at any point in time, which is then specifically applied to the production activity of a particular enterprise. Rather than relying solely on the general state of technical knowledge in society at any point in time, which is external to any one firm, the firm may capture some technological advantage through patents or trade secrets, reserving specialized and particularly relevant technical knowledge which they do not share with potential competitors.[19] The strategy of maintaining trade secrets keeps some technical knowledge internal to the firm.

Constraints imposed by the firm's capital equipment, such as the size of its factory, may be binding in the short run. For example, the specific design of the firm's capital installation, say of an assembly line or a steel mill, may be narrowly optimized for a particular application which was anticipated to be the most useful when the entrepreneurial plan was formulated and the capital installation was designed. Capital might be designed to be optimal either in light of the technical knowledge available when the equipment was designed at a certain point in time, or in light of what the entrepreneurial planner and the engineers and technical staff assisting them anticipated as the probable

---

19 Competitors can only uncover trade secrets through industrial espionage, unless the firm with the secret process or recipe sells the secret, licenses it, or voluntarily shares it with competitors or potential competitors. Patents give the patent holder exclusive legal use of the technology for a fixed term, but do not keep the technical knowledge secret. Patent holders generally license the use of the patented technology or process to their competitors. This enables the patent holder to capture a share of their competitors' revenue. The patented Bessemer process for producing steel was initially licensed to four British steelworks, but the steel produced was inferior, and Bessemer bought back his licenses. Stricter quality control enabled the Bessemer process to produce acceptable quality steel at a sufficiently low cost. Bessemer also used a trade secret—manganese nodules used as a catalyst in the steel converter—developed by Robert F. Mushet, one of his competitors. Bessemer purchased Mushet's patents and employed Mushet to implement and further refine the process. Without the trade secret, the value of Bessemer's initial patents was limited (Bessemer 1905, Anstis 1997).

future trajectory of the constellation of prices of the various alternative inputs. Entrepreneurial experimentation with substitution among inputs, or with input proportions, can bear only limited fruit if the installed capital now limits the extent to which inputs can be combined, thus limiting the extent of feasible substitutability among the inputs or factors of production.

Nevertheless, limited gains from substitution may still be possible, which were not anticipated when the capital combination was designed and installed. The knowledge gained from the entrepreneurial planner's experimentation in changing inputs and input proportions will be exceptionally helpful in specifying the characteristics of replacement capital when the time comes to swap out the old equipment. When the firm's capital combination acts as a technological constraint on resource substitution among inputs which would otherwise be desirable, this circumstance contributes to shortening the useful life of the capital. Although from a technological perspective its useful life remains unaffected, the capital's useful economic life is shortened because of potentially changed supply-and-demand conditions in the input markets, resulting in this capital now acting as a binding constraint and a limit on the firm's ability to substitute inputs in response to changes in input prices.

If input prices change to such an extent that a different combination of inputs would be both feasible and optimal, which constraints imposed by the capital equipment now make impossible to implement, the firm will continue producing with the less than optimal combination of inputs which their capital installation can handle. This imposes unfavorably high production costs on the firm, and the firm will not scrap its existing equipment immediately, but will generally retire the inefficiency-inducing capital sooner than it would have otherwise, and before the equipment has reached the end of its technologically useful life. To the extent possible, substitution among inputs is the principal economic strategy for responding to changes in input prices, using those resources more intensively when their relative price falls, and using other resources less intensively when their relative price rises. The ability of a firm to substitute among inputs will generally be limited in the short run by the technical constraints and requirements of their specific capital installation.

5.5 Intra-firm v. Inter-firm Impacts of Entrepreneurial Planning

Within a given firm, entrepreneurial planners have to be alert to the challenges and opportunities presented by changing market conditions and technologies, or at least those presented by their own changing perceptions of these challenges and opportunities. When a firm adopts and implements a new entrepreneurial plan, the new plan may introduce innovations which disrupt the market because these innovations have not been anticipated by others, or innovations which allow for a higher level of mutual plan coordination. Assume for the moment that an innovation is disruptive. This kind of innovation probably occurs less frequently in the real world, but is generally of greater interest. At first, an established product or industry initially serves an established consumer want. The status quo is comfortable, widely understood, and accepted among those who use or produce the product and otherwise interact with this industry. At some point, an alert entrepreneurial planner sees the potential application of a new technology or marketing technique, or identifies a new market niche for an existing product. The new product introduction must find favor with consumers. To do so it must offer them some added benefit, either in terms of a lower price or greater want satisfaction. If the entrepreneurial planner introduces a potentially disruptive innovation which is ultimately rejected by consumers, the only disruption is confined to their own firm.

In order for an innovation to be truly dramatic and disrupt an industry, the innovation must be embraced by consumers by offering significant benefits. It may be that the entrepreneurial innovation provides enhanced want satisfaction to consumers, or lower costs. The disruption the innovation creates for the consumers is always beneficial—if there were no benefits to consumers, they would not buy the product, or at best, would reject it after an initial trial. The disruptive aspects come from the impact of the new product introduction on the entrepreneurial plans of competing firms. The new product, once consumers adopt it, draws away market share from competing firms which have not yet adopted comparable innovative strategies, but instead are attempting to market the old and established products, but now with less success. These competing firms must always suffer in the short run, but the extent of the pain to competitors can only be proportional to the benefit received by consumers. If consumers do not benefit from a disruptive innovation, the status quo is never challenged or disturbed.

Eventually the competing firms which suffer the impact of a disruptive entrepreneurial innovation will adjust their own entrepreneurial plans to accommodate the changed market conditions. They may imitate the innovative industry leader, or offer alternative products with less dramatic and less disruptive adjustments or incrementally differentiated features. The entrepreneurial response to a disruptive innovation is always one which improves mutual coordination among the entrepreneurial plans of others (Kirzner 1996: 39-41). The introduction of a disruptive innovation is an exception to this general rule in the short run, but this exception operates only on competing firms. In the long run, innovations always improve the mutual coordination of entrepreneurial plans. Eventually competing firms observe the impact of the disruptive innovation which always benefits consumers, and learn to adjust to exploit the changed market conditions. Note particularly in the foregoing discussion that we have focused on examining the inter-firm impact of disruptive or Schumpeterian entrepreneurial innovation, and the intra-firm impact of coordination-enhancing or Kirznerian entrepreneurship.

Firms are organized to coordinate various activities of production, acquisition and processing of inputs, acquisition of output to be sold at retail for firms which only market output produced by others, distribution, marketing, etc. Each firm is organized to deliver a specific product or product line. Entrepreneurial planners who are alert to potentially unmet consumer needs will act accordingly and adjust their firm's activities to satisfy the unmet wants they are the first to perceive or suspect with innovative new products. To the extent the entrepreneurial planner's anticipation of consumer wants are correct, the firm benefits along with the formerly unserved or underserved consumers. If the entrepreneurial planner's anticipation of consumer wants turn out to be overly-optimistic or misplaced—an instance of Kirzner's Knowledge Problem A, the firm loses, and generally there is no benefit to the targeted consumer niche from this unsuccessful experimentation.[20] A limited number of consumers may benefit incidentally

---

20 See Chapter 2, section 2.1 for a more detailed discussion of Kirzner's Knowledge Problems A and B (Kirzner 1990).

as the unwanted new product output is sold off at a loss to the firm, but this is usually a one-time-only event.[21]

From the consumers' perspective, new products are constantly being introduced, often with extensive marketing and advertising campaigns which compete for consumer attention. The product and its marketing campaign aim at persuading consumers that the product will (a) satisfy latent wants so far unfulfilled by any product already on the market, (b) better fulfill wants which are already satisfied to some extent by existing products already in use by consumers, (c) satisfy existing wants just as well as existing products, but at a lower cost, or (d) any combination of (a) through (c). Consumers who are persuaded of the potential value of the new product will try it, but if the product does not live up to the promised or suggested benefits of the marketing campaign, this will be a one-time-only purchase. Any number of things may disappoint consumers in trying a new product. The problem may be less with the product's actual characteristics than with an overly ambitious marketing campaign which oversold the product. The new product may actually fulfill latent wants previously left unfulfilled, but if the price to the consumer is too high, exceeding the actual benefits to the consumer, they will never make a repeat purchase, unless the price is subsequently lowered or their preferences eventually change to better favor the product. The new product may

---

21 New product introductions often benefit groups beside the targeted market demographic. If a new product is advertised extensively to market group X, where it is rejected, but it is enthusiastically embraced by market group Y, whose purchases render the introduction a success, the entrepreneurial planner should rejoice in dodging a bullet. They might also take advantage of this fortunate success to reassess the value of their awareness, which would have been more effective if it had initially identified market group Y as the more likely target demographic. Entrepreneurial planners always act in the face of uncertain outcomes, and do not always succeed.

be better than established alternatives, and therefore can sell for a premium over the old products, but if the seller attempts to charge too high a premium, once more there will be no repeat business. This is an instance of Kirzner's Knowledge Problem A on the part of the seller, a problem of seller over-optimism. Or the seller underestimates the price premium consumers are willing to pay and does not charge a sufficiently high price. This is an instance of Kirzner's Knowledge Problem B on the part of the seller, a problem of over-pessimism. There is generally no mechanism to make the seller aware in this case that they could have charged a higher price and gained more revenue, and are thus simply leaving money on the table. At least the buyers benefit more and capture more consumer surplus in this case. The new product may meet consumer wants as well as the established product, but sell for a lower price. However, if the price is not sufficiently lower, that may not overcome consumer resistance against trying new alternatives.

5.6 First-order & Second-order Innovation

When one firm introduces a new product, competing firms do not have to be particularly alert to recognize the opportunities and challenges they face in contesting the new product in the market. This recognition is at least trivially a form of entrepreneurial alertness. As second-order innovators, the late entrant competitors have to assess the cost of producing the new product to compete against the first-order innovator. If they cannot figure out how to produce the product at least as cheaply as the first-order innovator, they cannot successfully contest the market, because their production costs will always be higher. Second-order innovators generally have a further advantage in that they are not subject to the same innovation risk assumed by the first-order innovator.

When the first-order innovator introduced the new product they were at least hopeful that there would really turn out to be a market for it at the price initially asked. The second-order innovator does not have to start from scratch, as it were, in experimentally setting and adjusting the asking price for the new product. This trial-and-error process has already been done for the second-order innovators by the first-order innovator, and by now it will be firmly established that buyers will pay for this product. Thanks to the first-order innovator, now there is a market for new entrants to contest. By the time the second-order innovators enter the market and attempt to contest it, the initial price has already been settled on. Until the market is contested by competing second-order innovators, the first-order innovator enjoys a monopoly, and can extract monopoly rents, provided they are willing to attempt to sell the product at the higher price (Figure 5.1).

The key feature of a monopoly or monopolistic-competitive product is that the product is sufficiently unique or differentiated from potential substitutes offered by competitors, that the firm can only sell a larger quantity by lowering the price. This results in the firm's marginal revenue (MR) falling below the demand curve. In contrast, for a perfectly competitive market, each firm is a price taker and can sell any amount without lowering the market price, thus the price P and marginal revenue (MR) are equal (P = MR). When the first second-order innovator starts selling the product in competition with the first-order innovator, that starts the competitive process of lowering the price and expanding output, but always starting from the first-order innovator's monopoly price, which may have been originally higher, and then will generally be lowered by competition with the second-order innovators'.

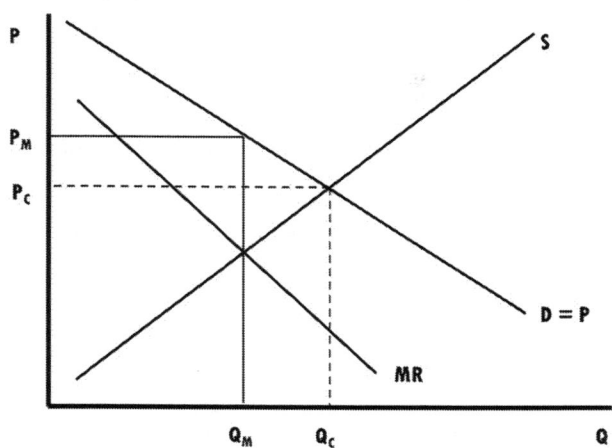

Figure 5.1 Monopoly and Monopolistic-Competitive Pricing

If the new product competes directly with established products for the same target consumers, but offers cost savings, second-order innovators can only contest this emerging market if they can match or exceed whatever share of those cost savings the first-order innovator passes on to consumers, by passing on an equal or greater amount of the savings on to the consumer. If the new product meets latent but unsatisfied consumer wants other firms may not be able to reproduce the product equally well, though the challenge and opportunity is to exceed the desirable characteristics of the first-order innovator's new product. The first-order innovator may maintain their market power through intellectual property protection; that is, patents and/ or copyrights, trademarks and other distinctive branding, or through trade secrets. If the new product meets consumer wants better than the old established products, the first-order innovator's pricing strategy becomes particularly significant. The new product can successfully be sold at a premium by the first-order innovator if they can persuade consumers it is better and more efficacious for satisfying their wants than the established product, but that creates greater opportunity for second-order innovators to undercut the first-order innovator's pricing. As long as the innovation is exclusively marketed by one firm, the opportunity to charge a monopoly price and extract monopoly rents is amplified (Figure 5.2); however, the greater the extent of the monopoly, the greater the incentive for imitators to contest the monopolist's exclusive market advantage. In other words, the greater the monopolist's advantage, the briefer it is likely to last.

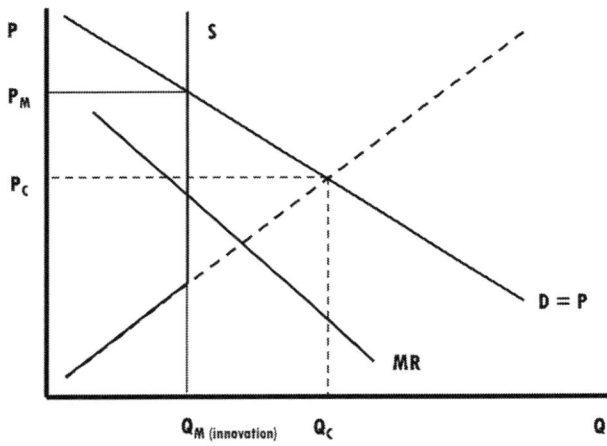

Figure 5.2 Monopoly Profits from an Exclusive Innovation

The market process account of the impact of entrepreneurial planning on consumers and their response to it focuses on the planners' efforts to anticipate consumer wants. The entrepreneur's goal is to present a new or existing product in such a way that it can be seen by potential consumers as either satisfying wants hitherto unknown to, and unrealized by, the consumer, hitherto unsatisfied, or satisfying well-established, known consumer wants, but now at a lower cost to the consumer. There is also some scope to market new or established products at higher price points, effectively converting a utilitarian good into a luxury one, or an inferior good into a normal one. Such a pricing and marketing strategy is strictly dependent on the vagaries of consumer behavior—sometimes it will work, and sometimes it will not, with the success of these attempts seem to depend as much on luck as on the implementation of the marketing strategy which accompanies the introduction of the higher priced version.

5.7 Schadenfreude—Lessons from Unsuccessful Entrepreneurial Plans

Alert entrepreneurs always pay special attention to, and seek to profit from, the marketing missteps of others. First-order innovators assume and are exposed to high market risk. Second-order innovators who copy the first-order innovators assume some risk, but the risk they face is generally an order of magnitude lower, as the first-order innovator has already paved the way for them. Alert entrepreneurs who are able to effectively dissect the reasons for failure of an unsuccessful attempt at first-order innovation will often find themselves now better positioned to construct a superior innovation or more successful marketing strategy. A first-order innovation which is rejected by one market niche may succeed wildly when targeted at a different niche, or merely when tweaked appropriately to address the actual wants and aspirations of the original target demographic.

Entrepreneurial strategies adopted and pursued by competing firms determine market organization, but only if, and to the extent that, these strategies succeed in meeting consumer wants (DiLorenzo 1994). If consumers reject some pro-offered entrepreneurial innovation, that will be because they saw no clear benefit provided, perhaps because the marketing effort failed to communicate benefits effectively to consumers, but at the same time this attempt also uncovers valuable information about consumer wants and the state of the market. Often a failed product would have succeeded if it had been marketed differently or to a different demographic. Other entrepreneurs who are alert to the information provided by entrepreneurial failures, whether their own failures or those of competitors, can benefit by constructing superior innovative strategies which are better attuned to the market realities uncovered through failure analysis. Products marketed unsuccessfully to one consumer niche may be ideal for addressing the wants and aspirations of a different niche. Or they may just be bad products. Failed product introductions engender post-mortem examinations, both internal and external to the firm which experienced the unsuccessful introduction. These studies are an attempt to extract useful information which can potentially inform subsequent attempts at introducing new products. Understanding why a new product introduction failed can inform alert entrepreneurs regarding how the product or its marketing campaign could be tweaked, how the product which failed to appeal to one market demographic might appeal more effectively to a different market demographic, etc. And in general, the more attention entrepreneurial planners pay to the previous failed attempts at introducing product innovations, whether the attempts are their own or their competitors', the wiser they become in the ways of innovation for the market.

Anyone can attempt to innovate, but the key to successful innovation is entrepreneurial alertness to opportunities to better satisfy the wants of others, both consumers and other producers. Alert entrepreneurs may be able to take advantage of the information they uncover through marketing experience by attempting further experimental plans seeking to address and exploit the information uncovered from analyzing failure. Each failure has its lessons. Successes also present lessons in that they can be imitated by second-order innovators, and may point the way to introducing a similar strategy aiming at a different market demographic, etc. Timing can be especially crucial, because an innovation attempted before the market is ripe for it, or without the appropriate marketing campaign to create buyer awareness and receptivity, may fail. This can act as a perceptual and institutional barrier, which must be overcome before the same innovation can be tried again at a time when it might have a better chance of success. Understanding that conditions and consumer preferences may change over time is an essential part of entrepreneurial alertness.

5.8 Ballpoint Pens—Bíró v. Reynolds

The ballpoint pen was invented by Hungarian-Argentine inventor László József Bíró (1899-1985). They were introduced in Argentina as a substitute for the then-conventional and ubiquitous fountain pens. Initially ballpoints occupied a particular niche market due to their utility—they did not smear and did not have to be refilled as frequently, but they were first marketed in the U.S. as a luxury novelty. American entrepreneur Milton Reynolds (1892-1976) reverse engineered Bíró's Birome pen, differentiating his product just enough to avoid infringing on Bíró's patents. Bíró was the first-order innovator with Reynolds coming in as a second-order innovator, but only in North America. Unlike Reynolds, second-order innovators in Italy and Britain licensed

Bíró's patents. However, Reynolds effectively introduced the product and the technology to the North American market. It remains unclear what form market adoption would have taken if Reynolds had not been there at nearly the beginning.

The first Reynolds ballpoint pens sold for what seems in retrospect the exorbitant price of $12.50 in 1945, comparable to the cost of many luxury fountain pens, though competition from new entrants quickly brought the price down (Rosenberg 1971). Reynolds' product introduction strategy captured initially high profits for approximately one year, and also made the product appear more attractive to and desired by consumers as a luxury good comparable to upmarket fountain pens. Because the Reynolds pen was relatively cheap to manufacture and did not incorporate any precious metals, his profit margin was especially high. Gimbels Department Store in New York sold $100,000 worth of Reynolds pens on the first day of sales in 1945. Once Reynolds lost their effective monopoly, ballpoints became cheaper and ubiquitous under the competitive pressures of many competing producers. Eberhard Faber, which had licensed the Bíró and Meyne Birome technology, marketed their Eversharp ballpoints to compete with Reynolds in the face of falling prices.

Reynolds stopped marketing pens in the early 1950s, once their product ceased to be a luxury good with a high markup, and they were no longer able to charge a high monopoly price. In retrospect, it appears Reynolds could have continued to extract value from the ballpoint market, by progressively marketing to less exclusive market segments at lower price points, throughout the 1950s and 1960s. The ballpoint pen offers an example of an initial market introduction of a luxury good with a very high markup. Reynold's initial monopoly price premium fell after a few years, though their first to market advantage was what enabled them to capture the temporarily higher profits in the first place. By 1950 the U.S. market was saturated, and consumers no longer perceived ballpoints as offering significant advantages over fountain pens in terms of convenience or efficiency. Bíró quickly regained his position as industry leader, licensing his patents to Eberhard Faber and Miles Martin, and ultimately selling them to Marcel Bich (1914-1994) for U.S. $2 million in 1953. Through licensing their original patents, the Bíró and Meyne company was able to contest markets beyond South America with less cost and risk, and ultimately captured a definite payoff by selling the patent rights. It cannot have been clear what the ultimate value of the original Bíró patents would have been in 1953 in terms of the future income stream they have since generated. There was and is no guarantee that a technological breakthrough will not someday make ballpoints obsolete, and there is no way to predict when or if this might happen.

As it turned out, by the 1960s disposable ballpoints came to dominate the market at significantly lower price points. The market for ballpoint pens rapidly became so competitive that if the Bíró/Bic product line was ever able to capture any price premium at all, it was very small. Bíró/Bic quickly regained such a large share of the market, combined with a strong reputation for high quality and reliability, that even a miniscule markup can account for tremendous profits. Markets for non-luxury ballpoints seem to be intermediate between perfectly competitive and monopolistically competitive markets. Some brands like Bic advertise extensively and may capture at least a small price premium, but these highly recognized brands have a number of more generic competitors which compete effectively on price.

5.9 The Last Studebakers

In 1962 the Studebaker Corporation hired designer Brooks Stevens (1911-1995) as an external consultant to try to revive their marque with three concept models (Hendry 1972, Foster 2008). By the late 1950s, Studebaker-Packard had first eliminated the Packard marque, which were no longer luxury limousines, but merely especially elaborate mid-size cars, and even discontinued their flagship Studebaker Hawk and Lark models, leaving only the expensive, high performance Avanti sports car designed by Raymond Loewy (Loewy 1979, Parissien 2013: 210-211). The Avanti was unfortunately announced and advertised long before it could be produced in any numbers, resulting in Studebaker having to turn away sales, squandering what little remaining reputation for reliability it still had, to say nothing of consumer goodwill. Stevens's concept cars were intended as revived Studebaker marques for the 1966 or 1967 model years, four to five years into the future. Studebaker was on its last legs by this time and even the Avanti would not stay in production that long. Ideally Stevens' prototypes would have enabled Studebaker to raise enough capital to at least resume production. Unfortunately, Studebaker also needed to reestablish their dealer network, which had collapsed when they had ceased production of Larks, Hawks, and Packards, and offered at best inconsistent distribution of Avantis. Studebaker's inability to supply enough Avantis to meet initial demand did nothing to reassure potential investors.

Stevens's sporty two-door Studebaker Sceptre concept was distinguished chiefly by its sleek and dramatic styling. It was a notably attractive car with a dramatic and innovative headlight assembly that stretched in a thin bar across the whole front of the hood underneath a subtle and futuristic chrome grill which resembled a giant electric razor

(Consumer Guide 1994: 160-165). The innovative LED headlights would not have been legal at the time, so it is interesting to speculate on what a production model would have looked like. A further innovation was that the c-columns were dark tinted glass rather than any opaque material.

The four-door Studebaker Cruiser would have been the company's flagship model, and featured rear suicide doors like the contemporary and highly admired Lincoln Continental. Stevens introduced the design innovation that the front and rear doors would be diagonally interchangeable; that is, the front driver-side door was identical to and interchangeable with the rear passenger-side door, as was the front passenger-side with rear driver-side. This feature would have provided beneficial scale economies in reduced tooling, requiring unique stamping for only two-door assemblies instead of four. Even the Continental's non-interchangeable rear doors required unique tooling for four different door assemblies, because the Continental's rear doors were shorter and otherwise different from the front ones. The Cruiser's unique design would have enabled a production run of every thousand cars to require two thousand right and left doors each, as opposed to the more conventional one thousand each of four different, unique doors, with each of the four requiring its own, unique tooling, stamping, and glass (Parissien 2013: 210-213). The Cruiser's front and rear bumpers were also interchangeable, providing additional production cost savings.

These advantages could have been more decisive for a car with a larger production run like the Ford Fairlane or Chevrolet Impala. Even if Studebaker had been able to obtain the financing they needed to go ahead with resumed production with the Cruiser and Sceptre, the production runs probably would not have been large enough to provide as great an advantage in the way of internal scale economies as could have been achieved by many of Studebaker's competitors (Kirzner 1963: 310-312). Lincoln would also have been hampered by similarly low production runs, but the cost savings for such an expensive luxury car might have offered more of an advantage, either if passed on to the consumer, or if simply retained by Ford, which often produced low runs of the Continental at a loss (Parissien 2013: 261-262). The Cruiser would have been a reasonably attractive sedan, but its relatively short hood and trunk would have readily distinguished it from the longer and sleeker Continental. The fact that the Cruiser would have shared the unique and readily identifiable suicide doors with a top-of-the-line luxury car that sold for around twice the price of most competing sedans might have enabled Studebaker to sell the Cruiser at at least some price premium. The Cruiser's cost saving features would either have made it more competitive or raised the firm's profit margin, or both. If Studebaker had marketed the Stevens design, competing manufacturers would have lost some market share and would have had to respond. Interestingly, by 1966, when the Cruiser would potentially have been introduced, Continental had abandoned the suicide doors, but it remains speculative whether this would have created more of an opportunity for the Cruiser to sell at a price premium. Many consumers liked the feature, and by the time the Cruiser could have been introduced, this would have been the only way to have them.

Stevens also produced a bizarre Cruiser-based hybrid utility vehicle, a unique cab-forward pickup. If this product had ever been marketed, it would have occupied a distinct, and probably very small, market niche. Steven's Cruiser and Spectre designs were attractive and advanced for their time. In all likelihood, if Studebaker had not already made a series of disastrous management missteps from which it could never recover, these innovative models would have found some favor with consumers and might have saved the company. As it was, Studebaker's obsolete and relatively inflexible manufacturing facilities and outdated capital installation held the firm back and imposed uncompetitively high costs through the 1950s. The company had refused to be absorbed into American Motors when Nash-Rambler had merged with Hudson in 1954. Studebaker was left largely in a position of responding to the Big Three's initiatives. Although each of the Big Three had to respond strategically to either of the other two, and to a lesser extent to AMC, they could generally ignore a small independent firm like Studebaker. Studebaker shut down their obsolete factory in South Bend, Indiana in 1963, and continued to produce Cruiser sedans in Hamilton, Ontario until 1966. The last Studebaker Cruisers had some features of Stevens's prototype, but none of the more revolutionary cost saving features.

5.10 Iridium Satellite Network

The Iridium Satellite Network was inaugurated as a Motorola subsidiary from 1997-2002 with an initial investment of $5 billion. The name was selected based on the initial design which called for 77 communications satellites, corresponding to the atomic number of the element iridium. Subsequent technological improvements enabled the network to operate with only 66 satellites (Fossa et al 1998). The initial Iridium Corporation went bankrupt because the product faced far lower demand than originally anticipated. Emerging cell phone technology proved to be far more economical and met the needs of the vast majority of prospective users at a fraction of the cost. The 2001 recession could not have helped, but the cost to Iridium subscribers was set at a high price point that ensured it could only appeal to a small market niche

(Lim, Klein, & Thatcher 2005). Iridium had not anticipated the growth in consumer demand for cell service which rendered the initial Iridium service highly overpriced and largely redundant. They had anticipated that they would enjoy a technological monopoly, pricing their service accordingly, only to discover that very few consumers were unable to take advantage of cheaper alternatives which had recently become available. Incidentally, Motorola was one of the two largest manufacturers of cell phones during this period, along with Nokia. Motorola's success in one area prevented it from succeeding in another.

The satellite network was reorganized with a new constellation of second generation IridiumNEXT satellites starting in 2017. It is now profitable. Recognizing that by this time there was a preponderance of cheaper and highly reliable substitute wireless phone and data transmission services, IridiumNEXT adopted a significantly lower pricing strategy and marketed the system more widely to explorers, mountaineers, journalists, and the military, all operating in places which are not covered by the International Maritime Organization's (IMO) geosynchronous Inmarsat satellite network. Among other things, the experience of the Iridium Satellite Network and the success of its second generation IridiumNEXT version illustrates the greater risk assumed by first order innovators, as well as the impact of this risk. When lessons learned from an initial failure are effectively internalized, a firm can respond with a more resilient, and ultimately less risky, plan.

5.11 Convair B-60

Because many aircraft have been either developed for military use, or share some part of their development costs with military counterparts, we have to be wary of applying lessons from defense contractor experience to the free market. The major difference is that there is basically only one consumer for a defense contractor's product, the government. In many ways airplane manufacture is an oligopolistic industry, and has become increasingly consolidated since the 1950s. Convair, now part of General Dynamics, was formed during World War Two through the merger of Consolidated Aircraft with Vultee Aviation. Convair's principal product during the war was the B-24 Liberator bomber, a more advanced next generation bomber design to follow the pre-war Boeing B-17. The Liberator's thinner, more advanced, and narrower aspect ratio wing gave it greater speed, range, and fuel economy, but if the B-24 lost power in all four engines, it would drop from the air like a rock. In comparison, the B-17's older and more conservative wing design produced greater lift and drag, and enabled the B-17 to glide for miles without engines.

Convair's B-36 was the largest aircraft of its time, with a 230-foot (70.12 m) wingspan, a 162-foot (49.42 m) overall length, and a tail height on the ground of 47 feet (14.25 m). 384 were built mostly from 1948 to 1956 at a cost of $3-4 million each. A six-engine prototype flew in 1944, but the B-36 was not produced in any numbers until 1948, to meet the new need to potentially deliver very large and heavy first generation hydrogen bombs. One problem with the B-36's innovative design was its unique pusher configuration, with its six propellers mounted at the trailing edge of the wing, instead of on the leading edge which is more typical. In the more conventional design, the propellers are mounted at the leading edge of the wing, and the prop blast forces heated air into the engine's carburetors. The B-36 forfeited this advantage, leaving its carburetors prone to icing, ultimately causing several engine fires and the loss of several aircraft. This is an example of an innovation for which the drawbacks outweigh the advantages, and which was not subsequently adopted by competing firms.

At roughly the same time, aviation technology was advancing rapidly and the first jet bombers were being introduced. The Air Force had contracted with several manufacturers to produce prototypes in a competitive flyoff, resulting in the North American XB-45, Convair XB-46, Boeing XB-47, and Martin XB-48. All but the B-47were straight wing designs. Although only the B-45 and B-47 were put into production, all the experimental prototypes generated a great deal of design, fabrication, and flight experience with high performance jet aircraft, which was thus widely diffused throughout the aerospace industry, offering potentially beneficial spinoffs for both military and civil aviation. There was plenty of innovative technology for entrepreneurial planners to be aware of. The most successful of these prototypes was Boeing's B-47 Stratojet, of which the Air Force ultimately purchased 2,032. With its six General Electric J47 engines, it required rocket assisted takeoff (RATO) to get into the air and reach altitude with its heavy bomb load, but its performance was comparable to that of contemporary fighter aircraft, though its load capacity and operating range were still nothing near those of the much larger and slower B-36.

When finally put into production, the B-36 was given a unique hybrid propulsion system, augmenting its original six piston engines with two of the B-47's J47 turbojets on the tip of each wing. The jet engines would only be fired up at altitude and provided the B-36 additional speed and range. The B-36 was already one of the largest and most complicated airplanes ever built, but production models had an incredible ten engines, with two separate fuel systems, one for aviation gasoline and one for jet fuel (JP-4).

Boeing was also asked to design a transitional swept-wing

piston-engined bomber, the XB-55, but this design was abandoned when the all jet B-47 proved so successful.[22] In 1946, the original proposal for what eventually became the Boeing B-52 had been with straight wings and six piston engines. The earliest B-52 design proposals from the mid-1940s were very similar to the B-36, with similar mission requirements and performance characteristics. The B-36 was selected for production because it was farther along in development. The original World War Two requirement for both planes was for a bomber which could strike Germany from North America in the event the Nazis had been able to occupy the UK. Over the B-52's protracted development jet engine technology improved so dramatically that Boeing ultimately adopted an all-jet design with swept wings. 744 B-52s were built between 1952 and 1962, with general production starting in 1955. As of 2019, 58 B-52s remain in service with the U.S. Air Force with 18 in reserve. All the others were scrapped, lost, or are on static display. With the introduction of the B-52, the slower B-36 became obsolete, however, with such an enormous investment of $3 million each, and the B-52 costing even more, approximately $9-15 million each, a way to extend the useful lives of the B-36 might prove beneficial.

Convair's solution was the B-60. It was based on their proven B-36 design, modified with the B-52's eight Pratt & Whitney J57 turbojet engines. As a strategic bomber, the B-60 had a number of shortcomings. The B-36's huge straight wings had been particularly thick, a good

---

22 The Soviet Union produced two large bombers which were roughly comparable to the B-52. The Myasishchev M-4 Molot (Hammer) or Bison had four large turbojets and was nearly as fast as the B-52, though it had a shorter range and smaller bomb load. The turboprop Tupolev Tu-95 Bear, which is still in use by the Russian Air Force and Navy, is slower than the B-52 but its range is comparable. Though larger than Boeing's XB-55 turboprop design proposals, the Tu-95 is similar in layout.

design choice for a slower plane, but not for a jet. The B-36's straight wings joined the fuselage at approximately the midpoint, a design choice which made sense for a straight winged plane. However, the jet B-60 had to have swept wings like the B-52. This resulted in the B-60's wings being placed very far back, providing some cost savings in that the majority of the B-36 and B-60 fuselage would be identical (Knaack 1988). B-60s were not necessarily intended to be built from scratch—some or all of the existing fleet of over 350 B-36s could have been converted to B-60s one by one.

The result of the problematic wing location was that the B-60's center of mass was very far ahead of its center of lift, making it difficult to control in flight, an especially undesirable characteristic for such a large plane. To attach the swept wings to the fuselage, the fuselage was changed as little as possible to keep down conversion costs, but this necessitated inserting a large triangular wedge at the trailing edge of the wing root, generating roughly twice the turbulence and drag, which were already bad because of the thicker wing. The deep root is fairly common among subsonic swept wing planes, featuring somewhat less prominently in the wing design of most commercial jetliners such as the Boeing 707, Douglas DC-8, and Convair 880, as well as most newer jetliners, but was not shared by either Boeing's B-47 or B-52, which were both faster as a result.

Given the design compromises dictated by the B-60's ancestry through the B-36, although it had a greater bomb load than the B-52, it was less stable and maneuverable, and with the same engines, was 100 miles per hour slower in the air. Mounting a thinner wing farther forward would have offered improved speed and control, but would have also required more extensive redesign and rebuilding of the B-36 fuselage, thus costing more. Rather than rebuild the existing B-36 force into B-60s, the Air Force opted to purchase more of the higher-per-forming B-52s, even though they were significantly more expensive.

Development of the B-60, much like Boeing's prop-driven XB-55, a transitional design which never advanced to the prototype stage, can be best understood as a relatively cheap insurance policy which would have been needed if the B-52 design had not ultimately worked so well. If Convair management and engineers had been able to present a more dramatic reworking of the B-36, the B-60's performance characteristics might have been closer to those of the B-52. Convair's strategy of crafting a proposal with the lowest possible conversion costs may have been dictated by the Air Force's program specifications, but this resulted in Convair losing the contract. Their decisions made sense and seemed optimal under the assumption that the B-52's performance would not be as good as it initially actually was. If Convair had known in advance how well the B-52 would perform, especially its airspeed and ability to climb rapidly to altitude, they would have been more likely to decide on a cleaner, thinner wing mounted farther forward. If implemented well, these design changes, though they would have cost more, would have improved the B-60's performance, competitiveness, and chances of success. However, entrepreneurial plans are always constructed in the face of an uncertain future which unfolds as the plan is implemented. Convair even offered to complete the additional B-36s which the Air Force continued to purchase until 1956, as higher performing and more advanced B-60s, but the Air Force was adamant they would rather spend up to three times as much for additional B-52s.

Aerospace engineers would have been well aware that a thinner wing would have generated less drag and would have enabled the aircraft to fly faster. In retrospect it appears that Convair's appraisal and evaluation was that the benefit of the cost savings which would have been provided by a less radical redesign and reengineering of the B-36 fleet, would more than offset any detrimental impact on performance. Also keep in mind that no one knew in advance how successful the B-52 would turn out to be, something which can only become evident in the fullness of time. From the Air Force's perspective, 100 miles per hour of additional airspeed would have made a significant difference in the ability of the B-60 to successfully complete and survive a strategic bombing mission against the Soviet Union. The B-52 would have been much more survivable in this hostile environment simply because of its greater speed and ability to evade enemy interceptor aircraft and air defenses. Until about 1955, the B-36's survivability depended on its ability to reach a much higher altitude than Soviet fighters or missiles.

The YB-60 could reach a maximum speed of 508 mph (411 knots, 818 km/h) at 29,250 ft (8,915 m), with a combat range of 2,920 mi (2,540 nm, 4,700 km) and a maximum range of 8,000 mi (7,000 nm, 13,000 km), a service ceiling of 53,300 ft (16,200 m), and could climb at the rate of 1,060 ft/min (5.38 m/s). The YB-52 prototype was over 100 knots faster, with a maximum speed at altitude of 628 mph (546 knots, 1,010 km/h) at 47,300 ft (14,420 m), with an unrefueled combat range of 3,576 mi (3,110 nm, 5,758 km). The only two YB-60s ever built had a wingspan of 206 feet (62.8 m), overall nose-to-tail length of 171 feet (52.1 m), and a tail height of 60 feet 6 inches (18.4 m). The B-52H, the only version still flying, has a wingspan of 185 feet (56.4 m), overall length of 159 feet 4 inches (48.5 m), and a tail height of 40 feet 8 inches (12.4 m). Earlier B-52s had a distinctive taller tail, 48 feet 8 inches (14.8 m) tall, which was reduced in height on the later model B-52G and B-52H versions to reduce drag and improve performance under conditions of extreme turbulence. The shortening of the tail was a response to tail damage in extreme weather conditions which had resulted in the loss of several B-52s and damage to others. The B-60s huge tail would have been even more vulnerable to turbulence.

Instead of the J57 turbojet, the final and most advanced 1962 H model of the B-52 was given a more advanced and fuel efficient Pratt & Whitney T33 turbofan engine.[23] As of 2019 the Air Force is currently considering re-engining its remaining B-52s. The T33 turbofans were already a major improvement over the J57 turbojets. Modern engines are far more fuel efficient than what was available in 1962, and new engines will give these 60-year-old planes a significantly longer unrefueled range.

The Air Force sought to replace the B-52 in the late 1950s with the North American B-70 Valkyrie. The B-70 would have flown at mach 3, over 2,000 miles per hour, at an altitude of 70,000 feet. Contemporary Russian fighters and air defense missiles would not have been able to reach or shoot down the B-70. The design was not just cutting edge, but would have required the industry to go a few steps beyond what was clearly known to be feasible, and would have advanced the state

---

23 The first generation jet aircraft engines were turbojets. Exhaust gases turn a turbine at the engine's trailing end. The aft turbine is connected by an axle to a forward turbine, the compressor, located just behind the engine's air intake. The compressor turbine produces and maintains high pressure in the combustion chamber where the fuel-air mixture is ignited. The turbofan, fanjet, or bypass engine is a refinement which allows up to about half of the air entering the engine to be accelerated by the first stage of the compressor. Some of the air accelerated by the compressor is allowed to bypass both the combustion chamber and the trailing turbine. Allowing this relatively cool air to mix with the exhaust gases expelled at the trailing end of the jet enables the engine to produce more thrust while burning less fuel. The major advantage of turbofan engines, which are used by most modern commercial airliners, is that they accelerate a larger volume of air to a lower exhaust speed, enabling them to generate greater thrust more efficiently. In comparison, a turbojet has to accelerate a smaller amount of air to a higher exhaust speed. This difference allows the turbofan to provide better fuel economy and greater operating range.

of the art in numerous ways. The projected cost of $750 million per plane was so prohibitive that the ability to acquire a sizable force of these planes was highly questionable. It has been argued that actual production costs could have been lower, because the development costs would have been spread over the whole production run. However, these costs per plane could well have turned out to have been even higher as design improvements and other enhancements were found to be necessary. Improvements in Soviet air defense technology also rapidly necessitated a low-level penetration strategy, for which the B-70 would have been far less suitable than the B-52. Two XB-70 prototypes were produced for a total program cost of $1.5 billion in 1962. The second, more advanced prototype, which incorporated a number of design and fabrication improvements based on experience gained with the first, was tragically lost in a 1966 accident. The surviving XB-70 is displayed in the Air Force Museum at Wright-Patterson Air Force Base in Dayton, Ohio.

CHAPTER 6

Entrepreneurial Planning & Business Strategy

Mises, Hayek, and Kirzner examined how prices transmit information, and how entrepreneurs compete to take advantage of available information and price signaling mechanisms to create and deliver superior market outcomes. As market outcomes are enhanced over time through the competitive actions of entrepreneurs, this allows both consumers and other entrepreneurs to better coordinate their plans and achieve increasingly higher levels of consumer and social well-being. Entrepreneurs compete to recognize and act on the most relevant information and exploit it to their advantage. They earn profits by better facilitating the actualization of others' wants and objectives. Each entrepreneur has a unique perspective on the massive volume of available market information, and not all of this information is shared equally widely. Some of this information is idiosyncratic proprietary knowledge such as trade secrets, but most of it is publicly available to any alert entrepreneur. Nevertheless, the quantity of information visible to each individual in society is always small compared to the total which is publicly visible. Kirzner in particular not only critiqued the static equilibrium model of perfect competition, but explored its limitations, and developed the market process account of how entrepreneurship contributes to real world competition.

Out of a publicly available information set which anyone can observe, the knowledge each entrepreneur is most alert to and aware of, is largely unique to that individual, determined by their unique history, experience, interests, and talents. Each entrepreneur is likely to specialize in some field of endeavor in which they have achieved the greatest success in the past. Recognizing the central role of entrepreneurs in guiding and carrying out market process helps us understand how market exchange allows for generating and using the essential information which alert entrepreneurs use to improve on past market outcomes. Without alert entrepreneurs competing in a market economy, this information would otherwise be useless, inaccessible, and meaningless. Competitive markets subject the experimental innovations of entrepreneurial planners to strict and unyielding profit-and-loss incentives (Ikeda 1994). Market competition privileges those innovations offering economic benefits to the firm's prospective customers, but puts at a disadvantage those equally well-meaning but unsuccessful attempts that purport to offer promised benefits which subsequently fail to materialize. Competition also punishes those who fail to innovate at all by leaving them behind.

Market participants only benefit to the extent they correctly anticipate the plans of others—offering a new product for sale provides no benefit at all to anyone if no one buys it. Even for a consumer, anticipated benefits cannot be realized if the consumer wants to buy a product which is not offered for sale. Similarly, production plans which call for combining various inputs to produce a certain amount of output cannot be carried out if the necessary inputs are unavailable, or cannot be acquired at a sufficiently low cost to ensure the enterprise turns a profit. The perceived benefit of a prospective innovation must always be strong enough to overcome the natural forces of sloth, inertia, and resistance to change. Although entrepreneurial planners always face the risk that the strategy of avoiding change may turn out not to have been the best possible strategy, it is often the most comfortable and easiest strategy to pursue, and discounting the possible risks of stagnation in continuing to do whatever is most familiar seems to come naturally. In the face of an uncertain and unfolding future, we cannot know that our present course of affairs will always be the best response, but it is always an easy response requiring no further effort or strain of decision. One simply continues as one has been doing.

The attempt to formulate an optimal response in the face of an unknown and uncertain future is always fraught with the need to acquire sufficient intelligence and information, which may not yet be available, since the future the entrepreneurial plan will seek to address has yet to unfold before us. In the face of the high cost of acquiring, processing, and interpreting the necessary information, the risk of error, and the difficulty of confidently making decisive and authoritative choices in an environment of overwhelming uncertainty, we often default to merely continuing what we have done in the past. The natural tendency to continue the prevailing state of affairs is a major strategy for responding to uncertainty, though it may not always be a successful strategy. Success or failure of an entrepreneurial plan can only be uncovered in the fullness of time—it cannot be preconceived or predetermined, which is why the most successful entrepreneurial planners constantly adapt their plans to meet changing conditions as they arise.

6.1 Innovative Strategy & Market Organization

Entrepreneurs compete with each other as buyers in one market and sellers in another. Recall the distinction between first-order and second-order entrepreneurial innovation. A first-order innovator does something as a response to a business opportunity they are the first and initially the only one to perceive, or at least they are the first to act on. A first-order innovation is something essentially new, not an imitation of an established competitor or a strategic response to their behavior. Market organization is largely determined by the responses of second-order innovators.[24] Clearly it is much easier to differentiate products from those sold by competitors when the firm produces a good for sale than when the firm merely engages in arbitrage. Entrepreneurs can shape the way inputs are combined in production and can target their final product at the preferences of underserved consumer niches which have been so far unperceived—and therefore underserved—by other entrepreneurs.

Market organization is determined by the strategic interaction of feedback and response among entrepreneurial planners and the consumers who demand final goods and services. Firms are designed by entrepreneurial planners, subject to institutional constraints imposed by the legal-regulatory environment (Foss 1997). Firms are also designed to overcome limits on how efficiently information can be processed. Imagine the coordination difficulties which would be faced by a mass of freelancing independent contractors the size of even a small firm,

---

24 See Chapter 7 for a more detailed discussion of how entrepreneurial planners bring about different kinds of market organization: perfect competition, monopolistic competition, oligopoly, or monopoly.

let alone a large one the size of General Motors or General Electric.[25] In designing a business firm, an entrepreneurial planner is able to capture important strategic advantages from having preferences and expectations which differ from his or her competitors, but also benefits from correctly understanding and anticipating behavior and responses of others, particularly of potential competitors. Because entrepreneurs attempt to coordinate their plans and expectations with those of other entrepreneurs—who may be suppliers of needed inputs or purchasers of the firm's output—as well as with consumers, successful innovation is contingent on innovators' unconventional and unanticipated offerings being met with the response which the innovator correctly anticipated. However, whenever this advantage is based on innovative firm organization, the advantage will generally only be temporary, because firm organization typically cannot be concealed from potential imitators. Innovative entrepreneurs have an automatic advantage over merely imitative managers, though through adaptive, second-order innovation, entrepreneurs can benefit further because they can avoid most of the risk willingly assumed by the truly creative entrepreneurs who are the

---

25 In a classic article on the theory of the firm, Coase (1937) attempts to explain why firms exist and argues that firm organization reduces transactions costs, including the cost of processing information. Information processing burdens increase exponentially with the number of different individuals involved, but the more efficient and streamlined information transmission streams created by the internal hierarchy of a business firm makes most of these information processing streams unnecessary. If individual workers interacted directly with one another, the level of coordination and efficiency they could achieve would be limited, and would also be severely hampered by the high transactions cost which would be required for them to interact as independent agents. A firm enables workers to achieve the level of social cooperation necessary to support complex and mutually coordinated production plans under the direction of an entrepreneurial planner. Information processing burdens help explain why firms cannot grow without limit, and why central economic planning, where the whole economy would be managed as a single large firm, cannot work (Klein 1996).

first-order innovators.

If an idiosyncratic entrepreneur with especially unique and uniquely valuable or correct expectations is aware of the different expectations held by competing entrepreneurs, they will then be in a better position to act on their advantageous situation. This will be much less the case when the idiosyncratic entrepreneur is less aware of what are the more mainstream expectations of potentially competing entrepreneurs. Then the idiosyncratic entrepreneur will be in less of a position to realize or take advantage of the unique benefits they alone enjoy, because if they mistakenly think everyone else thinks as they do about the coming future, they will not see any advantage to act on. In fact, when an idiosyncratic entrepreneur with unconventional or innovative views of the market or of their business opportunity set mistakenly believes their idiosyncratic views are more widespread, they may mistakenly anticipate benefiting from external scale economies.[26] These external scale economies may never come into existence if no one else acts on the unique, and uniquely correct anticipations which actually belonged alone to this one visionary entrepreneurial planner (Tarko 2013).

Once they discover their views are not sufficiently widespread or current to provide the hoped-for benefits, the uniquely visionary innovator in this case might still succeed by proselytizing their idiosyncratic views among the industry. Entrepreneurs who are most alert in

---

26 Scale economies result when the unit cost of production falls with increased output. This can be due to spreading the fixed costs over more units of output. Scale economies can be internal or external to the firm. External scale economies result when the suppliers and specialized labor needed for a particular industry tend to congregate wherever that industry is concentrated—the scale economies this creates benefit all competing firms and potential new entrants. Internal scale economies result from the production technology, fixed costs being spread over more units of output, or the market power of a larger firm in being able to command or negotiate a lower price for inputs on more favorable terms.

one area or direction may be less so in other areas—sometimes to the point of seeming to wear blinders. Imagine, for example, a stock market speculator who employs technical market analysis. The speculator watches for a particular configuration in the price of a stock charted over time; that is a familiar and characteristic pattern in the charted price of the stock and when they observe this pattern, the market analyst takes that as a signal to implement a particular strategy to buy, or perhaps to sell.[27] If their first experience in attempting to follow this strategy had failed, in most cases they would have abandoned it at that point. If instead the strategy succeeds initially, it may indicate a profound and underlying truth about the market, or it may be merely a coincidence. As long as a particular strategy continues to succeed and chalk up additional gains for technical analysis, the speculator is happy, is making money, and each success in a sequence of successful applications of the strategy will further confirm the speculator's belief in the strategy's efficacy and the validity of technical analysis. The first time the strategy loses money, the speculator may take the loss as an utter and complete disconfirmation—it proves that technical analysis and the related strategy do not always work. However, in many cases, speculators will just assume that their recent loss is no more than a

---

27 Technical analysis attempts to predict market upturns and downturns based on patterns in past data (Schalbackers 1930, Edwards, Magee, & Bassetti 1948). Two particular patterns which a technical analyst might try to identify in stock charts would be the so-called "head and shoulders" or "aborted head and shoulders" configurations which would then be taken as a strong indication of a likely market downturn for the stock under consideration. Upside-down versions would be taken as indicating likely market upturns. Computer analysis is more sophisticated, automates the search function, can react faster, and monitor larger numbers of stocks, but does not necessarily have any greater validity. Applying a trading algorithm appears to substitute an objective and unvarying condition for a subjective trading decision, but the design of the algorithm necessarily incorporates subjective judgement.

bewildering and unfortunate anomaly, a black swan which occurs very rarely. The speculator will then continue the strategy until a few more losses have been chalked up, and perhaps quite a few.

It is something in the nature of speculative markets that the behavioral environment often seems to go through phases. A technical strategy which seems effective in a booming market may not work as well, or even at all, in a bear market. Markets are complicated things, and sometimes our experience suggests regularities which turn out to be nothing more than illusions. The most alert entrepreneurs must probably be especially on their guard against this kind of phenomenon because they may be particularly susceptible to identifying apparent patterns which are really not there at all. We have an instinctual tendency seize on these apparent regularities to help explain things which are too complicated to admit simpler explanations.

When consumers find a new product marketed, they must be convinced they will receive some additional benefit, whether tangible or intangible, to justify substituting the new product for their previously established choice. This benefit may be a lower price, or actual short-comings of the old product may have been addressed by the new product. Advertising can be useful in informing and persuading potential consumers of the new product's proposed additional benefits or lower cost. If the new product is sufficiently better, especially if it will signal affluence or some other indicator of superiority or desira-bility, the consumer may be persuaded to pay a higher price. Again, advertising and marketing strategies can now come into play to help establish and reinforce the perception of the product as one that signals affluence and therefore justifies the price premium. Consumers will also pay for various markers of virtue, such as all-natural, organic, free trade, dolphin safe, green, fair trade, etc. Each of these claims can be featured prominently in advertising the product.

The key to capturing the higher profits of a monopolistic-competitive market is effectively differentiating the product from other alternatives and potential substitutes. The product may be unique and occupy a unique market niche, or it may be basically the same as many alternative substitute brands. Even so, it can still be marketed and branded in such a way as to suggest that a price premium is justified, as for example, a luxury product, a signal of affluence, targeted toward a specific demographic market niche, etc. Sometimes this differentiated branding strategy succeeds, but sometimes it does not. Brand names for domestic products can be chosen to suggest the same qualities and origin as the most expensive and highly regarded imported product. For example, a mediocre domestic wine could be branded with a name suggestive of a French origin, with most of the label even written in French, as long as there is no explicit and fraudulent claim that the wine is actually from any region of France. Apart from the taste or quality, the label makes the product a better substitute for French wine to many consumers. A cheap and unappealing perfume can be watered down to reduce its overpowering scent, reducing the cost of production by further stretching the production run. Now, at least potentially, the product can be marketed at a premium.

Whether consumers will reward such stratagems in the market will remain to be seen, and can only be discovered by trying them. There can be little doubt that an appropriate marketing strategy can greatly enhance the chances of success of any strategy to differentiate a product from alternative substitutes. At a minimum, advertising must inform consumers of the new brand's special characteristics and features, along with its supposed benefits.

The entrepreneur must combine available resources in an attempt to anticipate and satisfy consumer wants. The value of the firm's productive resources, as well as its goods-in-process, and finished inventory stocks, are captured in the value of the firm considered as a going enterprise. Entrepreneurs must imagine creative ways to fulfill consumer wants, imaginatively outdoing potential competitors in fulfilling consumers wants better and more completely. The most successful entrepreneurs often succeed because they provide an innovative product which satisfies consumer wants better and more completely than by providing what consumers might have asked for if given a chance—as the famous quote commonly misattributed to Henry Ford says, "If I had asked my customers what they wanted, they would have asked for a faster horse." To implement an entrepreneurial plan, entrepreneurs must visualize and implement a roadmap to completion to acquire the necessary resource combinations, combine them in a production process, and market the output attractively to the target market demographics, and then perhaps implement strategies to broaden their market niches, once established. Entrepreneurial planners are likely to face little competition, at least initially, if their vision of a potential product differs very dramatically from that envisioned by potential competitors—these are the planners who enjoy the greatest advantage as entrepreneurs. Their innovations will create the largest short run disruptions to the plans of others, but provide even greater benefits in terms of greater social cooperation and mutual plan coordination in the long run (Kirzner 1996: 39-41, Lewin 1997).

In constructing an entrepreneurial plan, often the entrepreneur must justify every assumption to numerous individuals who might be supervisory or advisory within the firm, and confirm every detail with numerous other individuals, who may contribute unique insight and help refine and improve on the entrepreneur's initial vision.

Entrepreneurs may conduct extensive market research to help design the product, or determine how it can be marketed, and what advertising media should be used and will be most effective. Strategies which fail or merely disappoint can be revisited and revised, and new strategies can then be devised which are based on accrued experience and better information.

Market research can inform any stage of developing an entrepreneurial strategy, but should be designed specifically to access or generate the precise latent information which is most vital to the firm's task at hand. Survey data might inform a strategist concerning what consumers are willing to pay for various features being considered to be added to an existing product. Those features that can be added at an increased cost of production which is still lower than the extra price which can be successfully charged will pay for themselves in higher profits, and will generally justify charging a higher price for the product. Those new features that would cost too much to add should be foregone, but an alert entrepreneur will remain alert to alternative, lower cost ways of providing either the same precise feature, something very similar which may cost less, or something else completely different which may yet serve the same purpose for consumers.

Entrepreneurs should always be attracted first to the newest products which are most dramatically different from established substitutes. Though introducing new products means greater risk and uncertainty than with producing and selling more familiar product offerings, the more a new product is differentiated from established substitute products, the greater the extent of the initial monopoly the producer will temporarily enjoy. If the new product introduction is successful, the firm captures monopoly profits until the first imitative competitor can enter the market (Kirzner 1963: 310). Then competition will start to lower profits, but the original firm can attempt a further round of innovation, and if they do this often enough, will have gained reputation and credibility for succeeding with the target consumer audience.

6.2 The de Havilland Comet

In the early years of jet aviation, Britain had a tremendous head start. No one individual has a better claim to having invented the jet engine than Air Commodore Sir Frank Whittle. Nevertheless, the first practical jet aircraft was the German Messerschmidt Me-262, which had two small turbojets. It was introduced so late in World War Two that it could not be produced in sufficient numbers to have much impact. Several were shot down by slower propeller-driven Allied fighters, though the Me-262 was always highly regarded for its performance and successful technological innovation under the most difficult constraints imaginable.

The first passenger jet, the de Havilland Comet, was a truly cutting edge design—perhaps too much so. It operated at greater speed and higher altitude than any other aircraft of similar size up to that time. Its critical design flaw was the punched rivet holes around its passenger cabin's sharp-cornered rectangular windows. The rectangular windows were not unusual for the time, and can be found on many other planes of the era, such as the Douglas DC-3 (C-47) and DC-4 (C-54) airliners. The Comet's larger fuselage was made of sheet aluminum which was generally no thicker or stronger than that of any other contemporary propeller-driven aircraft, though very few were anywhere near as large as the Comet. No other commercial airliner of the time could fly as fast or high, and therefore their airframes were not subjected to the same levels of stress as the Comet, particularly the extreme stresses from cabin pressurization at altitude. Pressurization cycles subjected the Comet airframe structure to stresses similar to inflating and deflating a very thin skinned aluminum balloon. These cycles created unanticipated high stresses at the rivet holes around the windows. The fabrication process of punching the rivet holes to attach the window frames created small hairline cracks and served to make the aluminum skin even more brittle around these points. Cracks would spread as the plane approached altitude and the inside cabin pressure greatly exceeded the outside pressure. Subjected to such high stresses at points of particular structural weakness on the airframe, Comets started splitting open in the air with no survivors.

After four mysterious and catastrophic failures in 1953 and 1954, the Comet fleet was grounded. The subsequent investigation was unprecedented, and uncovered the role of metal fatigue in structural failure, something which had not previously been suspected or antic- ipated (Cohen 1955). The Comet was redesigned with cornerless oval windows, which did not create undue stress through pressurization cycles. A thicker skin made of a stronger aluminum alloy was also used on later Comets, and the new rivet holes were drilled rather than punched through the aluminum, which was less likely to start the fatal hairline cracks. In addition, the redesigned oval window frames were glued to the skin as well as being riveted, providing additional strength, and preventing any hairline cracks from spreading (Atkinson, Winkworth, & Norris 1962). Such redundant approaches to fabrication have become standard. Air ace Eddie Rickenbacker, then president of Eastern Airlines, visited de Havilland's Comet plant before the accidents and professed to be appalled by the original rectangular window design, but his concerns went unheeded until the crashes, though one wonders if the account in his memoirs is not an instance of selective memory (Rickenbacker 1967).

The redesigned Comet 4 debuted in transatlantic service in 1958, only one month before the first Boeing 707 flight. The Douglas DC-8 became available in 1960. By this time, the Comet was now significantly more expensive to operate than its newer and more modern competitors. BOAC and de Havilland had to face the risk of first-order innovation. Before the accidents and grounding, they enjoyed the monopoly pricing power of a first-order technological innovator. The technical knowledge gained through the Comet accident investigations was instrumental in ensuring the success of the next generation of jet aircraft. Competing firms, particularly Boeing and Vickers-Armstrongs, successfully incorporated lessons learned to successfully implement less risky, second-order innovations.

From 1952 to their grounding in 1954, de Havilland used most of its production to supply BOAC. Numerous orders from other airlines, including Pan Am, were cancelled during the grounding. The Vickers-Armstrongs V-1000, a larger turbofan jetliner derived from the Vickers Valiant bomber, which would have had a layout similar to the Comet, was cancelled by the British Ministry of Supply in 1955. The V-1000 would have competed with the Comet and the 707, and the availability of an alternative plane would have enabled BOAC to continue jet service without disruption. BOAC ordered fifteen more modern and fuel-efficient Boeing 707s in late 1956, around the end of the Comet grounding, though they were not delivered until 1960. Once de Havilland introduced the larger and redesigned Comet 4 after the grounding, more advanced competitors, such as the 707, prevented the firm from regaining its market share. Boeing, Douglas, and Vickers-Armstrongs, which ultimately produced the VC-10, all benefited tremendously from the technical data developed by the accident investigations. If de Havilland had not faced any competing firms, it would have been entirely natural to resume their industry leadership after the grounding.

Because of the more competitive and contested nature of the airliner market, de Havilland's competitors were able to take better advantage of the breathing space offered by the Comet grounding, as well as benefit from the technical data uncovered by the investigation. At the same time the state of technology was advancing especially rapidly. The case of the Comet illustrates the dangers and risks to which first-order innovators are exposed. In this case, the financial rewards accrued mainly to second-order innovators, particularly Boeing, which was also a strong technological innovator. De Havilland's management, though they would certainly regret the loss of life due to the accidents, was among the most entrepreneurial in the industry, and could have no regrets regarding their path-breaking contribution to advancing aviation, which they probably valued more than any financial returns.

6.3 Designer Jeans

Designer jeans still sell for a premium over conventional jeans, but few would argue that conventional jeans are not a good, even near perfect, substitute. Each introduction of a new line of designer jeans and related apparel seeks to address, and perhaps even create, a different market niche and reach a different consumer demographic. After the initial introduction of the first few designer brands, diminishing returns to successive further introductions of new brands began to set in. Designer jeans were a product and marketing strategy which successfully transformed a utilitarian product, blue jeans, into a luxury product commanding a higher price and markup, and offering sellers greater profit margins. New introductions continue, because part of the appeal of such luxury products is their perceived exclusivity, their higher cost to signal consumer affluence, and their rarity or lack of ubiquity.

In certain social circles, one cannot stand out if one wears the same relatively mundane and common brands of designer jeans as one's peers. One can stand out better with a new, unusual, or uncommon brand of designer jeans, which may signal the wearer as being affluent, fashion-forward, or particularly hip. However, except for affluence, one can potentially signal precisely the same things, as well as a superficial lack of relative pretension, by wearing normal, non-designer jeans. The value of the product comes partly from its exclusivity and luxury cachet, which are maintained through the high price and markup.

Designer jeans are an example of a familiar product which sells in a monopolistic-competitive market. These products have to be differentiated from one another and extensively, even extravagantly, advertised to create brand awareness and inform potential consumers of their special design and features. The interplay between intra-firm and inter-firm entrepreneurial innovation is especially interesting because it is more or less continuous. When any firm introduces a new model or pattern, it must advertise extensively and incur significant marketing and distribution expenses, which have to be recouped by sales. Competing firms can respond with either new designs or merely new marketing campaigns. Any time a new brand of designer jeans is introduced, production and marketing generally continues as long as revenues are sufficient to cover the costs. For this kind of product, marketing costs are by far the largest. Brands should be discontinued once their sales fail to generate sufficient revenue to cover these costs, including the extravagant marketing costs.

6.4 Marketing Strategy: the RCA Berkshire Festival Series

The most typical strategy for new product introductions is to offer the consumer cost savings or technological advances, or both. For example, the picture quality of a contemporary flat-screen television is much greater than what was possible with the highest-end plasma screens of a mere ten years earlier, and at a fraction of the cost, which continues to fall as screen size continues to increase and picture quality improves. Back in 1948, RCA's top-of-the line Berkshire Festival Series radio came in a huge mahogany Baker Furniture cabinet designed to mimic Baker's largest, top-of-the line breakfront, and included a state-of-the-art record player and a 29-inch rear-projection black-and-white television. This flagship unit retailed for around $4,000 at a time when that would buy a Cadillac or at least two ordinary cars! Only 1,000 were produced and owners included conductor Sergé Koussevitzky and the Shah of Iran. Koussevitsky endorsed the product in RCA advertisements. Most of the price was for the very high quality radio receiver, incorporating the latest military technology designed to take advantage of RCA's wartime experience as a prime defense contractor. The large TV screen was particularly noteworthy for the time considering that the largest cathode ray tubes which could be manufactured in 1948 had only a 4-inch diagonal. The product did not sell in great numbers, but was never intended to. Less expensive models in the Berkshire Festival Series product line, most of which lacked the TV, sold well, though they were also extremely expensive luxury items (Lewis 1991).

In many respects, the way a product is marketed and packaged is as important as its physical characteristics. Advertising presents the consumer with information about what is offered for sale. Apart from the straightforward information about the product and its intended applications, advertising may also attempt to appeal to consumer aspirations and differentiate the product from competitors' to create a monopolistic-competitive market. This enables the differentiated product to capture monopoly profits. With a broad range of substitute products, distinctive advertising contributes to building a so-called mystique for a particular marque or brand, distinguishing it at least psychologically from alternative substitutes. RCA's extensive advertising of their product line, including the Koussevitsky endorsement, helped them market the lower-cost, higher-volume models, which incidentally provided RCA a higher profit margin. The omnipresence of saturation advertising attempts to strengthen such a mystique and perhaps build it rapidly. Consumers may respond as desired, or not.

6.5 The Ford Edsel

When Ford introduced the Edsel in 1957, they had been planning this innovative new product line for almost ten years. Ford introduced the Edsel with an unprecedented marketing campaign, including a yearlong series of print ads in prominent publications, each highlighting a single innovative feature, but leaving the car's overall appearance and design cues a tantalizing mystery. The campaign culminated in an hour-long variety show on television. The two-year marketing campaign drastically oversold the Edsel, which when finally revealed, was at most, just another car (Daines 1994).[28] Consumers disliked the name intensely, an unsurprising outcome which had been anticipated and well appreciated, both by Ford's marketing consultants, as well as by the Ford family. The family would have vetoed the use of the name if Ford had recently become a publicly traded corporation (Deutsch 1976). The Edsel was dramatically different in engineering and styling from anything else offered by American carmakers, though all Edsels shared the prominent tail fins which were typical of the era and not distinctive at all.

One difficulty with the original Edsel concept was that they were intended to be marketed as a high quality product and produced in a dedicated factory. Ford had identified a gap in Ford's product line between the moderately upscale Mercury and the luxury Lincoln. The original need for the Edsel was for a marque to compete directly with Chrysler's Dodge and GM's Buick and Pontiac divisions. Late in the design process, Ford adopted the cost-saving expedient of producing all Mercurys, Edsels, and Lincolns in the same plant for a newly formed MEL division (Parissien 2013: 196-197). The consolidated production facility sought to exploit internal scale economies, but the approach introduced quality control issues for the first Edsels. Because the Mercury, Edsel, and Lincoln product lines shared very little or no common tooling, the only economies came from proximity of operations within the same plant—essentially, the Edsel benefitted, if at all, more from external scale economies than internal ones.

---

28 This suggests the introduction of the Segway in 2001. Prior to its unveiling, the Segway was kept under strict secrecy, only offering enticing and ludicrously overblown hints that it would literally transform civilization and be the biggest thing since the internet or the PC (Kamen 2003). Once revealed, it instantly became unclear what the actual market for this bizarre novelty product would be.

Ford's pricing strategy for the Edsel was also problematic. Although it is impossible to say how well alternative pricing approaches might have worked out, the prices for the entry-level 1958 Edsel Ranger ($2,484-$2,643) were comparable to the most expensive Ford division product, the Fairlane 500 ($2,410-$3,138), as well as the entry-level Mercury Medalist ($2,547-$2,617). The next higher priced Edsels, the Pacer ($2,700-$2,993) and Corsair ($3,311-$3,390) competed directly with Mercury's Monterey ($2,652-$3,081) and Montclair ($3,236-$3,597). The top-of-the-line Edsel Citation ($3,500-$3,766) also competed with the Mercury Montclair. The most expensive Mercury, the Park Lane ($4,280-$4,405) was priced above the Edsel Citation. Lincoln prices started at $4,334, with the 1958 Continental priced between $4,802 to $4,927. Edsels were priced to compete against other Fords, especially against Mercury, not against Buick or Pontiac.

Producing so many different MEL products sequentially over each model year created initial quality control problems which impaired Ford's ability to rapidly build a reputation for the new Edsel as a high quality, well built product (Bonsall 2002). Similar problems were not documented at the time for contemporary Mercurys and Lincolns, perhaps because these were more familiar, less exotic products, and Ford workers in the MEL division found it easier to produce them to relatively higher quality standards. If Mercurys and Lincolns had similar design or production flaws, these shortcomings were less critical given their more conservative and less innovative design, engineering, and styling. Also, the established Ford marques already enjoyed strong reputation for quality, which the newly introduced Edsel had to build from scratch. Quality control issues were alleviated quickly if not solved completely, but the Edsel was never able to recover from its initial poor reputation (Dicke 2010). Even in the face of the 1957-1958 recession, the Edsel remains the most successful new marque roll out in automotive history in terms of units sold (Daines 1994). Essentially Ford got what they had hoped for. Nevertheless Ford was disappointed with sales, and eliminated the Edsel in 1960 after a drastic redesign which ultimately became the modestly selling Mercury Comet.

6.6 Widescreen Cinema

Cinema technology was introduced in the early 1900s by technological innovators including Thomas Edison (1847-1931). Color filming was introduced as early as the 1920s, but it was expensive and cumbersome, and was used only for a limited number of films, and usually only for select scenes in those. For example, Cecil B. DeMille's *King of Kings* (1927) features limited scenes in two-color Technicolor. Restored versions are exceptionally vivid, with deeply saturated color which suggests old master oil paintings. Synchronized sound was introduced next by Warner Brothers with *The Jazz Singer* (1927), which features several synchronized songs, but only about two minutes of sound dialog, commencing with Al Jolson's famous line, "wait a minute, wait a minute, you ain't heard nothing yet." Most of the film is silent with intertitles like contemporary silent films. In 1931, Warners contracted with Technicolor to produce several films each year in color, but the initial success did not justify the greater expense of color filming—the only results of this contract were two horror films starring Lionel Atwill and Fay Wray, *Dr. X* (1932) and *The Mystery of the Wax Museum* (1933).

The industry developed two approaches to filming in color. Technicolor's original process employed standard black-and-white film, with the image split with a prism so it could be filmed on two, and later three, separate strips of 35 mm black-and-white film. Each film register had to be very precisely synchronized. The split images would be exposed through different primary color filters. The film exposed through a particular filter produced a black-and-white image that was then printed in the same color as the corresponding filter. When combined this produced a full color positive image. Technicolor developed color-fast metallic dyes to print these images in bright, deeply saturated, though not necessarily very natural color—their cyan red dye was particularly orange-balanced. Peculiarities in the technology's spectral balance could be compensated for by carefully selecting and adjusting the color schemes for sets, costumes, makeup, and lighting. The Technicolor Corporation provided a consultant for each film to advise the filmmakers on the use of their process and the color schemes of the production design. In Hollywood this was often Natalie Kalmus, the ex-wife of Technicolor president Dr. Herbert Kalmus.

The alternative approach was to use film with a granular matrix consisting of elements for the three primary colors, such as with Eastman Kodak's Eastmancolor and Agfa's Agfacolor, sometimes called Ansco Color. Because the film had to have all three primary colors embedded in the same 35 mm celluloid matrix, the grain density could not be more than about one-third as dense as with the finest grained black-and-white film used for Technicolor. Because they were cheaper and easier for the film studios to use, Eastmancolor and Agfacolor replaced the original Technicolor process in the 1950s. The banquet scenes at the end of Sergei Eisenstein's *Ivan the Terrible Part Two* (1946, but not released by Mosfilm until 1958) were filmed on Agfacolor stock which had been seized from the Nazis (Sklar 2002: 247). This was the first color filming in the Soviet Union. Initially single film color processes suffered from serious defects in picture sharpness and resolution, because it was technically difficult to produce as fine grained a film as with Technicolor.

By the early 1950s, American film studios were facing the competitive external threat from television, and most film executives clearly anticipated that this would only worsen for them over time. One thing which the studios could already offer was color, because color televisions and broadcasting were still uncommon. The other advantage was that the first-generation television sets were small, and a movie theater could easily offer a significantly larger screen, along with such still-uncommon amenities as air conditioning and stereo sound.

Twentieth Century-Fox introduced CinemaScope with *The Robe* (1953), the first modern widescreen film. This process used anamorphic Hypergonar lenses patented by Henri Chrétien (1879-1956), first to compress the wider filmed image onto conventional 35 mm film, and again during projection in the theater to un-squeeze the image for the wider CinemaScope screen. In comparison with the original theater screens they replaced, CinemaScope screens were typically higher, and over twice as wide (Sklar 2002: 315-316). Most installations attempted to make the new widescreen as large as technically feasible given the dimensions of the theater auditorium and proscenium. The original standard aspect ratio, the ratio of film width to height, had been set at 1.375:1 in 1932 by the Academy of Motion Picture Arts and Sciences. CinemaScope offered a wider 2.55:1 aspect ratio, and if, as most were, the theater's new screen was higher than its original Academy aspect ratio screen, the picture size could be over five times as large. The best installations of the new, wider screens fully engaged theatergoers' peripheral vision from most seats.[29] Fox obtained licensing fees from any studio which also used this patented process, which ultimately included every other studio except Paramount and RKO, as well as many independent producers.

Fox also received rental income on their inventory of Bausch & Lomb CinemaScope lenses. Each production required at least one and usually several of these lenses for filming, and each theater needed two lenses for projecting the film. Each lens produced rental income for Fox. The original lenses were complex, expensive, and cumbersome to manufacture, and Bausch & Lomb was unable to satisfy the whole industry's demand. Fox's willingness to exploit their monopoly position created an opportunity for Panavision, which was founded in 1954 to help supply theater owners who were willing to pay $1,100 for each Super Panatar lens, rather than rent Bausch & Lomb lenses from Fox. The Panavision lenses were cheaper to produce, lighter and less cumbersome, easier to use, and technically superior in that they produced less optical distortion. Interestingly, Panavision's current business model, much like Fox's in the 1950s, is that they only rent their inventory of cameras and lenses.

It remains debatable how much difference widescreen actually made for the studio's bottom lines, and how much time they may have bought the studios in the face of the dramatic social changes of

---

29 Originally, CinemaScope provided four magnetic sound tracks which were chemically bonded to the celluloid on either side of the left and right sprocket holes. To provide sufficient space for sound recording, the sprocket holes were reduced, so-called "Fox holes." Later, Fox confronted the fact that many theater owners were reluctant to invest in expensive modifications to their sound systems, so Fox also offered an alternative standard monaural magoptical sound track on the right side of the film. Because this cut into the image printed on each frame, it reduced the CinemaScope aspect ratio from 2.55:1 to 2.35:1. Modern widescreen films have a 2.40:1 aspect ratio.

the 1950s, 1960s, and 1970s. What is interesting is how the different Hollywood studios brought different approaches to entrepreneurial planning in response to this new technology. Fox had introduced CinemaScope, and the process had to be licensed from them. Once Fox entered the market in 1953, all their films were in CinemaScope from 1954 to 1967, except for a few higher-budget films like *South Pacific* (1958) and *Cleopatra* (1962) which they filmed in the 70 mm Todd-AO widescreen process. Virtually all of Fox's output was also now in color. Fox developed its own in-house color processing subsidiary DeLuxe. This enabled Fox to avoid delays and constraints which might have been imposed if they had continued to rely solely on Technicolor for processing and prints. Most other studios would continue to rely on Technicolor for additional prints when they could not satisfy exhibitor demand in house, and Fox would also occasionally continue to use Technicolor when DeLuxe was overburdened. Like MGM's Metrocolor division, DeLuxe also processed film for other studios, and the choice of the subsidiary name, which does not reference Fox in any way, may have been intentional to avoid discouraging competing studios from using their service and providing Fox an additional revenue stream.

Fox was able to extract some income from competing studios which had to rent CinemaScope lenses from Fox, but this led the other studios to explore alternative technologies, or merely alternative lens suppliers like Panavision. Fox also received income from each theater, who also had to rent lenses from Fox. Furthermore, the costs of installing a new screen and sound system had to be borne exclusively by the theater owners.

Among the Hollywood studios, Paramount was the principal holdout and refrained from adopting CinemaScope. Recognizing that most existing theaters would be relatively expensive to convert for widescreen, they commissioned Technicolor to develop the VistaVision process. This enabled Paramount to avoid paying licensing royalties to Fox. VistaVision was more expensive, but the added cost was borne by the studio rather than theater owners. Paramount's first experiment was to persuade theater owners to install larger screens depending on the dimensions of the theaters—with 1.66:1, 1.85:1, and 2:1 aspect ratios being the most common. They first used these large screens for George Stevens's *Shane* (1953), which had been completed in 1951 but never released. They felt a western would not be too compromised by being viewed in different theaters in a variety of different aspect ratios. Once Paramount concluded that some of the benefits of CinemaScope could be obtained at lower cost, they went to Technicolor and asked them to develop a high quality color process which would not need anamorphic lenses. Theater owners had to pay for the new screens, but with their less extreme aspect ratio, VistaVision screens usually cost less to install than the wider CinemaScope screens, and many theater owners appreciated the cost savings. Warner Brothers and MGM also made a few films in VistaVision, but it was more expensive and the added cost was borne by the studios, so was not used nearly as frequently as CinemaScope. Technicolor had a financial interest in having as many films as possible made in their proprietary processes, which were VistaVision, and later Technirama, and Techniscope. Paramount abandoned VistaVision by 1960 because it cost about $80,000 extra per film. After 1960 Paramount switched first to Technirama and finally to Panavision. By using VistaVision, Paramount was covering more of the costs of their high quality widescreen process, which Fox and the others successfully transferred to the theater owners.

VistaVision incorporated Perspecta Sound with a single optical monaural track. This system was much cheaper for theater owners to install than CinemaScope's magnetic stereo system. A Perspecta decoder utilized three bass ranges to steer the music tracks to left, center, and right speakers. The bass ranges for Perspecta encoding were unobtrusive, but not subaudible. All dialog was monaural with Perspecta, though because of Vista Vision's less extreme aspect ratio, this was not as glaring a defect as for CinemaScope films. Perspecta Sound was inherently compromised and vastly inferior to magnetic stereo, but it simulated a dimensional effect for music and some sound effects, and it was an improvement over unenhanced monaural sound.

MGM was the largest and most profitable Hollywood studio throughout most of its history. Their response to CinemaScope was to adopt the technology aggressively. Most of MGM's major releases of the fifties were in CinemaScope and color, usually Eastmancolor processed in-house by Metrocolor.[30] Unlike Fox's DeLuxe, the Metrocolor trade name made the subsidiary's ownership obvious, but MGM's corporate culture viewed that as a plus, a source of status and prestige which lesser studios should be willing to pay for. MGM also occasionally used Agfacolor instead of Eastmancolor. Director Vincente Minnelli was especially fond of Agfacolor's softer palette, and used it for *Brigadoon* (1954) and *Lust for Life* (1956). MGM apparently felt less threatened by its competitors. Unlike CinemaScope's standard magnetic stereo sound, MGM generally used Perspecta Sound, which was not well suited to widescreen. This provided a cost advantage in that more theaters could book MGM's CinemaScope films than Fox's.

MGM actually did develop its own widescreen process, MGM

30 MGM's first CinemaScope film was *Knights of the Round Table* (1954). It was filmed in Eastmancolor processed in house by MGM as "Color Magnificence." Until they adopted the Metrocolor service mark, MGM color films generally credited Eastmancolor, such as with *Forbidden Planet* (1956).

Camera 65. This was a 70 mm process[31] using Panavision anamorphic lenses, which was significantly more expensive than more conventional 35 mm processes like CinemaScope, and would only have been used for more expensive films. MGM made two films in this process, Edward Dmytryk's *Raintree County* (1957) and William Wyler's *Ben Hur* (1959). Warner Brothers also adopted CinemaScope for most major releases, with Eastmancolor processed in-house as Warner Color. George Cukor had already filmed significant portions of *A Star is Born* (1954) when Warners executives decided to make it their first CinemaScope release, significantly adding to the cost of that film.

United Artists' occasional major releases were in CinemaScope and color. Most of UA's releases were in 1.85:1 spherical widescreen, with many in black-and-white. The major minors, Universal and Columbia, were thriving and gaining market share throughout the 1950s. Universal International released occasional major films in CinemaScope and Eastmancolor, but nearly always credited "Prints by Technicolor." Universal did not have in house processing facilities. Most Universal releases in the fifties were in 1.85:1 spherical widescreen, whether in

---

31 Conventional film is 35 mm wide, including the sprocket holes and soundtracks. 70 mm film was used for Todd AO/Dimension 150, Ultra Panavision 70 (aka MGM Camera 65), and Super Panavision 70. Of these 70 mm processes, only Ultra Panavision 70/MGM Camera 65 used anamorphic lenses to squeeze and un-squeeze the image. The MGM Camera 65 trade name referred to the 65 mm of printable width on 70 mm film. Five mm were taken up by sprocket holes and sound recording surfaces. The non-anamorphic widescreen processes, Todd AO and Super Panavision 70, used spherical lenses and would be projected onto large screens with a 2.20:1 or 2:1 aspect ratio. Todd AO was developed by American Optical Company for producer Mike Todd and offered ultra wide-angle lenses which could capture up to a 120 degree field of vision, as well as six track stereo sound. When the process was expanded with 150 degree lenses, it was renamed Dimension 150. Super Panavision 70 was Panavision's version of Todd AO.

color or black-and-white. By the sixties, most Universal releases were in 2.35:1 Panavision. Columbia also released occasional major films, like *Bridge Over the River Kwai* (1957) and *The Guns of Navarone* (1961) in CinemaScope and color, and *Lawrence of Arabia* (1962) in 70 mm SuperPanavision 70. As with Universal, the vast majority of Columbia releases were shot in 1.85:1 spherical widescreen. Disney shot its first live action film in CinemaScope, Richard Fleischer's *20,000 Leagues Under the Sea* (1954).

Once-proud RKO was literally falling apart since Howard Hughes gained control in 1948. In his first year as chairman, he dismissed 700 employees and reduced the studio's annual output from 30 films to nine. Hughes also shut down production for six months to have all the remaining employees investigated for Communist sympathies. Hughes elected not to use CinemaScope as he did not want to help finance Fox. He purchased the rights to a cheaper and technically inferior widescreen process called Superscope which offered a 2:1 aspect ratio. Later versions of this process provided the same 2.35:1 ratio as CinemaScope, and were called RKO Scope 235 or Superscope 235. Superscope was adequate for black-and-white filming, but in color it exhibited noticeable grain problems because it used a smaller area of the 35 mm film. This process eventually became the basis for Technicolor Italia's Techniscope process. Usually it was used to keep down costs, but some directors felt its grainy picture was desirable for westerns.

Hollywood in the 1950s was an oligopolistic industry. The 1948 Paramount antitrust decision forced studios to divest their theater chains, enabling the smaller studios to compete more effectively. Fox was challenging MGM for leadership, and except for Paramount and RKO, the other studios largely adopted Fox's technical innovations. Paramount and Warners held their own in terms of market share, with

United Artists a few steps behind. Columbia and Universal gained market share along with Allied Artists, formerly Monogram, while RKO and Republic went bust.

CHAPTER 7

Entrepreneurial Strategy & the
Emergence of Market Organization

Entrepreneurial strategies determine market organization, at least to
the extent the market rewards entrepreneurial plans because and to the
extent that they allow consumers to better satisfy their wants. Perfectly
competitive markets, with large numbers of similarly-sized producers
and little or no product differentiation, arise because entrepreneurs
entering these markets imitate established small enterprises. Monopolistic-competitive markets arise because entrepreneurs imitate and
respond strategically to each others' branding, advertising, and product
differentiation (Kirzner 1963: 308-309). Entrepreneurs cannot imitate
a competitor's brand, unless their plan is merely to profit from buyer
confusion, but typically their strategy is to offer new alternatively
branded products which consumers will accept as being of equal or
higher quality as established brands, or better meeting the needs of a
targeted consumer niche.

Pricing strategy comes into play here—in some cases a higher price can successfully be charged because it helps signal to buyers "this brand is better or of higher quality than the established substitute." Monopolistic-competitive markets result from entrepreneurs who excel at second-order innovation; for example, in marketing strategies or responsive actions aiming at gaining strategic advantage, but first-order innovation plays an important role as well, as there are more dimensions for it than in perfectly competitive markets.

Oligopoly arises where entrepreneurs achieve a certain degree of market concentration through successful competition, and then imitate, respond to, and evoke strategic responses from, other major players. One firm with significant—often dominant—market share initiates a first-order innovation, perhaps founding the industry, and then the relatively small number of competitive partners, each with relatively high market share, contribute second-order innovations. First-order innovation, when it occurs, will have a greater impact here because of each firm's relatively high market share.

Monopoly arises when one enterprise, perhaps through employment of trade secrets or patents, grows through successful competition to the point where the firm's size acts as a barrier against potential competitors, or the firm successfully seeks a government-enforced grant of monopoly privilege. Monopoly arises competitively through first-order innovation, but can be preserved through second-order innovation, including the achievement of government protection to preserve monopoly rents indefinitely. Once a temporary monopolist successfully obtains an extension of their monopoly rents through government coercion, they have locked in some of the short-run market disruption their innovation has introduced, and they effectively delay and limit the longer- term benefit of greater cooperation and mutual coordination of entrepreneurial plans (Kirzner 1996: 39-41). Consumers and other producers will take advantage of the monopolist's new product, but because government coercion limits their ability to bring their plans into the highest possible mutual coordination, the benefit of the monopolist's product is also limited. What limited benefit there is will be disproportionately captured by the monopoly firm, as long as they benefit from discriminatory regulation.

7.1 How Innovation Spreads

The first-order innovator who first appears as a buyer of input resources initially enjoys a monopsony input market, where they are the only buyers of the input resources used to produce their product, until other competitors choose to imitate them. Alert second-order innovators exercise entrepreneurial awareness when they realize that they can imitate the first-order innovator, and how they can actually implement this imitative process in a manner which makes the best use of the second-order innovator's comparative advantage and special areas of competence. Second-order innovators avoid much of the risk assumed by first-order innovators. Robinson (1933: 220) shows how monopsonist buyers use their market power to purchase lower quantities of inputs at lower prices than would prevail under competition. Similarly, until and unless imitators appear, this same first-order innovator enjoys a monopoly in the market where the product is sold to consumers or other final users. If the first-order innovator can maintain entry barriers, for example, by successfully lobbying for protective regulation, their market advantage can be preserved, but otherwise competing entrepreneurs will be attracted, both by the below-competitive-market monopsony input prices in resource markets, as well as the above-competitive-market monopoly output prices in the firm's product markets, eventually reducing the first-order innovator's profit margin.

The sequence of events is as follows. First, the first-order innovator, guided by their entrepreneurial awareness of (a) the potential market opportunity, and (b) their unique knowledge and intuition about how the product might be provided and marketed, introduces a new product which finds acceptance from consumers; in other words, the new product introduction succeeds on the market. If the product does not find favor with consumers, there will probably not be any imitation of the failed first-order innovator. However, assuming the product meets consumer needs, initially the first-order innovator has a monopoly over sales, and may further benefit from being a monopsony buyer of any input resources which can only be used to produce this particular product; that is, those resources used to produce this product and for which there is no other use. Next, entrepreneurial awareness is exercised by the second-order innovators, who observe what the first-order innovator has done, seeking to piggy-back on the successes or failures of the first-order innovator. The second-order innovators may find various marginal improvements which may be made to the first-order innovator's product, production methods, or marketing strategies. Second-order innovators may introduce cheaper production methods, or employ less costly inputs. They may successfully attempt to substitute cheaper inputs for more expensive ones. They may identify unreached market demographics or new market niches which the first-order innovator neglected or overlooked, or they may devise successful strategies to reach these market niches better than the first-order innovator, essentially tailoring the product to better appeal to or meet the needs of specific target demographic.

At any stage of innovation, the attempted introduction of new products, innovative production or marketing methods, etc., all innovators always face uncertainty and assume risk. If what they attempt fails, they pay the price of market competition. This is why entrepreneurs need to pursue not the most glamorous or most widely recognized opportunities, but those where they can apply their own, most distinctive information advantages and specialized knowledge to meet the needs of others and offer new and previously unforeseen opportunities to increase social cooperation and mutual coordination among the entrepreneurial plans of others (Kirzner 1996: 39-41). Ideally, the entrepreneur has studied their product and its potential market. They are intensely aware of the strategies tried by others in the industry, know what has failed and what has succeeded in the past, and can apply this knowledge effectively to construct and implement new strategies to address the specific consumer need that they are the first to infer, conceive of, or anticipate. Because entrepreneurs are not omniscient, some will fail. Because some entrepreneurial planners succeed and others fail, start-up financing for new projects has to be carefully rationed by financial intermediaries and venture capitalists. The information of financial investors is at least one step further removed from the realities of the product markets—generally their expertise is more in financial markets—and inevitably they ration credit in too conservative a manner.

Entrepreneurial planning aims at extracting profits as a share of the benefits the entrepreneur creates by enabling others, both consumers and other producers, to bring their entrepreneurial production and consumption plans into better mutual coordination. Entrepreneurs profit if they are able to introduce the product differentiation which distinguishes monopolistic competition from pure competition—thus entrepreneurs organize markets. Imitative second-order entrepreneurs erode the first-to-market advantage of the initial first-order innovator, and strategic responses to preserve monopoly profits may result in creating oligopolistic markets or preserving monopoly markets over the long run. Entrepreneurs may seek to preserve their monopoly profits, perhaps by obtaining regulatory advantages, or may move on to earn temporary monopoly profits elsewhere. Their strategy is to move from one emerging market to the next, initially earning temporary monopoly profits, but abandoning each market as imitative new entrants begin to erode the original monopolist's profits with their second-order innovations and the attendant competition successful imitation provides.

7.2 Alternatives to Perfect Competition

The neoclassical, comparative-static, general equilibrium model of perfect competition was supplanted by alternative models which were both more specialized and realistic. Edward Chamberlin (1933) and Joan Robinson (1933) introduced the monopolistically-competitive model as an analytical advance beyond the model of perfect competition, but only under the same comparative-static, general equilibrium conditions which assumed away the possibility of dis-equilibria, or any role for market process. By the 1930s, the theory of perfect competition had become highly formalized, as the initially loose and non-descript conceptions of competition in the economics literature were gradually purged of their latent vestiges of process thinking, rendering analysis both simpler and more formal, but always at the expense of essential realism.

John M. Clark (1955, 1960) made pioneering efforts to promote a dynamic understanding of competition, though the profession largely ignored him, even though criticism of the static-equilibrium understanding of perfect competition continued to proliferate after 1960. Nevertheless, contemporary mainstream microeconomics continues to prefer the sterile formal elegance of competition as a final equilibrium, arrived at instantaneously and without the participation of any economic agents, over the messy dis-equilibrium reality of competition as market process driven by both competition and coordination among entrepreneurial planners (see, e.g., Silberberg 1978: 209-211).

The familiar model of perfect competition contrasts starkly with the more subtle, less formalized, conception of entrepreneurial competition and market process. Market process explains how entrepreneurial producers anticipate and respond to consumer demand and changing market conditions, without relying on unrealistic assumptions about pre-existing market organization—in reality market organization emerges after the fact, through the strategic interaction of entrepreneurial planners, and the strategic responses of second-order innovators to the actions of first-order innovators and other second-order innovators (DiLorenzo 1994). Entrepreneurs face profit-and-loss incentives—gaining profits when they correctly anticipate future market conditions and act on those anticipations, but suffering losses when their plans fail (Ikeda 1994). Market process subjects entrepreneurs to this unrelenting discipline, because any profit-seeking innovator in this speculative environment faces the pressure of imitative arbitrage by competitors, eroding and eventually eliminating the original profit opportunity. Market organization—whether perfect competition, monopoly, monopolistic competition, or oligopoly—emerges from market process, as a product of entrepreneurs' speculative efforts to uncover entrepreneurial profit opportunities and to act on, capture, and preserve them as long as possible.

Perfect competition's assumption that individual producers are price takers who are unable to influence the market price removes any role for, or any possibility of, entrepreneurial experimentation with price adjustments. However helpful it has been for economists to examine this static-equilibrium result devoid of entrepreneurial action, its real world applications are severely limited. Real markets feature competition among innovative entrepreneurs, and assuming away entrepreneurs' innovative, speculative, and profit-seeking behavior, strictly limits the ability of our economics to explain market process in the real world. The reality is that the market price arises because entrepreneurial planners are constantly experimenting with price adjustments, both to see if they can get the immediately local market closer to equilibrium, and to test whether the underlying equilibrium may have changed. The market-clearing price changes whenever market supply and demand conditions change. Even when entrepreneurial price-setters know market conditions have changed, and can use the comparative statics analysis of microeconomics to determine which direction the equilibrium price and quantity should move, entrepreneurs still need to experimentally change the price in an attempt, as it were, to feel out the new equilibrium. Market equilibrium in this sense should be understood less as an actually realized target—or even one which could potentially be reached and more of a hypothetical and idealized target which would clear the market in principle.

Neither are formal models with such limited applicability likely to be especially fruitful in offering guidance for policy or regulation, and the resulting policy has not been conspicuous by its success—generally leading to further intervention to correct problems introduced by the original intervention. Market process generates the pattern of resource allocation and productive activity in real markets, creates the constellation of market prices, and results in the actual satisfaction of real consumers' wants. In contrast, the focus of mainstream neoclassical microeconomics is on whether competition is present as a formal state of affairs—in other words, whether arbitrary formal conditions are met, which is largely irrelevant in reality and cannot inform effective policy.

Government regulation restricts what entrepreneurial planners can do, and prevents innovations and innovative products from being offered to the consuming public. Innovations which do not benefit consumers will be rejected by them, and therefore cannot result in profits being earned by the entrepreneurial planners. Some government regulation prevents innovations from being subjected to a market test. This kind of regulation necessarily lowers welfare and consumer satisfaction. Regulations which lower the cost of asserting property rights and internalize external costs are beneficial and welfare-improving (Ikeda 1998: 43-45). The stronger the environment for property rights, the better the institutional support for entrepreneurial discovery.

Mises (1949: 354-376) and Kirzner (1963: 286-290) emphasize that monopoly of supply or of any one factor necessary to supply a particular output, is a sufficient, but not necessary condition for the emergence of monopoly prices. In addition, consumer demand for the output must be sufficiently inelastic that the monopolist, oligopolists, or monopolistic-competitors can increase their revenue by raising the price and offering a lower amount of the output for sale. Furthermore, the prospective price-setters must be willing and able to do so. This is easy for a true monopolist, though the high monopoly profits earned by such a firm would generally attract new entrants, which would erode the monopolist's original profits. It is entirely plausible for a monopoly firm to sell their product at a lower price above the perfectly competitive one but below the theoretical monopoly price. They may do this because they are willing to accept lower revenue than what they could receive with the higher monopoly price, which acts as an upper limit on what they can charge in the market, simply because they want to avoid the high economic profits and monopoly rents, all of which will attract new entrants. A firm may also avoid charging a higher monopoly price to avoid regulatory attention. New entrants will compete against the monopoly firm, lower prices toward the competitive outcome as a lower limit, and thus drive down the monopoly's profit margins. The monopoly may find it optimal, or at least beneficial to trade lower profits in the short term for lower visibility to potential competitors. The longer the firm can go without attracting either regulatory attention or competition from new entrants, the longer they can preserve their limited monopoly profits. It may be more desirable to a monopoly firm to earn more limited monopoly profits for a longer period of time, as opposed to earning higher monopoly profits for a shorter period of time, because the higher profits will attract competition faster, and so destroy the firm's monopoly power.

The problem with oligopoly is that a relatively small number of large firms all with high market share facing the same market demand would generally find it more difficult to successfully coordinate their collusive strategies to achieve monopoly profits. If they succeed, they face the problem of cheating from within the oligopoly cartel, as well as creating the incentive for new competitors to enter the market. Monopolistic-competitive firms can compete on many margins to differentiate products and marketing strategies. They seek to capture market share from each other, but also face incentives to expand the market for the industry's product.

Robinson (1933: 57) describes a situation which may occur with multiple monopolistic equilibria facing the firm. In her hypothetical example, the demand curve facing the firm is highly elastic in some regions and highly inelastic in others. As a result, the firm's marginal revenue curve has a number of distinct local maxima and minima, such that the continuously increasing marginal cost curve intersects it at multiple output levels. In this environment, monopoly firms would have several distinct stable, though sub-optimal, equilibria. Only entrepreneurial experimentation could uncover this situation if it ever existed in reality, and that would be sufficient to overcome it.

7.3 From Market Process to Market Organization

Markets self-organize through market process, which offers an account of how entrepreneurial planners drive markets to self-organize, and over time, to achieve a higher level of coordination among myriad producers and consumers. Entrepreneurial planners compete to better satisfy consumer wants. This is the competitive principle of consumer sovereignty, and entrepreneurs profit only to the extent consumers reward them with profits, sales, and their business, but entrepreneurs have no real concept of organizing, or intention to organize, markets in a particular way. Entrepreneurs simply respond to and exploit incentives as they find them. The way markets self-organize can be characterized as being subject to fits and starts, because entrepreneurial innovation can disrupt the anticipation of others as well as disrupt established entrepreneurial plans which have already been started and put in progress, though just as often, entrepreneurial innovation makes possible a higher level of coordination among entrepreneurial plans.

Some of the case studies discussed above in Chapters 5 and 6 illustrate different kinds of market organization. Ballpoint pens initially commanded high price premia in geographically-segmented monopoly markets. Even today, the industry leader captures a modest price premium through extensive advertising and differentiation. Satellite phone service was unable to successfully capture monopoly rents due to cheaper competing substitute products. Designer jeans and consumer electronics have to pursue differentiation strategies and advertise extensively to capture even modest monopoly rents. In an oligopolistic industry, the actions of any one firm typically has to be taken into account by all its competitors.

7.4 Perfect Competition

A perfectly competitive output market is characterized by large numbers of similarly sized producers with little or no differentiation among the products sold by competing firms. Perfectly competitive markets arise because the new entrepreneurs entering these markets imitate established small enterprises, and succeed chiefly through this strategy. Alternative strategies either have not been tried because no alternative to mere rote imitation has occurred to anyone, or because all the entrepreneurs who have attempted such innovative strategies have failed in the past, finding that they were not rewarded by con- sumers. In other words, the differentiation strategies which were tried in the past failed because they did not contribute to better satisfying consumer needs. For example, product differentiation has either never been attempted, or when it has been attempted, consumers have rejected it—consumers either do not desire product differentiation, or they do not desire the precise form of differentiation they were offered in the past. An entrepreneurial innovator may yet succeed in designing the precise and precisely successful differentiation strategy which will meet consumer needs and be rewarded in the market. To do this, they will have to avoid past, unsuccessful differentiation strategies, unless market conditions, for example, consumer preferences, have changed to allow unsuccessful past strategies to succeed now or in the future, and successful entrepreneurs will have to rely on a deep, meaningful understanding of consumer wants and aspirations, including how these may have changed over time.

However, it may simply be that in this market every producers' output is a perfect substitute. If this is the case, and accurately reflects consumer knowledge and belief, the added costs of product differentiation cannot be successfully passed on to consumers, because consumers do not and will not see these added costs as justified or beneficial. Often, however, the product can still be successfully differentiated, either in general, or to a specific target marketing niche. For example, some part of the output may be particularly rich in a certain mineral or chemical which makes that part of the output particularly beneficial for certain specialized applications, though it may offer no general benefit to the vast majority of users. In this case, the chemical rich output could be marketed at a premium to users whose specific application particularly benefits from that chemical. This would effectively reserve part of the output of an otherwise generic product, for the exclusive use of consumers who would benefit most from the special properties of the reserved output.

7.5 Monopolistic Competition

Advertising faces the task of informing potential consumers of both the specific properties of the chemical rich version of the otherwise generic product, as well as its benefits for specific applications. Generic appeals that our brand is better for all applications because it is richer in property X, and everybody recognizes the benefits to everybody of more property X in any conceivable application, tend to strain credulity. A firm trying this approach will be likely to lose credibility and would have greater difficulty selling their product at a premium. A firm which markets their version of the otherwise generic product as being specially formulated for certain applications where property X offers specific benefits will build credibility with consumers, and is more likely to succeed in being able to charge a premium to the target demographic which actually benefits from the output which is richest in property X. The premium captured in the output price just needs to be lower than the value of the benefit as perceived by the target users. This target demographic would particularly benefit from a specific property in which the reserved output is particularly rich, and are willing to pay a premium to have that part of the output set aside for them, since it meets their needs especially well. Clearly, advertising plays a vital role in making consumers aware of the special properties and benefits to be obtained from this differentiated output.

An alternative approach to differentiating otherwise generic output in a competitive market is when two or more otherwise completely generic outputs could be combined to create a unique and uniquely desirable compound or composite product. The composite product can then be marketed to what is essentially a new set or subset of consumers compared with those who originally consumed each component separately, though the various sub-groups of consumers or market niches may overlap, and likely do. As an example, an otherwise undifferentiated good can be combined with a delivery service for which some consumers would hopefully be willing to pay more. Now the product is actually differentiated, but simply by combining it with another product, the delivery service. Any two goods for which a synergistic effect can be observed or suspected may be potentially differentiated this way. Consumers will either reward the innovator or not. Marketing is essential to inform potential buyers of the availability of these new compound offerings, along with specific details, requirements, parameters, benefits, and synergies they may have in combination. Whenever a product or product combination has failed to succeed with consumers in the past, that does not suffice to demonstrate it cannot succeed in the future or for all time. The time may be right, or a more appropriate and effective marketing strategy, perhaps to a different market demographic, may make all the difference.

There is no first-order innovation in a perfectly competitive market, only second-order innovation. First-order innovation, when it occurs, creates a new industry by introducing a new product. New product introduction in a perfectly competitive industry may substitute for or complement the original product. Generally, if production of the original product generates waste and an innovator finds some use for these byproducts, the whole industry can be affected. A familiar example is the natural gas (methane) which is found in virtually all petroleum deposits. Originally there was no use for this dangerous waste product, but once the necessary infrastructure was provided to deliver natural gas to consumers for cooking and heating, natural gas went from being a hazardous nuisance to a valuable commodity. Now, increases in the price of natural gas cause more oil to be pumped, and vice versa. Sometimes the natural gas, which was originally a valueless and undesired waste product, is more valuable than the petroleum pumped from the same well.

Monopolistic-competitive markets arise in the first place because entrepreneurs imitate and respond strategically to each others' branding, advertising, and product differentiation strategies. In these markets the products are similar enough that they are still fairly good substitutes, though not necessarily perfect ones. Sometimes, the products in a monopolistic-competitive market are otherwise generic, but are the subject of narrowly specialized marketing campaigns and advertising which appeal to narrowly defined market niches and demographic groups. Advertising attempts to address specific uses and technical applications and appeal to specific market niches. Entrepreneurs cannot imitate their competitor's brand, unless their plan is merely to profit from buyer confusion—for example, labeling domestic wine so it appears to have been imported. More typically the strategy of a monopolistic competitor is to brand and advertise their otherwise relatively generic product as meeting certain narrowly defined needs, suggesting the specific brand meets the targeted needs especially well and better than competing alternative products, and perhaps targeting a very narrow demographic niche. The key to successfully appealing to consumers is to understand the wants and aspirations of the targeted demographic, or through especially evocative advertising to successfully inspire its members to adopt and embrace such wants and aspirations.

Successful monopolistic-competitive sellers enjoy limited monopoly power, meaning they can charge a higher price than would prevail under perfect competition, defraying the added costs borne in differentiating their product from those of their competitors, and from associated marketing and advertising expenses (Geroski & Mazzucato 2003). Monopolistic-competitive firms need to be able to defray any additional expenses they incur in advertising and differentiating the product, and these added expenses need to be successfully passed on to the consumer. These added expenses include, for example, the additional packaging and carrying costs of offering the product in a variety of different sizes, stocking each of them for distribution and retail, and offering a product line which includes a variety of differentiated versions of the original generic product to appeal to as many target demographics as possible. Competitive markets are criticized because these added costs are seen as wasteful and unproductive, and would be eliminated in any more enlightened, progressive socialist nirvana directed by scientifically advanced and public-spirited technocratic dictators. However, the fact that in the real world consumers are willing to reward innovators for providing differentiated products sufficiently demonstrates that these innovations of monopolistic competition do in fact better satisfy peoples' needs, and the information provided by advertising would not be provided otherwise, or otherwise be made available, to the consumer (Geroski & Mazzucato 2003).

The higher price successfully charged by a monopolistic-competitive supplier is always justified, but only to the extent the product meets the specific needs of certain consumers in the demographic market niche. There are many dimensions for entrepreneurial innovation in a monopolistic-competitive market, such as major or minor changes in product characteristics, marketing to specific applications or uses of the product, marketing to demographic niches, etc. Members of a target demographic niche have to be offered added value which they can perceive and accept as beneficial, thus justifying their paying a higher price. These new differentiating characteristics may not offer similar benefits to groups other than the target demographic. It is also possible that the product is relatively generic, but is marketed differently to different groups of consumers. Today, the image presented in a multi-media marketing campaign might intentionally attempt to portray a very different impression, identify different applications, uses, properties, aspirations, etc. through traditional media, in sharp contrast to the image portrayed on new media, because these marketing vectors generally reach different age groups. Even within new media, an ad for LinkedIn or Facebook might be very different and target an older age group, than ads for Instagram, Twitter, Snapchat, or other platforms which typically reach younger demographics. Generally, as new media platforms emerge and enjoy at least a passing vogue, the newer the platform, the younger the age demographic.

New media also attempts to utilize browser history data to target ads to the purportedly most receptive consumers. These efforts have so far yielded mixed reviews. Search for something online, and count on it that you will be deluged with unsolicited ads for that product. This generates revenue for social media platforms, but it also wastes advertising hits specifically—though unknowingly—targeted at consumers who are particularly unreceptive because they recently purchased the precise product social media is still wasting time and effort, though only virtual effort, in trying to sell them. This is a particularly wasteful strategy which (a) strictly limits the value and benefits of social media to the consumer, and (b) wastes the seller's advertising budget on a market demographic which is optimized not to buy the product, because they just did, though perhaps from your competitor. Advertising effectiveness decreases with the ubiquity of ads—like network television, social media platforms should maximize ad revenue by charging advertisers more for limited but focused penetration which is more likely to garner and merit consumer attention.

7.6 Oligopoly

The strategic interaction among the several oligopoly firms charac-
terizes an oligopolistic product market. This kind of market consists
of a small number of large firms, each of which has captured significant market share. Consumers can shop around for price savings
among the limited number of firms. Shopping around is not likely to
be prohibitive because of the relatively small number of firms, and
the oligopolists can either compete to undercut each other, or they can
collude to maintain uncompetitively high prices. Successful collusion
means that the oligopolists in the industry act together as if they were
a single monopoly firm, and apportion the available market demand
amongst each other. This is generally illegal, unless done at government behest and with government sponsorship.[32] Introducing product

---

32 TACA, the Transatlantic Conference Agreement, is a government-sponsored
shipping consortium headquartered in Crawley, UK. It was founded in 1992 as
the TAA (Transatlantic Agreement) and renamed TACA in 1994. TACA effectively has a license from several governments to collude in the public interest to
maintain stable freight-carrying prices over transatlantic routes. Participating
firms are A.P. Moller-Mærsk, Atlantic Container Line (ACL), Nippon Yussen
Kaisha Line (NYK Line), Mediterranean Shipping Company (MSC), and Orient
Overseas Container Line (OOCL). The collusion to set prices would ordinarily be
prosecutable under U.S. antitrust legislation, and that of several other countries,
but the U.S. Maritime Administration's sponsorship, along with that of other
governments, protects TACA and its participating firms against prosecution in
U.S. courts under the common law doctrine of entrapment by estoppel. The
principle is that if a government official asks you to do something in the public
interest, or even under the pretext that it may serve the public interest, you
cannot be held criminally or civilly liable, even if the action would otherwise be
a criminal offense. More broadly, an individual cannot be prosecuted for relying
on the representation of a government official that an act is legally permissible.
Civil plaintiffs may have recourse against the government in this case. In 1998
the EU fined TACA 564 million DM for antitrust violations, but the sentence
was overturned in 2003 by the European Court of Justice. For more discussion
of TACA see Mulligan & Lombardo (2008) and Lombardo & Mulligan (2010).

differentiation or extensive advertising by one oligopoly firm may enable it to capture market share from its partners, as long as the firm is not trying to pursue a collusive strategy in concert with its oligopoly partners (Geroski & Mazzucato 2003). The real goal of entrepreneurial marketing, strategy, and differentiation should be to expand the size of the market by reaching new consumers. Entrepreneurial innovations, for example new product introductions, expanding or diversifying the firm's product line, product differentiation, etc., which expand the size of the market may not be seen by oligopoly partners as violating any informal collusive compact. Successful market-expanding innovations may actually provide external benefits to otherwise passive oligopoly partners—thus such strategies pursued by one oligopoly firm do not raise any kind of alarm and do not call for a defensive strategic response from the other oligopolists. The best thing the competing oligopoly firms can do in this case is enjoy the added sales and revenue.

When oligopolists compete to contest market share from one another, the market will approximate a perfectly competitive one. Oligopoly firms will typically practice product differentiation by offering differentiated product lines, which compete with those offered by their oligopoly partners. The large size of the firms in an oligopolistic market is liable to generate internal scale economies which would not be possible in either a perfectly-competitive or monopolistically-competitive market. Since some part of the scale economies can be passed on to consumers, and competitive pressures should result in this happening, a non-collusive oligopoly market may actually provide greater consumer surplus than either monopolistic-competitive or perfectly-competitive markets.

7.7 Monopoly

Monopoly, the fourth and most extremely concentrated form of market organization, arises when one enterprise, perhaps through employment of trade secrets or patents, grows through successful competition to the point where the firm's size acts as a barrier against potential competitors, or the firm successfully seeks a government-enforced monopoly grant. Monopoly arises competitively through first-order innovation, but can be preserved through second-order innovation, including the achievement of government protection to preserve monopoly rents indefinitely. Entrepreneurial innovators can supplant an established monopoly by offering alternative products which serve the same purpose, either better or at lower cost to the consumer. Monopolies generally seek to preserve their privileged position as long as possible, and on as many fronts, and through as many strategies as possible. However, there is no monopoly on entrepreneurship. Entrepreneurs should be alert to opportunities offered by monopolies' relative unwillingness to anticipate, cater to, or satisfy consumer wants.

Monopoly firms may suffer from x-inefficiency because they are insulated from competition and may not employ available resources as efficiently as they would have to under the pressures of competition, and thus will not operate at the same level of capacity or efficiency as they would in perfect competition (Liebenstein 1966). Monopoly firms may find it advantageous to use resources to lobby for preferential regulation which acts as a barrier to entry, protecting the established monopolist from having to face competition from new entrants. Pursuing this strategy may preserve the firm's monopoly power for some time, while costing the firm less than it would to operate at the competitive optimum or to use the same resources spent lobbying the government for regulatory protection on developing innovative new products, cost-saving production techniques, etc. This behavior by a monopoly firm can also act as a barrier against competition from potential new entrants.

A large monopoly firm may benefit from both internal and external scale economies (Kirzner 1963: 310-312). Internal scale economies are internal to the firm. External scale economies are external to the firm per se, but internal to the industry—a monopoly firm can still capture these economies because the monopoly firm is the entire industry. Examples of external scale economies include clustering of input or support providers and ancillary services, and labor market congregation of workers specialized for that industry. These circumstances would make it relatively more difficult to locate a start-up competitor in any other location than where the large monopoly firm is located, and any start-up locating elsewhere would also face significantly higher costs, which would act as a natural barrier to entry for any firm which would hope to potentially compete against an established monopoly. Internal scale economies make it more likely that a firm will be a monopoly, and once its market share becomes large enough, it will capture any external scale economies as well.

Market Process & the Business Cycle

The three chapters of Part Three develop an account of how entrepreneurial planning and market process normally contribute to sustainable coordination of the economy's complex arrays of flexible and interdependent entrepreneurial plans. These plans coordinate productive activities over time to satisfy consumer wants while accommodating experimentation which leads to improved coordination, higher levels of production, lower cost, and introduces new products. However, under expansionary government policy, we will see that entrepreneurs are driven to construct an expanded network of production plans which become increasingly fragile, resulting in numerous and widespread plan rigidities which limit the flexibility and sustainability of many plans. This impairs the market's ability to keep entrepreneurial plans in mutual coordination. This market process account of the business cycle will provide Austrian business cycle theory with more explicit microeconomic foundations. This section will also demonstrate how the business cycle, which is often presented rhetorically as a fatal shortcoming of a free market economy, actually results from the socialization of money and credit media, financial risk, leverage, and public debt, presenting more of a critique of socialism than of capitalism.

Chapter 8, Sustainable & Unsustainable Coordination of Entrepreneurial Plans, discusses the mutual plan coordination which entrepreneurial planners create and compete against each other to improve and enhance. The role of interest rates and financial markets in providing and allocating financial capital to fund business expansion and extend entrepreneurial plans is introduced. The interest rate needs to reflect the actual time preference of people in the economy for the plans funded by borrowing to be sustainable, capable of being completed, mutually coordinated with the plans of others. Real consumers actually decide, based on their own time preference, how much of their income to save and how much to consume.

Chapter 9, The Business Cycle, presents a market process account of how monetary expansion results in unsustainable investment and the parallel inability of entrepreneurial plans which are misaligned with the time preferences of people in the economy to remain in mutual coordination. The discoordination and mutual incompatibility of entrepreneurial plans formed in an environment of artificially low interest rates triggers a recession when expansion becomes unsustainable.

Chapter 10, Keynesian Stabilization Policy: Cause or Cure?, provides a critique of the most popular public policy responses to recession.

CHAPTER 8

Sustainable & Unsustainable Coordination of Entrepreneurial Plans

Productive activity in a market economy is coordinated through prices and the voluntary exchanges between buyers and sellers. We have already seen how this process allows prices to emerge in the first place, and how entrepreneurial planners contribute to continuously adjusting prices in response to changing economic conditions and newly discovered opportunities to better satisfy consumer wants. The more advanced an economy, the greater the number of mutually beneficial exchanges and the greater the diversity and complexity of economic activity. We can observe that economic activity generally tends to expand in both diversity and complexity as the economy grows, but the problem of the business cycle is to explain why this growth is not always steady. Economic expansions are punctuated by periodic economic downturns or recessions of varying length and severity. The periods of expansion between two recessions also seem to vary, typically not lasting not much more than about ten years. Sometimes recessions occur more frequently. One way to frame this most important problem in macroeconomics is to observe the insight from market process; that economic expansion comes from successful entrepreneurial planning, which needs to be mutually coordinated in a sustainable way with the plans of others. Recessions occur after the late stages of an expansion result in entrepreneurial planners engaging in numerous productive activities which are ultimately unsustainable because these plans cannot all be coordinated. A recession occurs when many entrepreneurial planners throughout the economy are engaged in activities they will not be able to complete.

8.1 Installed Capital Limits the Flexibility of Entrepreneurial Plans

Charles W. Bischoff (1942-) distinguishes between uninvested financial capital and installed physical capital: the "putty-clay" model (1969)[33]. In his formulation, "putty" capital is uninvested savings which helps

---

33 Some of the insights of Bischoff's putty-clay model were already captured by Cantillon and Turgot. The distinction between financial capital, which Bischoff calls putty capital, and physical or installed capital, which Bishoff calls clay capital were already fully developed in various forms throughout the macroeconomics, capital theory, and finance literatures. However, the distinction between financial and physical capital was frequently muddled from the earliest days, if only because financial capital can always be readily converted into physical capital, but physical capital cannot generally be converted back into financial capital, except at a loss. Many economists who felt the distinction could be taken for granted seem to have failed to appreciate how critical the distinction actually is between financial (putty) and physical (clay) capital. Bischoff's key insight is that physical, installed, or clay capital is always less flexible, and generally suffers from rigid constraints on the extent it can be reallocated once it has been installed for a specific, forward-looking entrepreneurial plan. At a minimum, financial or putty capital will always earn the same market return offered by the financial sector on various savings instruments, but the physical clay capital can potentially earn a higher return. Otherwise no one would ever convert their financial putty capital into physical clay capital. The potentially higher return on physical clay capital will be realized if and only if, once installed, this physical capital is used as originally envisioned by the entrepreneurial planner. A further condition which must be satisfied to realize the return originally expected is that the entrepreneurial planner's initial expectations with regard to future market conditions over the course of the plan must either turn out to be accurate, or market conditions must turn out by chance to be even more favorable. If market conditions turn out to be less favorable than what was originally antici- pated, the return on physical capital employed in the plan will actually be lower. If that results in the lower return being sufficiently unfavorable, the entrepreneurial planner may attempt to reallocate the installed clay capital to the next best use. Now the clay capital installed for the original entrepreneurial plan will be used in some manner different than what was originally envisioned, and for which it was spe- cifically acquired, designed, optimized, and installed. Except due to extraordinary good fortune on the part of the entrepreneur, the return on this installed physical capital will generally now be lower, because the design and installation was techni- cally optimized for the use and application originally intended. To a certain extent these technical operating characteristics either cannot be changed at all, or require additional investment for any modification.

clear the financial markets for loanable funds, where accumulated household savings provides the supply of loanable funds, and the desire of firms and entrepreneurial planners provides the demand for loanable funds to finance new entrepreneurial plans or investment projects[34]. In each time period in Bischoff's model, worker-consumers earn wage income by selling their labor services to the firms. In addition, various households might also earn rental income from the land they own, or interest income in the form of lease payments on the capital equipment they lease to firms, or income in the form of entrepreneurial profits for the entrepreneurial planning, talent, or management services they provide to the firms. Then the households divide their total income between consumption spending and the amount they set aside and do not spend on current consumption, but save for the future. This amount which is not spent on consumption is the household's savings.

The financial intermediaries of the banking system pay us interest on our accumulated savings. The higher the interest rate the banks offer us, the more we save, and the less we spend on present consumption. The banks take our savings deposits and lend them to firms and entrepreneurial planners to finance their productive activities. The banks charge interest on these loans, ensuring the interest rate they charge is greater than the rate they pay depositors, so they can simultaneously afford to pay interest on deposits and capture profits for the bank. Bank profits come in the form of the spread between the low interest rate they pay us on our savings deposits, and the higher interest rate the banks receive for loans. From the perspective of a borrowing firm

---

34 In this context, an investment project means the same as an entrepreneurial plan. Both expressions refer to forward-looking productive activities which entrepreneurs might finance out of their own savings or might borrow funds at interest to finance.

or entrepreneurial planner, the interest rate the firm pays to the bank, which is higher than the interest rate paid to savers, must also be lower, or at least no higher than the return the entrepreneurial planner expects to realize on the project they seek to finance through the loan.

This "putty" capital is denominated in money, and consists of financial assets like bank account balances, certificates of deposit, corporate stocks and bonds, etc. In contrast, "clay" capital is what the borrowing firms purchase with the more liquid, uninstalled "putty" capital. Capital becomes the less liquid, "clay" capital once it is purchased, installed, and exists in the form of productive physical assets in the form of factories, steel mills, railroad lines, trucks, earthmoving equipment, locomotives, rolling stock, tools, equipment, etc. Each item of "clay" capital is expected to yield a definite return in currently operating entrepreneurial plans, and is far less liquid than the original un-invested "putty" capital. "Clay" capital can be reallocated, but only to a limited extent, and only at significant cost—it possesses the property Ludwig Lachmann (1906-1990) called "multiple-specificity," in that each item of physical capital can be used in a variety of different ways, but its physical form limits its substitutability for other uses (Lachmann 1947, 1956, Horwitz 2000: 47-51).

For example, a locomotive can be sold from one railroad to another. But a switch engine is a poor substitute for a road engine, even though they are both locomotives. A switch engine is small and its design is optimized for moving small numbers of rail cars short distances in a rail yard. A road engine is larger and more powerful to pull a whole train over intercontinental distances. Even within the category of road engines, the largest and most powerful are optimized for use in mountainous regions. For airlines, the route length, and to a lesser extent the climate and altitude of the operating airfields dictate which aircraft are best suited. Certain planes are more economical to operate over long routes than shorter ones. Airlines can realize internal scale economies by operating a standardized fleet consisting of larger numbers of a smaller variety of different model planes, but this can limit their ability to compete over a variety of different route lengths; that is, short, medium, or long distance routes. Consider Southwest Airlines, which only operates Boeing 737 variants. Southwest's ability to compete on longer and international flights is relatively limited because it is strictly constrained by what the various versions of the 737 can economically do. The Southwest fleet is not as uniform as it may appear at first, because newer versions of the 737 have larger, more powerful, and more fuel efficient engines, a longer fuselage, and a greater wingspan.[35]

But compare this to any legacy flag carrier[36] airline, such as American or Delta. Through a series of mergers and consolidations, the largest U.S. airlines have inherited a bewildering hodgepodge of different aircraft, necessary to serve on their much greater variety of short domestic, long domestic, and overseas routes. Consider also their merger history. When American merged with US Airways in 2013, it acquired a completely different, very large fleet of exceptionally

---

35 As this is written, the latest version of the Boeing 737, the 737 Max has been grounded following two disastrous accidents which caused a complete loss of life of everyone on board each plane. This situation is reminiscent of the Comet grounding from 1954-1958 after several catastrophic accidents. See Chapter 6, section 6.3.

36 The U.S. flag carriers were Pan American and TWA (Trans World). Although privately owned and not government- subsidized apart from compensation they received for Civil Reserve Air Fleet commitments, these two airlines were licensed by the U.S. government to operate international routes negotiated by treaty. They ceased to be flag carriers after U.S. airline deregulation in 1978. Delta acquired most of Pan Am's routes and assets after Pan Am's bankruptcy in 1991. TWA was acquired by American in 2001.

diverse and different aircraft types. This is not the fleet an airline the size of the current American Airlines would have chosen—if it had been offered a choice. In some cases an airline's choice between two aircraft for a similar route profile will be somewhat arbitrary if their operating characteristics are sufficiently close. However, after a merger or consolidation, the merged fleet now often has two or more different types for any given route profile, greatly compromising any internal scale economies in maintenance and operations costs which could have been obtained with a larger number of just one type for those routes. Ideally, such a large airline with a highly diverse route system would need three types of aircraft; small planes for short routes, medium for medium routes, and larger for longer routes. They would ideally select planes with the sizes and internal configurations which are most appropriate for the routes flown by the airline in each category, which would generally be those with the most fuel efficient engines.

Multiple specificity of capital (Lachmann 1947, 1956) helps explain why the very chaotic and diversified aircraft fleets inherited by the largest legacy carriers put them at a competitive disadvantage compared to smaller, more nimble airlines with newer, more fuel efficient fleets, which were designed and selected to be better optimized for those airlines' route structures. In addition, the less diversified a fleet an airline can operate with, the lower will be its maintenance costs. Capital equipment is always designed with a specific use in mind. Entrepreneurial planners must expect the return on the clay capital they select for their firms, which they purchase with putty financial capital, to be at least as high as the return on financial assets such as government bonds, which were also available to the entrepreneurs when they entered into their production plans. The entrepreneurs must also be able to convince financial intermediaries and other sources of venture capital that their expectations are reasonable, and are highly likely to be successfully realized. The actual return on installed capital may be much lower, as expectations may be disappointed, or plans fail to proceed as anticipated.

8.2 Plan Maintenance & Changing Market Conditions

Entrepreneurs observe prevailing market conditions while understanding that conditions may always change due to unforeseen circumstances and events. Entrepreneurial plans are always predicated on a deep, complex, and interwoven tapestry of complementary and interlocking, interdependent entrepreneurial plans formulated and implemented by others. These plans are needed to provide the required inputs and the anticipated constellation of prices which the entrepreneurial planner takes as the underlying working assumptions on which they base the entrepreneurial plan which they construct in turn, obtain financing for, and then carry out. Even the smallest deviation from one of an entrepreneurial plan's underlying assumptions—if an input price is too high, or the available quantity of the input is less than needed, or the selling price of the finished product turns out to be lower than anticipated, etc.—can wreak havoc with a sufficiently sensitive plan. In this case, frustrated expectations can mean the difference between successful profit making and bankruptcy. The best entrepreneurs are exceedingly knowledgeable regarding such things as input availability, prices, and the demand conditions prevailing for the output they seek to produce. They seek less to merely command an encyclopedic knowledge of market conditions than to successfully manage and adapt their entrepreneurial plans over time in the face of an unknown and unknowable future which unfolds before us, but the entrepreneur's deep encyclopedic knowledge of the market is produced as a necessary byproduct of their entrepreneurial alertness.

As a best entrepreneurial practice, an entrepreneurial plan will have as much flexibility written into it as possible, whether the plan is literally committed to writing or is merely implicit in the conduct of the firm. Alert entrepreneurs know market conditions may change, and indeed that they do change all the time, rendering conditions different from what was originally assumed when the plan was first conceived (Leijonhufvud 1981: 265). While one innovative entrepreneur seeks to disrupt the market in one area, others seek to disrupt it elsewhere. Not all succeed, but some do. Nevertheless, an entrepreneurial plan is partly built on subjective expectations which are in principle unique for each individual, but also partly built on the inflexible physical data of objective engineering relationships (Mises 1957: 378). Our understanding of these inexorable relations of the natural sciences may change due to advances in learning or technology, or be overcome through substitution among inputs, but the underlying physical limitations are constraints which cannot be overcome. Entrepreneurial alertness to new ways to satisfy new or existing consumer wants is the only truly inexhaustible resource constraining the evolution of market conditions.

The onset of a recession shakes up established entrepreneurial plans which have already been started and are now in the process of being carried out. At the start of a business downturn, some entrepreneurial plans which have already been started will not be able to be completed because they depend on other plans which are failing or being abandoned. Because all entrepreneurial plans are part of a complex web of interdependent relationships, the failure to complete any one entrepreneurial plan as anticipated results in ripple effects of plan failures throughout the economy as other plans which depended on the first are disrupted and now can no longer be completed as originally intended. The onset of a recession marks a structural shift from a bull market environment characterized by euphoric and unsustainable over-optimism to an equally extreme bear market environment characterized by melancholic over-pessimism.

The same kinds of investment projects which did not always receive the most sober and critical due diligence in the deliriously over-optimistic days of the boom are now evaluated after the bust in a more depressed speculative ambiance which has turned much more strictly against risk taking. Some of the most valuable technological advances will be delayed many months or years because of this general atmosphere of recessionary pessimism. Some advances may be forgone entirely, being completely forgotten by the time a recovery makes it possible to finance them. Entrepreneurial planners who were not sufficiently or appropriately cautious during the expansion, having been caught with their pants down at the start of the recession, now overreact by becoming dramatically more risk averse during the recession, and well into the recovery. The overcautious behavior of some entrepreneurs opens opportunities for those who are better able to gauge the risk and potential return of prospective investments during the recession, provided they can find the financing they need.

At the start of a recession, expectations about future market conditions generally shift systematically from optimistic to pessimistic, and entrepreneurial decisions about whether and where to invest "putty" capital are reevaluated. Often, a project which would have been easily and enthusiastically funded without too much scrutiny during the boom will now be delayed until the end of the recession. At the onset of a recession, however, "clay" capital, which is already installed, now generally cannot realize as high a return as what had been expected. Due to the newly unfavorable business conditions, all the items of installed clay capital now generally face a much lower expected return in their original intended use than what the entrepreneur anticipated when they made their allocation decision, designed the capital installation, purchased the equipment, and implemented the plan.

During the course of a recession, installed clay capital may be abandoned completely, or may be used exactly as called for in the original production plan, but most commonly, clay capital is used during the recession in a modified production plan which is designed to make the best use possible of the clay capital in the recessionary environment. Generally, the original entrepreneurial plan put in place prior to the start of the recession was predicated on higher expected demand for the firm's product. This now has to be changed in light of new expectations; for example, that the selling price and sales volume will be lower until the recession is over. In addition, most input prices will also fall due to the decreased demand for input resources which results from the recession's general contraction of business activity. This will actually help the firm's profit margins, but this favorable circumstance is normally more than offset by the lower sales revenues most firms earn during the recession.

The firm's installed capital was predicated on the more optimistic pre-recession expectations of the firm's output price and sales volume. Cutting output generates additional excess capacity. If the capital installation can be subdivided, some units of clay capital might be sold off or leased to other firms. Or the firm could potentially use its excess capacity to produce a different output where that would be profitable given the newly less favorable business conditions. In the absence of a happy accident, in most cases the firm's profits and fortunes will be diminished for the duration of the recession. When facing numerous changes in other firms' complementary production plans, entrepreneurs adapt and attempt to achieve as high a return as they still possibly can, on those investments they have already committed to (Garrison 2000: 74). Generally, this return will be lower than the return they optimistically expected to realize in the original production plan, but higher than the return that would actually be realized if the firm's production plan was carried out exactly as originally intended.

The problem with the original, pre-recession entrepreneurial plans is generally with the over-optimistic expectations about market conditions, which are now systematically less favorable overall. The technical capabilities embodied in the pre-recession entrepreneurial plans are not the problem, though they may be mistaken or incorrect in certain isolated plans, but will generally never occur systematically throughout the economy. If anything, the ever-advancing state of technical knowledge contributes to constantly lowering costs of production and constantly increasing output, as well as creating new markets for new products. The improvement in technology which occurs while a given entrepreneurial plan is being carried out will almost always make it easier for entrepreneurial plans to succeed.

The physical clay capital available to any given firm to reallocate was generally intended for a different production plan, predicated on a different interest rate, for a given and now changed financial maturity corresponding to the useful life of the installed capital. So whenever clay capital is reallocated, the return typically falls below what it was previously expected to be in the original production plan with the original capital combination. This newly lowered return is generally still strictly higher than what the return would be given the newly changed business conditions, if the entrepreneurial planner neglects to reallocate the clay capital and install it in a new combination for a new entrepreneurial plan. Generally, the return on the new plan will be lower, otherwise recessions would boost productivity and output, but still higher than the actual return on the original unmodified plan.

In Keynesian terms, there is a liquidity constraint[37] on clay capital, in contrast to uninvested financial putty capital. If they could, entrepreneurial planners would take their funds directly out of installed clay capital and invest these funds in higher yielding government bonds or other financial assets, but these funds are tied up in illiquid physical assets. These physical assets can still be sold but generally cannot command as high a price now that their productive yield has become less competitive. Lachmann (1947, 1956) recognized that installed "clay" capital is multispecific—meaning that it can be used for a specific variety of different specific purposes (Horwitz 2000: 47-49). Unfortunately, even though there is no liquidity constraint on financial putty capital which is always measured in money terms, the return on investment opportunities generally becomes much lower during a recession than before the unsustainable boom which preceded the recession, or than what returns were previously expected to be.

8.3 Constraints Imposed by Financial Capital: Time Preference & Term Structure

It is less obvious that multispecificity and heterogeneity are also shared to some extent by uninstalled financial or "putty" capital. This insight is the basis for the segmented markets (Culbertson 1957) and

---

37 Keynes 1936: 106-107.

preferred habitat (Modigliani & Sutch 1966) theories of term structure, the relationship between the return on financial assets and their
time to maturity (Thomas 1997: 138-154, Van Horne 1998: 83-100).
In the more basic pure expectations theory (Fisher 1896, Lutz 1940)
and liquidity premium theory (Hicks 1946: 146-147) financial instruments with different maturities are assumed to be perfect substitutes,
so the supply of and demand for different maturities of financial assets
all have infinite elasticities of substitution;[38] that is, they are perfect
substitutes. For example, according to the pure expectations theory of
term structure, a one-year treasury bill, reinvested or rolled over every
year for ten years, should always have the same return as a ten-year
treasury bond over the same time period, as long as the expected future
returns are the same over the ten-year period. If financial instruments of
any particular maturity did have a higher yield, the higher yield would
make those bonds more desirable as a store of value, their price would
be bid up by savers trying to capture the above market returns, and the
higher bond price would drive the return on these bonds down. In other
words arbitrage equalizes the returns on assets of different maturities.

Under the pure expectations theory, market arbitrage is assumed to
ensure that only the differences in expectations about future interest
rates enable financial assets of different maturities to have different
yields. The liquidity premium theory recognizes that individuals' desire

---

38 The elasticity of substitution between instruments of different maturities a
and b measures how responsive the demand for bonds of one maturity is to
changes in the price of bonds of different maturities. The price of bonds is
inversely proportional to interest rate or return on the bond. The formula is

$$e_{sub} = [dQ_a/Q_a]/[dP_b/P_b] = dQ_aP_b/dP_bQ_a = [(Q_a^1-Q_a^0)/Q_a^0]/[(P_b^1-P_b^0)/P_b^0]$$
$$= d\log(Q_a)/d\log(P_b).$$

The substitution elasticity is one for perfect substitutes, which are completely
interchangeable, and zero for two things that cannot be substituted.

for liquidity—easier convertibility into cash—means lenders will demand, and borrowers will be willing to pay a premium in the form of a higher interest rate or return for any less liquid, longer maturity assets. The higher return is necessary partly to offset the greater default risk of the asset's longer exposure to market risk; that is the extra risk imposed by having to wait for the borrowed money to be returned (Fisher 1959).

In contrast with the pure expectations theory which assumed savings instruments and loans of different maturities are perfect substitutes, the segmented markets theory treats different maturities as being completely non-substitutable; that is, financial instruments with different maturities are assumed to have zero elasticity of substitution. In this view, the market for one-year financial assets is completely separate from the markets for six-month or two-year assets, or from those of any other duration or maturity. The arbitrage which equalizes return on instruments of different maturities in the pure expectations theory is assumed not to operate in the segmented markets theory, because of the assumption of rigid market segmentation. Never mind that shorter term assets actually can be rolled over to borrow or lend money for an equivalent time period. Rolling over one-year bills for ten years is equivalent to buying a single ten-year bond, in terms of the amount loaned or borrowed. Which is more advantageous depends on how interest rates actually change over the ten-year period. Which appears to be more advantageous before the fact depends on the expected returns on the different instruments and how interest rates for the different maturities are expected to change over the ten-year period. If expectations are not fulfilled, the actual outcome will generally be different.

The more realistic preferred habitat theory assumes substitution elasticities across maturities are low, but that if one maturity actually offers a sufficiently higher yield than others, or is simply expected to before the fact, arbitrage among instruments with different maturities would attract investment demand until the difference in returns and interest rates was minimized. However, in general, the differences among returns on instruments of different maturities would never be entirely eliminated. The preferred-habitat theory recognizes that differences in interest rates for different maturities will generally never be eliminated because there is generally never a perfect match between the maturities for which the savers want to save and borrowers want to borrow. It is the savers who supply loanable funds, make bank deposits, and buy bonds, and the borrowers who demand loanable funds, take out loans to finance their investment projects or entrepreneurial plans, or sell bonds. Market arbitrage brings down and minimizes the differences among different maturity interest rates, but can never eliminate them entirely.

Here entrepreneurial arbitrageurs are alert to the profit opportunities which exist whenever financial assets with different maturities have sufficiently different rates of return. They can reduce the information imbalances and asymmetries which are indicated by the different returns, but generally diminishing returns set in before a perfect equilibrium can be reached. The market process consists of profit seeking entrepreneurial planners continually adjusting the market toward this dynamic equilibrium which is continuously redefined by the decisions and actions they take. The prevailing term structure of interest rates determines resource allocation among early, middle, or late stages of production, in accordance with consumers' time preference and available investment alternatives.

If market arbitrage has resulted in a certain market interest rate on savings, loanable funds, or investible resources at a certain spread above the interest earnings on financial assets such as savings deposits and government bonds, this signals a profit opportunity to alert entrepreneurs. Entrepreneurs compete to formulate entrepreneurial plans which will allow them to borrow from financial intermediaries at this available market interest rate, and earn the highest yield they can contrive, over and above the prevailing market interest rate. If an entrepreneur cannot formulate such opportunities, they should not borrow, but loan their own funds to other entrepreneurs who can create investment opportunities with the potential to yield above market returns with the highest apparent probability of success. This in turn enables lenders to earn higher returns with less effort. Automatically, the incentive structure of the loanable funds market ensures that only entrepreneurs capable of implementing the highest yielding plans, or who believe in and can successfully convince others that their plans will in fact be the highest yielding with the highest likelihood of success, will be borrowers. Everyone else will be a saver-lender.

8.4 Asset Valuation & the Return on Investment

It is important to realize that under the inexorable profit-and-loss discipline of the market, entrepreneurial plans may subsequently fail, and often do, simply because they were based on and assumed unrealistic or unrealized expectations. The institutional structure requiring entrepreneurs to convince lenders or other third parties to part with their money to invest in any proposed entrepreneurial plan in return for a share of the profits should generally help improve outcomes. The process of convincing lenders and venture capitalists to invest or finance the investment expenditures which are necessary to implement an entrepreneurial plan ensures that loanable funds advanced on credit are rationed to the highest yielding and most plausible opportunities, offering the greatest apparent likelihood of success, at least before the fact. However, the nature of this market discipline and credit rationing may result in overly conservative financial appraisals which may unfortunately also prevent some valuable and particularly innovative plans from ever being financed or attempted.

Entrepreneurs use the putty funds they borrow to install clay capital equipment and complementary means of production in order to put the entrepreneurial plan in motion. The entrepreneurial planner's objective is to realize the greatest yield surplus above the loan interest rate they will have to pay back to the lenders. Once the production plan starts to be implemented, in the process of implementation, the value of the resources coordinated by the more successful entrepreneurial plans; that is, the market value of these enterprises as going concerns, will be bid up until the yield on the enterprise's resources falls to match the market interest rate. In contrast, less successful firms see their value bid down until the yield on those firms' resources *rises* to match the market yield. This is part of the market discipline which rewards successful entrepreneurs and penalizes the less successful.

8.5 Coordinating Production: the Role of Prices & Interest Rates

Firms' entrepreneurial plans have to mesh successfully with those of one another in the sense that they must coordinate their activities. For example, for plan A to be completed successfully, any inputs required for plan A must be produced at a sufficiently low cost as the output of some other plan B, which must in turn be able to receive its inputs at a sufficiently low cost as the output of plan C, etc. Every entrepreneurial plan is always predicated on a very precise and specific set of combinations of complementary plans which must be completed on time and as anticipated by each entrepreneur. Similarly, all the output produced by each plan must be purchased by some consumer or other buyer[39] at a sufficiently high price, so that continuing all of the production plans has been justified, and continues to be justified going forward. These chains of linear causal sequences are actually better understood as a complex multidimensional web of interdependent input-output relationships. These relationships can only be considered static or stable in the absence of disruptive entrepreneurial innovation. By disrupting the market in the short run, entrepreneurial planners who introduce successful innovations improve the mutual coordination of entrepreneurial plans in the long run (Kirzner 1996: 39-41).

Entrepreneurial plans are coordinated through price signals which are set by the innovations and adaptive responses of entrepreneurial planners in a competitive market. If, for example, an iron ore mine is depleted, the steel producers who previously depended on it as a source of ore must now go to an alternative, more expensive source. The alternative can be assumed to be more expensive, either because the depleted mine was initially chosen because it was the lowest cost source of iron ore, or because alternative mines are farther away, therefore imposing, at a minimum, higher transportation costs. Assuming that the steelmaker faces a perfectly competitive market and is a price taker,

---

39 For example, other producers may purchase capital equipment produced by another firm as part of their entrepreneurial plans, or any firms' output may be purchased by another firm as an input into their production process, in addition to direct retail sales to the final consumer. The ultimate objective of all productive activity is the satisfaction of consumer wants, along with the profits which are earned in exchange.

then raising the price of their output is not an option, because doing so would simply drive their customers into the hands of competing steelmakers. If the steelmakers make no adjustments to their production plan, they will earn lower profits because of the higher cost of one of their inputs; in this case, of the iron ore.

Provided it is technologically feasible, one alternative response might be for the steelmaker to adjust their production methods so that they use iron ore less intensively and other resources more intensively—substituting one input for another in production. For example, the firm might experiment with using more coal, to fire their blast furnace at greater heat or for a longer time, in order to extract more molten iron from a given amount of the iron ore. If this is technically feasible and succeeds, the firm's profits will still be lower than what they had been when the iron ore was still cheap. However, the steelmaker's response of economizing on the use of iron ore when it becomes more expensive saves them from having their profits lowered by as much as they would have fallen if the firm had not responded by adjusting production at all.

In terms of borrowing and servicing the debt incurred to set up the firm, firms can only borrow if they can successfully convince lenders that the return on any prospective investment will be at least high enough to allow the borrowers to service the interest and pay back the debt. Occasionally lenders will get this calculation wrong, usually due to an appraisal of the firm's prospects which turns out after the fact to have been too optimistic, but the occasional and random errors like this only discipline lenders to be more careful in the future. Lenders generally respond to loan defaults by more closely and carefully scrutinizing each new prospective loan and the associated entrepreneurial plans the loans are sought to finance. Much like successful entrepreneurial plans, every successful business loan is built on the past experience of failed loans, which are always invaluable learning experiences for the banks and other financial intermediaries, though expensive. Unfortunately, this knowledge and experience tends to date rather badly as the economy develops technologically, new possibilities are opened up by the introduction of new complementary products and technologies, and the boom-and-bust cycle continues to repeat. As long as interest rates are steady and accurately represent savers' time preference, the economy builds a sustainable capital structure.

If interest rates rise, consistent with higher time preference by savers; that is, less patience on their part to delay immediate gratification, this requires an adjustment to a higher yielding but still sustainable capital structure. If savers' time preference rises, that means they are more impatient to enjoy immediate consumption, and divide their current income into a combination of consumption and saving which now becomes more balanced toward immediate consumption than before. In this situation, interest rates have to rise to better reward savers, because they would prefer to spend that money. If savers' time preference falls, that indicates they are more patient and will delay satisfying their own wants, now dividing their current income into a combination which is more balanced toward saving. Now the greater abundance of savings allows interest rates to fall.

With higher interest rates consistent with higher time preference, less income is saved, and the financial system has fewer loanable funds available to finance new ventures and new entrepreneurial plans. Entrepreneurs who seek to borrow must pay a higher interest rate, and so can only seek to finance higher yielding ventures and entre-preneurial plans with higher expected yields. A new startup project may still fail because it does not prove as productive as anticipated by the entrepreneurial planner who conceived it and carried it out, but the higher interest rate means this economy will have fewer startups, though the smaller number which succeed in this environment will have to be more successful and faster growing. The higher interest rate imposes a higher threshold rate of return which an investment project, whether a new firm or an expansion of an existing firm's activities or product line, will have to match or exceed in order to be a success—and as a result fewer investment projects succeed in this more competitive, higher interest environment.

With lowered interest rates consistent with lower time preference, less income is consumed, and more is saved. More loanable funds are now available, and are offered at a lower interest rate to fund new ventures and new entrepreneurial plans. Entrepreneurs will still seek to borrow funds for all the projects they would have at a higher interest rate, but with the differences that (a) the lower market interest rate makes those projects even more profitable, and (b) the lower interest rate also makes additional projects appear feasible which only offer lower anticipated rates of return. So more new ventures and entrepreneurial plans will be financed. As before, a new startup project or entrepreneurial plan may still fail because it does not prove as productive as anticipated by the entrepreneur who conceived it and carried it out, but the lower interest rate means this economy will have more startups.

Furthermore, the larger number of new investment projects which succeed in this environment will not subsequently need to be as successful or high yielding as before. Many entrepreneurial plans can still succeed even though they actually provide a lower rate of return and grow more slowly than a successful enterprise would have had to in the higher interest rate, higher time preference environment.

The lower interest rate now imposes a lower and less competitive threshold rate of return which an investment project, whether a new firm or an expansion of an existing firm's activities or product line, will have to reach in order to be a success—as a result more investment projects succeed in this less competitive, lower interest rate environment. The lower interest rate is the criterion of success or failure, and it has now become a less stringent and demanding condition. Although the existence of all these lower yielding projects brings down the economy's average rate of return, more projects will be financed, and the economy will expand.

Over time, interest rates and the underlying rate of time preference can change in either direction, and these changes only bring about a wholly sustainable transition toward either investment at the expense of consumption expenditure[40] in the case of lower interest rates, or toward consumption at the expense of investment in the case of higher interest rates. Either movement of interest rates is sustainable, as each brings about a rebalancing of the economy's productive activity to favor either consumption or investment; that is to favor either consumer goods at the expense of producer goods or vice versa. This shift results in each case in a sustainable reallocation of resources in favor of either producers or consumers, as long as the process of transition is consistent with the change in overall time preference by savers—meaning this market interest rate reflects the natural rate of interest. The business

---

40 Investment goods, otherwise known as physical capital, capital equipment, or clay capital can also be described as producer goods. Producer goods may be used to produce other lower-order (Menger 1871) producer goods, or first-order consumer goods. It is often convenient to divide all production into consumer goods and producer goods. In general, consumer goods satisfy our wants immediately, while producer goods potentially satisfy our wants in the future and over time.

cycle arises when the banking system artificially decouples interest rates from consumer time preference—once this happens, the interest rate, an important and indispensable economy-wide price signal, is now communicating disinformation and causes some of the coordination among entrepreneurial plans to become unsustainable (Horwitz 2000: 6).

CHAPTER 9

The Business Cycle

The problem of what causes, and what can prevent, the business cycle is the central and most important problem of macroeconomics. Without recurrent recessions, the economy would just expand more or less steadily. Recessions are the stumbling blocks to unimpeded economic progress and ever-expanding human happiness, flourishing, and prosperity. Entrepreneurial plans have to be mutually coordinated to be successfully completed, benefit consumers, and earn profits. As long as this mutual coordination can be established and maintained, the economy can continue to expand. However, whenever the economy experiences any kind of unsustainable expansion or an inability to maintain the mutual coordination among entrepreneurial plans, the economy has to retrench and reallocate resources to activities which can be sustained.

9.1 Austrian Business Cycle Theory

O'Driscoll (1977), Garrison (1985, 1989, 2000), and Ioannides (1992) reframe the Austrian business cycle (ABC) theory of Mises and Hayek in terms of the transmission of the information used by entrepreneurial planners in implementing and maintaining their plans. Hayek's view of the economy's general equilibrium was as a state of mutual plan compatibility, mutual coordination, or dovetailing among the otherwise independent plans of many different actors. In any state of sustainable coordination, firms produce the appropriate combination of inputs required by other producers, along with consumer goods which satisfy people's wants directly, and all output is offered for sale at prices which are feasible and sustainable, so that the output from each firm finds a ready buyer. Whenever prices of individual products are maladjusted and do not allow markets for those products to clear, the discoordination this introduces is minor and transient, lasting only as long as it takes for the prices to adjust to clear the markets. Products which are desired and technically feasible to produce, but cost too much to produce, are outside the feasible business opportunity set, until or unless market conditions change or the state of technology advances to sufficiently lower production costs. Capital markets where savings are lent and borrowed determine the market interest rate by coordinating entrepreneurs' expectations of future consumer wants with the physical production necessary to satisfy those wants over time. Sustainable production is coordinated with future consumer demand and saving through the time preferences of the consumers who indirectly finance sustainable productive activity through saving.

Entrepreneurs compete to improve this intertemporal coordination among the numerous production plans, and in the absence of government interference or expansionary policy, this results in an absence of any widespread or systematic discoordination. Isolated discoordination will generally be present as individual entrepreneurial plans are experimental and do not always succeed, and at any point in time, some fail. Some innovations may not be rewarded and meet with success, and other, successful innovations may cause the unchanged entrepreneurial plans of others, which have succeeded for some time past, to fail now if left unadjusted in the face of newly introduced competing products or innovative techniques. These coordination failures are minor, random, transient, and self-correcting. The worst outcome from this kind of discoordination is that an individual firm goes bankrupt because its entrepreneurial planners were unable to adapt their pre-existing plans in the right direction or to the necessary extent. The more alert entrepreneurs still succeed and are rewarded because they are aware of the possibility of this happening, and respond to it appropriately.

Expansionary government policy, specifically monetary expansion, however, prevents the natural maintenance of entrepreneurial plans from being sustainably kept in mutual coordination. Expansionary policy increases production activity to a level and a combination of activities beyond what can be sustained over the long run. Increasing the money supply results in financing additional production activity and resource use, including labor employment and investment in capital equipment, beyond what is sustainable, and simultaneously bids up the cost of these scarce resources beyond their sustainable values. The principal motivation for expansionary government spending is deficit finance, which enables politicians to buy votes without the downside of having to raise taxes. Initially and for some time into an unsustainable expansion, everything will appear favorable in the macroeconomy, because as a result of expansionary policy, output, employment, and nominal incomes all rise. Unfortunately, at some point the unsustainability spreads widely enough throughout the economy to become critical. Mutual plan coordination becomes increasingly more difficult to sustain as an artificial boom progresses. Eventually it becomes too difficult to maintain all these plans in mutual coordination, and restore those which have been disrupted by entrepreneurial innovations to their original state of higher coordination (Lewin 1997). At this point, many half-completed plans which have already been started have to be abandoned or modified.

Each plan depends for its success on the successful completion of numerous other entrepreneurial plans, either to provide input resources at a sufficiently low price, or to purchase the output at a sufficiently high price. At some point the economy reaches a stage where some plans can no longer be completed as originally intended. These partially completed plans require the output of certain other plans of other entrepreneurs, and at this point some of the other plans are already being scaled back or abandoned. Every time the plans of one entrepreneur fails, all the other entrepreneurial plans are still at work generating stocks of goods-in-process which will now not be adequate to complete the all the plans of other entrepreneurs. To some extent goods-in-process can be substituted for one another, but this substitutability is always limited. The strain this puts on the economy's ability to maintain an increasingly layered and interdependent set of entrepreneurial plans in mutual coordination grows exponentially throughout the expansion which precedes a recession. Every time an entrepreneurial planner recognizes the unsustainability of their own plans and scales them back, a ripple effect of additional discoordination spreads throughout the economy, and when the mutual coordination of entrepreneurial plans can no longer be sustained in the short run, a recession starts.

By lowering the interest rate, expansionary policy gives entrepreneurial planners misleading signals, and provides more investment funds than are actually justified by the savings of others in society. Increasing the money supply depresses interest rates without simultaneously lowering people's time preference. In this case, although interest rates fall because of an increase in the money supply, people do not change their preferences for immediate consumption as opposed to saving. Although people's preference for saving and consumption has not changed, the lower interest rate influences their choice of how to divide their income into consumption and saving. Consumers are not becoming more or less willing to defer satisfying their wants by saving, and cannot be made to do so by monetary expansion and lower interest rates. In other words, their time preference is not falling, and so does not justify the lower interest rate. In fact, in response to the lower interest rate which now rewards saving less, people will save even less and consume even more. An expansionary monetary policy makes consumers behave as if their time preference has risen;that is, as if they had become more impatient and less willing to delay immediate gratification. They save less of their income because the interest rate which is their reward for saving, has gone down and—which is the flip side of saving less, they consume more, increasing demand for final output.

In the face of the price inflation which normally accompanies monetary inflation, the incentive to consumers is to save even less, because the real interest rate will be even lower. Simultaneously, consumers spend more on consumption goods, because rising prices will make their spending have less purchasing power in the future. Thus, they will spend more on consumption goods today at today's lower prices, as an alternative to spending the same amount in the future when they expect prices will be higher because of inflation.

In an inflationary environment, consumers will also purchase stocks of durable consumer goods as a form of saving, because consumers' expectation is that these real assets will hold their value better than financial assets like savings account balances, certificates of deposit, or bonds, which are denominated in dollars of falling value (Horwitz 2000: 129). Inflation also makes it necessary for entrepreneurial planners to revise their plans more frequently, and makes it more difficult for them to keep their plans mutually coordinated. The need to revise entrepreneurial plans more frequently, and the lower signal value of inflationary prices and interest rates, introduces vastly more entrepreneurial errors throughout the economy. Furthermore, the artificially low interest rate and greater availability of loanable funds ensures that entrepreneurial planners systematically overinvest in longer-term, higher order activities, which are the most difficult to reallocate and profitably salvage resources and installed capital from (Horwitz 2000: 123-126).

When the unsustainability of entrepreneurial plans becomes sufficiently critical, many plans have to be abandoned and the resources and goods-in-process already tied up in those plans must be liquidated. At the start of a recession, resource prices collapse as these gluts of resources and goods-in-process which were urgently acquired based on unrealistic expectations are now revealed to be unneeded and unwanted. Partially processed resources and goods-in-process are offered for liquidation at whatever fire sale prices they can command at this point. The overexpansion fueled by below market interest rates generates more unsustainable economic activity in the short run, but when the economy adjusts, many of these unsustainable entrepreneurial plans which were started during the boom will not be able to be completed as anticipated, or coordinated with the plans of others. Stocks of resources which were mistakenly acquired throughout the economy when they appeared to be needed now have to be liquidated because there is a glut.

The boom phase of the business cycle has generated partially processed resources and goods-in-process which no one is now willing to purchase at the originally anticipated price, and which cannot now be used in complementary production plans, because many of the production activities outlined by those complementary plans are being abandoned. Although entrepreneurs attempt to reallocate available resources to their next best uses, these widespread gluts of unwanted goods, services, and clay capital cannot generally command the prices they did when it was anticipated they could be used in the original set of mutually coordinated production plans. There is generally no way most of these resources can ever attain the value they were expected to sell for, when they were acquired for use in entrepreneurial plans which were set up during the overly optimistic days of the unsustainable boom. The value added of these input resources and goods-in-process in their next best uses is always lower, and as the optimism of an unsustainable expansion gives way to the pessimism of a recession, the next best value may be extraordinarily low in comparison. Prices of these resources collapse.

9.2 The Market Interest Rate & the Onset of Recession

The interest rate puts a price on what borrowers have to pay if they borrow to enjoy immediate gratification beyond what they could afford today on their current income, as well a price which rewards savers for deferring their gratification into the future. If people on average are patient and content to save, the relationship of saving to borrowing will result in a low interest rate, as people save more of their incomes and consume less. If people on average are impatient and desire immediate gratification, then the relationship of saving to borrowing results in a high interest rate, as people save less of their incomes and consume more. Investment spending, which finances all processes of production, is funded primarily through borrowing at this market interest rate.

If the government prints additional unbacked fiat money, more money is deposited in the banking system and becomes available to borrow. The additional supply of loanable funds allows interest rates to fall below what they would have been if the size of the money supply had been kept fixed. The lower interest rate on loans now makes borrowing cheaper, but the lower interest rate on deposits rewards saving less. Given people's original and unchanged time preferences, people respond to the lowered interest rates by saving less and consuming more. Because the lower interest rate makes the cost of borrowing lower, firms also borrow more for investment purposes, to expand business activity and production. Ordinarily this would not be possible, except that now, because the government is creating more fiat money and loanable bank deposits, it has increased the amount of money in circulation, and with it the amount available to be loaned to entrepreneurs. So instead of people having to substitute investment for consumption or vice-versa, both investment and consumption can increase together. This creates a business cycle boom which is both artificial and unsustainable.

The boom which precedes a recession is always a real phenomenon, though it is never sustainable, which is why it always collapses into a recession. In spite of its origin in an expansionary monetary policy, the unsustainable boom results in an increase in real goods and real assets being produced, and demand for labor increasing, thus lowering unemployment and increasing real output. Before interest rates were lowered below the natural rate, the original entrepreneurial plans were in a high state of mutual coordination throughout the economy. The lower interest rate lowers the cost of borrowing, triggering a systematic expansion of any activity in the original plans which would have been financed by borrowing, because it is now relatively cheaper to borrow.

Cantillon effects occur due to the injection of newly created money being concentrated in certain sectors of the economy. The real impact of expanding the money supply is always focused on whatever the people who receive the new money spend it on. This increases demand for certain kinds of output at the expense of other kinds, resulting in more of that output being produced, and then being sold at a higher price. As the additional amount of new money spreads further throughout the economy, other prices are also driven up, though to a lesser extent the farther one looks from the point and time of the original injection of new money. The industries which produce products bought with the new money expand at the expense of the rest of the economy. Other industries contract because the general increase in prices results in consumers being unable to buy as much real output as they could before, a phenomenon known as forced saving (Horwitz 2000: 114-115). Cantillon (1755: 155, Bordo 1983: 242) was the first to identify real effects of inflation and understand why they would be focused on particular sectors of the economy.

But in addition, new investment projects suddenly become affordable. These are projects which had been marginal and less competitive because they have lower expected yields. This additional investment did not appear feasible at the original, higher rate of interest which prevailed before expansionary monetary policy lowered the interest rate. At the lowered interest rate, some of these additional, lower yielding projects now appear attractive. These projects were not financed or entered into as long as the natural rate of interest prevailed, but now that interest rates are lower, lower yielding projects now appear to pay off. As the economy expands, plans become more complicated, requiring a higher degree of mutual coordination, and stretch out over longer time periods. This way it becomes more difficult to maintain an increasing number of different plans in mutual coordination. Entrepreneurial plans are always predicated on the successful completion of numerous other plans, and maintaining this mutual coordination is always necessary to ensure that any particular plan can be completed successfully.

At some point this process of expanding the circles of mutual dependency and plan coordination reaches a breaking point. The natural interest rate which would normally have coordinated plans in accordance with consumer time preference; that is, the relationship between consumers' desires for consumer and producer goods, or in other words for immediate as opposed to future satisfaction of their wants, is no longer available to coordinate the greater number of more complicated plans which are eventually rendered unsustainable. Eventually the artificially low interest rate finances plans which are too complicated and too dependent on other, contingent plans, to bring them all simultaneously to completion, and the collapse of each enterprise has a ripple effect on all its suppliers, employees, shareholders, and customers, throughout the economy. Once this point is reached, a recession starts.

Entrepreneurial plans are always speculative and it is inevitable that at any given time, some will fail, and some will be unsustainable or otherwise incapable of being brought to a successful conclusion. Nothing in the economy works to make these failures and sustainability problems occur all at once and normally they occur at random. It is only the economy-wide signaling mechanism of the market interest rate, which normally serves to coordinate entrepreneurial plans throughout the economy, that can create a *coordinated* unsustainability and disruption which is the business cycle.

9.3 How Entrepreneurial Planners React to the Lower Interest Rate

In formulating a new entrepreneurial plan, or in maintaining one which is already in progress but has to be modified, the firm's decision makers have to borrow to start a new venture, or expand or modify an existing one. Even when entrepreneurial planners do not have to borrow, they often have to consider the return they can get on any idle funds. If the interest rate falls due to expansionary monetary policy, entrepreneurial planners will still finance the investment projects they would have borrowed for at the old, higher interest rate, but now that the interest rate is lower, they will seek to borrow more, and finance additional, lower-yielding projects. The lower interest rate means that more projects will be pursued by entrepreneurial planners throughout the economy. Some of these projects will be lower-yielding, and the average yield will be lower than what it would have been if only the more select, higher-yielding projects had been financed at the higher interest rate.

This makes the economy larger, producing more output and employing more workers, but it drives a wedge between saving and investment. Saving falls at the lower interest rate, while investment spending rises, as does consumption spending. The only way investment can rise while saving is falling is because the money supply is being increased—the added new money has to go somewhere.

These things would happen and create an unsustainable structure of production where interdependent entrepreneurial plans cannot be successfully completed or kept in coordination with one another, even if the expectations of the entrepreneurial planners were static and did not respond to the expansionary monetary policy. Unfortunately, the expansionary policy creates additional distortions. Businesses expand, unemployment goes down, consumption and investment spending increase—the only thing that does not appear to be moving in the right direction will be savings. In the lower interest rate environment, some of the firms' new investment spending will have a lower expected return, all the way down to the lower interest rate. But the real effects of monetary expansion, Cantillon effects focused on particular, booming industries where expansion is localized, helps bias the entrepreneurial planners' expectations of what the returns will be on the investment projects they contemplate.

Real expansion, however unsustainable, makes many expected returns more optimistic than they really should be. Entrepreneurial planners mistakenly view the unsustainable boom as a period of unprecedented prosperity which they expect to see sustained. Experience appears to support their perceptions as long as the boom lasts, but once a correction starts, the unsustainability of many of the lower yielding plans, which in reality have even lower sustainable yields than what the overoptimistic entrepreneurial planners had expected, becomes obvious.

9.4 The Hayekian Triangle

Hayek introduced the Hayekian triangle diagram (Figure 9.1) to illustrate ABC theory (Hayek 1935: 39). The goal of production is the satisfaction of human wants, so the economy's total output of consumer goods is the height of the triangle. Producer goods are part of the economy's output, but do not satisfy wants directly. The base of the triangle is production time, which passes as consumer goods are produced. The division of the stages of production into early, middle, and late stage goods, is also due to Hayek, and corresponds to Menger's (1871) distinction between higher order (early stage) goods and lower order (late stage) goods. In Menger's terminology, consumer goods are first order goods. The division of the production structure into a sequence of manufacturing operations is due to Garrison (2000), who used it as an illustration, but the diagram applies equally well to all production in the economy. The slope of the Hayekian triangle represents the interest rate. Value is added at a rate determined by the rate of interest as producers process raw materials and other productive resources through successive stages of mining, refining, manufacturing, distribution, wholesale, and finally, the retail sale of consumer goods to the final users.

The market interest rate, which determines the slope of the Hayekian triangle, arises through market arbitrage and negotiation between high time preference borrowers and low time preference savers, and ultimately reflects the time preferences of the various individuals in the economy. The lower the interest rate, the lower the reward for saving. If this results in savings being in short supply compared to the amount people want to borrow at low interest, there will be a credit shortage which is resolved by raising the interest rate. The higher the interest rate, the greater the reward for saving. If this results in savings being more abundant than the amount people want to borrow at high cost, then that results in the interest rate falling. The lower the equilibrium interest rate, the cheaper it is for entrepreneurial planners to borrow to purchase producer goods (capital equipment) and other productive assets, and expand their production activities. Within limits determined by the available technology, a lower interest rate results in a flatter Hayekian triangle, but because the economy will be accumulating producer goods which improve productivity, the height of the triangle can be made higher, because an economy with more producer goods becomes capable of producing more output, including more consumer goods.

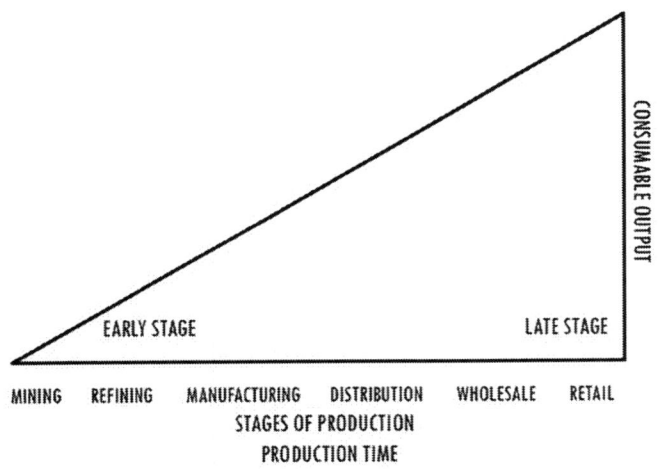

Figure 9.1 The Hayekian Triangle

In principle, any interest rate, and therefore any slope of the triangle, can be sustainable. The height of the triangle, consumer goods produced and consumed each time period, is determined by the economy's total output, which generates the economy's total income, minus the amount saved. More is saved the higher the interest rate, that is, the greater the reward for saving. Hayek used this diagram to demonstrate the unsustainability of an expansionary monetary policy. If we increase the money supply, the newly injected money enters the economy through bank reserves and deposits, so banks suddenly have more to lend, causing the interest rate to fall below the natural rate, which was market determined and reflected the time preferences of individuals. With a lower interest rate, entrepreneurial planners find that they can borrow more cheaply. They will still borrow to finance all the high-yielding projects that they would have borrowed to finance at the old, high interest rate, but now they will also borrow for additional rounds of lower yielding projects as well. This extends the structure of production, making the Hayekian triangle flatter. These lower yielding investment projects are added throughout the economy at all stages of production, but where they are added to the earliest stage, they extend or lengthen the production structure by adding lower-yielding early stage activities. These will take longer to result in final consumer goods, offer a lower return, and extend the base of the Hayekian triangle (Figure 9.2).

Because the lower interest rate rewards savers less, and because this is not a market interest rate accurately reflecting savers' time preferences, when consumers divide their income into consumption and saving, under the influence of the artificially low interest rate, they choose to save less and consume more. The increase in the money supply which was responsible for lowering the interest rate provides the additional funds to purchase the producer goods required to expand business activity and extend the production structure, even though people save less. Unfortunately, the production structure which exists as a legacy from before the increase in the money supply cannot simultaneously satisfy the economy's increased demand for both producer and consumer goods. There would be no sustainability problems if the interest rate had changed naturally, because the economy can substitute producer goods for consumer goods or vice versa. However, with a lower interest rate from expansionary monetary policy, the economy simultaneously faces increased demand for both producer goods and consumer goods. To satisfy the increased demand for consumer goods, entrepreneurial planners raid the middle stages of the production structure, bringing unfinished, and half-finished goods to market early. The unsustainability of this strategy can be seen through the bottleneck it creates in the middle stages. There is no technically feasible way to keep transforming goods of higher order into goods of lower order at the amounts demanded. Once entrepreneurial planners run out of goods in process they can bring to market early, the economy's unsustainability becomes critical, and a recession starts. Middle-stage production can only be looted for so long before its critical role in providing the throughput which connects early stage and late stage activities makes the economy's structural deficiencies critical.

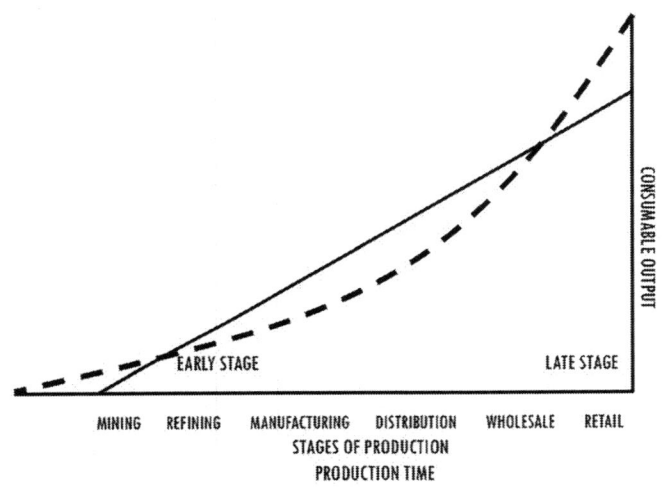

Figure 9.2 Hayekian Triangle for an unsustainable expansion

9.5 The Financial Instability Hypothesis

In framing his Financial Instability Hypothesis (FIH), Keynesian economist Hyman P. Minsky (1919-1996) classifies heterogeneous firms in three categories, according to the relationship between their cash flow and debt (Minsky 1975, 1982, 1986, 1992).

(1) *Hedge finance units* generate cash flow through their regular and ongoing business activities which is sufficient to cover both the interest and pay down the principal on their debt. This condition can be seen as

reflecting the discipline not to borrow more than their cash flow justifies, at least in normal economic times.

(2) *Speculative finance units* have borrowed so much, that although the cash flow generated by their normal business activities is sufficient to cover the interest payments on their debt, it is not adequate to pay down or pay back the borrowed principal. Finally,

(3) *Ponzi finance units* have already borrowed so much they cannot even cover the minimum required interest payments on their debt. In Minsky's Financial Instability Hypothesis any protracted period of prosperity leads eventually either to a progressive acceptance of greater risk on the part of some firms, or a mistaken under-evaluation of the true market risk to which the firms are exposed, on the part of others.

As the expansion phase of the business cycle wears on, the psychology, mindset, and attitude of entrepreneurial planners becomes increasingly more optimistic and more risk tolerant. For so long the market has been booming and many entrepreneurial planners have met with unqualified success in everything they have attempted for as far back in the past as they can remember. To some extent, the apparent increase in risk tolerance is misleading. The protracted prosperity of the expansion phase of the business cycle increasingly lulls entrepreneurial planners into a misleading sense of security as the negative impact of the last recession recedes in their memory. For many entrepreneurial planners, their risk tolerance may not actually have increased, but they now mistakenly and over-optimistically under-assess their real exposure to market risk. It has been so long since the last recession that business decision makers and entrepreneurial planners forget what the last recession was like, and the view that recessions are a thing of the past grows in popularity.

This progressive under-assessment of risk applies both to perceptions of specific investment projects or entrepreneurial plans, and of the general state of market and business conditions. This over-optimism or euphoria results in and from businesses increasing their investment spending and purchases of producer goods during the expansion phase of the business cycle, requiring the firms to take on more debt. As firms borrow more and the unsustainable expansion continues, these increasingly over-leveraged firms expose the financial sector to greater default and market risk. For every firm which has borrowed to finance unsustainable business activity which cannot be kept in mutual coordination with the plans of others, there is a bank or other lender which is more exposed to default risk than they realize. And until the recession actually starts, banks continue to lend. As a result the actual risk-adjusted returns to investment are lowered systematically and economy-wide as the progressive expansion of borrowing for investment continues. The economy becomes increasingly dominated by speculative and Ponzi finance units as hedge finance units, which normally make up the bulk of the economy, take on increasingly higher levels of debt. A given firm may find itself financially overextended merely by failing to meet the sales or earnings expectations which they assumed to justify their present borrowing levels, as well as by aggressively pursuing additional investment finance by borrowing.

Higher degrees of leverage are widely seen as being entirely normal and necessary for economic growth as the expansion phase of the business cycle continues. The more prudent and conservative approaches to lending and borrowing are progressively abandoned by more and more firms and entrepreneurial planners. Once the Ponzi finance units reach levels of indebtedness where they can no longer borrow in the increasing amounts they need based on their fixed collateral, they find that they are suddenly forced to sell off assets to make interest payments. Once the economy reaches a critical threshold of Ponzi finance units, this creates an oversupply of assets being offered for sale, and the glut of oversupply which occurs at this point causes a collapse in the price of the assets the Ponzi finance units are trying to sell off to raise cash. These can be physical assets or securitized claims to the firm's cash flows or other income. The resulting collapse in asset prices triggers debt deflation, a financial crisis, and a shortage of liquidity. Because the distribution of Minsky's FIH categories is highly sensitive to fluctuations in the firms' earnings, a crisis state can be brought about by a deceptively low critical mass of Ponzi and speculative finance units. Furthermore, since speculative bubbles are often localized in particular industries, we would expect to see different degrees of over-leverage develop in different sectors. A sufficient degree of speculative and Ponzi finance concentrated in a particular industry may be sufficient to drive a financial crisis which will then spread to most or all other sectors.

The FIH is a Keynesian explanation of the business cycle, but it has a highly interesting relationship with ABC theory, which depends on monetary expansion to drive the period of expanding and unsustainable prosperity which precedes a recession. According to Minsky's FIH, long periods of economic expansion make borrowers and lenders alike more willing to engage in activities for which they systematically underestimate the actual risk. The macroeconomy becomes increasingly unsustainable as protracted prosperity, stability, and economic growth naturally lead entrepreneurial planners to progressively underestimate their exposure to risk and the risk of potential investment opportunities. This drives a wedge between the risk-adjusted return on investment anticipated before the fact, which determines borrower and lender behavior, and the actually realized risk-adjusted return after the fact. It appears quite clear that this process is amplified and made significantly worse by expansionary monetary policy which ABC theory puts forward as the cause of the business cycle. Minsky's FIH helps flesh out some of the missing detail of the malinvestment liquidation phase of ABC theory, and it turns out that the two views are surprisingly complementary (Prychitko 2010).

9.6 FIH Research & Empirical Studies

The FIH has been further developed (Dos Santos 2005, Dos Santos & Zezza 2008), but only a few studies have tested Minsky's theory against real world data. Sethi (1992) developed a model of firm behavior based on the FIH where information constraints, transactions costs associated with accessing and processing new information, and the dynamics of learning all contribute to the progressively unwise acceptance of over-leverage and investment expansion, both on the part of firms which borrow and the financial intermediaries which lend to them. His computer simulations were able to mimic business cycle behavior better than the rational expectations models which are more common in the empirical business cycle literature, when the rational expectations forecasts and agent expectations were not publicly observable, but had to be discovered through observation over time.

Silipo (2011) examines whether asset portfolios start taking on more overvalued risky assets over the course of a business cycle expansion. As entrepreneurial planners become more optimistic, they become less averse to risk, or simply under-assess the risk they expose their firms to. This eventually results in the assets they use for loan collateral becoming over-valued (Minsky 1982). As the volatility of capital asset prices falls over the course of a business cycle expansion, standard valuation techniques lead agents to conclude that assets are undervalued based on expected cash flows. Actual cash flows have been increasing and may be over-assessed over the course of an unsustainable expansion, while cash flow volatility is increasingly likely to be under-assessed as the expansion progresses. If entrepreneurial planners wrongly perceive their risk exposure as being lower than it actually is, then risk-adjusted returns are systematically misperceived as being greater than their true underlying values. Asset valuations are thus systematically biased upward during a business cycle expansion, which sets the stage for a correction. To borrowers and lenders caught up in the euphoria of an extended boom, these inflated asset values seemingly justify higher credit limits, more borrowing and lending, greater investment spending, and economic expansion. In the absence of having experienced recent losses which would make them more cautious in the face of this unjustified euphoria, lenders and borrowers become increasingly likely to mistakenly conclude that cash flows justify increasingly higher debt levels.

As the steadily growing cash flows of the boom continue, entrepreneurial planners' recollection of past recessions, financial crises, and market volatility tends to recede in the dim mists of time. This results in capital asset prices rising beyond what is justified by current cash flows, the levels of debt which are considered normal and acceptable increasing in relation to the firms' income streams and collateral requirements (Minsky 1982: 144), and lenders requiring less collateral of lower quality. All these transformations of the financial sector contribute to making the economy more fragile and less sustainable. It also makes it more likely that any liquidity crisis will spread rapidly and catastrophically. As investment spending and profits increase during the expansion phase of the business cycle, this contributes to the transformation of the financial structure from an initial one of transparent and robust simplicity dominated by Minsky's hedge finance units, to one of increasing complexity, with networks of hidden dependency, concealed weakness, and fragility (Minsky 1982: 111, Silipo 2011: 443). In many ways the mutual dependency and weakness of financial interconnections, which enables a financial crisis to spread, is an open secret, which investors and financial experts manage to ignore.

Silipo examines 1991-2009 data leading up to the 2007-2009 recession, and among his conclusions are "that investor confidence and risk appetite shaped the business cycle more than monetary policy and the cost of borrowing (Silipo 2011: 447)." Risk measures such as the Goldman Sachs Risk Aversion Index fell steadily over the expansion and rose abruptly at the onset of the 2001 and 2007-2009 recessions. In addition, leading up to the financial crisis in late 2007, bank asset holdings more than doubled, but the majority of this balance-sheet expansion occurred in increasingly risky assets (Silipo 2011: 448-449), including derivatives and securitized debt. Leading up to the crisis, more and more banks decided to follow the example of industry leaders by investing heavily in higher-yielding, high-risk mortgage-backed securities rather than lower-yielding, low-risk conventional lending. Wachovia National Bank was among the last to do this, achieving bankruptcy as a reward.

Minsky (1987) cites debt securitization, where banks sell off their loan portfolios in the form of bonds or other financial securities, as a vector which spread and increased financial fragility, because it helped banks avoid the traditional regulatory constraints on the growth of liquid assets, bypassing reserve requirements, central bank regulation, and monetary policy. Securitized debt instruments, including mortgage-backed securities, were structured to include as many low-quality mortgages as possible while still receiving AAA or Aaa ratings from the bond rating agencies. As financial obligations become increasingly layered through securitization, the economy becomes more vulnerable to the inevitable liquidity crises which must occur eventually at some location. Highly-layered obligations, made possible through extensive and unregulated securitization, ensured that any minor or localized liquidity shortage would spread rapidly from bank to bank and sector to sector, given the fragile and interdependent financial structure (Minsky 1982: 132). Silipo observes that expansion-generated portfolio transformations also shrink the financial system's domain of stability, making liquidity crises more likely to occur. At some point, one becomes inevitable.

One feature of the 2007-2009 great recession which does not strictly fit the FIH is that the liquidity crisis occurred among those households and financial institutions which had run up the highest levels of indebtedness, rather than among the relatively less indebted corporate sector (Silipo 2011: 452). This explains why the crisis occurred in the overextended financial sector, as opposed to the corporate sector. Silipo also observes that interest rates rose along with the amounts borrowed, although generally borrowing should fall as the cost of borrowing rises. This could only happen due to an increase in loan demand (or a decrease in supply, which can clearly be ruled out), and one of the possible causes of such an increase in demand is an increase in borrower confidence. Such an increase in confidence may now appear to have been completely unwarranted, but it seems quite plausible that too many people in the finance industry simply forgot about the last crisis, or had not been working in the industry that long ago. The flight to quality[41] which Minsky (1982: 131) predicts, clearly occurred

---

41 A flight to quality occurs when lenders and investors suddenly perceive that they are exposed to significantly higher risk than they had previously realized. Lenders such as banks respond by lending only to the safest, most creditworthy borrowers. During a recession, this can make it difficult for entrepreneurs to raise funds for business expansion, delaying (or even preventing) recovery. Investors rebalance their portfolios away from riskier assets like corporate stocks toward low-yielding government bonds. During the 1930s, banks which had been eager to lend to finance unsustainable business expansion in the 1920s held a large part of their reserves in low-yielding U.S. Treasury bonds, which did not contribute to a speedy recovery. During the 2010s, the U.S. Federal Reserve System paid interest on bank reserves, rewarding banks for refraining from making the loans to businesses that would have contributed to a faster recovery.

once debt deflation started the crisis as a response to greater uncertainty by profit-maximizing, risk-averse banks (Silipo 2011: 453). The Federal Reserve System allowed the monetary base to quadruple, though the measures of the money supply only increased by a comparatively moderate factor of about one-third by May 2012, because banks were suddenly more reluctant to lend their dramatically increased level of reserves. Silipo's study is noteworthy as one of the few empirical examinations of the FIH.

Most applications of the FIH use computer simulations. Keen (1995, 2013) used simulation studies to reproduce the dynamics of the expansion and collapse. In addition to increasing risk and instability over the course of an expansion, Keen also shows that over the expansion phases of the cycles, the labor share of total income fell, non-financial business incomes stabilized, and financial-sector income rose. Chiarella and Di Guilmi (2011) observe that in the stock market, each agent forms unique expectations which determine the market valuation of financial assets, taking advantage of the market's range of available expectations to stand in for the range of firm and entrepreneurial planner capabilities, and the range of physical and financial assets each firm possesses. In addition, to model the demand for money, they model money supply measures as being linked to and partially determined by the total amount of financial assets, rather than a fixed multiple of the monetary base, an approach which is supported by the recent monetary literature (for example, Binner et al 2010) and recent experience. Their simulations effectively mimic the business cycle over a variety of conditions. They conclude, "The economy can be stabilized by reducing its capacity to create endogenous money and the maximum debt ratio allowed (Chiarella & Di Guilmi 2011: 1167)."

Both Keen (2013) and Chiarella and Di Guilmi (2011) rely on a conventionally negative Phillips curve[42] tradeoff between inflation and unemployment for their FIH models, arguing that price level increases lead to, or perhaps are caused by, reductions in unemployment. A number of recent studies have shown that either this relationship is exactly reversed—inflation actually lowers employment, even in the short-run—or that the dynamic between inflation and employment is more complicated. Increases in the price level may result in moderate, though temporary, increases in employment and real economic activity, but also result in larger permanent losses of jobs and real output over the long run (Niskanen 2002, Reichel 2004, Moghaddam & Jenson 2008, Mulligan 2011), as ABC theory predicts. If increases in prices over the course of an unsustainable expansion are driven by increases in the money supply, or less directly by increases in risk tolerance, the fact that these ultimately result in negative economic growth, lends support to both the FIH and ABC theory.

Further empirical evidence indicates that increasing the money supply decreases employment in the long run (Mulligan 2011a, 2016). When the money supply is increased, this extra money and bank credit primarily affects the earliest and latest stages of production, but not the middle or intermediate stages (Mulligan 2014a, 2017). Historical data for the Bank of Amsterdam shows that monetary expansion used

---

42 The Phillips curve (Phillips 1958) is a hypothesized negative relationship between the inflation rate and the unemployment rate. This purported relationship was identified by New Zealand economist A.W.H. Phillips (1914-1975). The idea that there was a tradeoff between inflation and unemployment was attractive to Keynesian policy makers and politicians. The Phillips curve was initially criticized by Phelps (1967) and Friedman (1968). See also Herbener (1992). More modern empirical research demonstrates that the relationship between inflation and unemployment is positive (Niskanen 2002, Reichel 2004, Moghaddam & Jenson 2008, Mulligan 2011)—in other words, inflation causes higher unemployment, or vice versa.

to finance the Netherlands' wars in the 1700s contributed to price instability and inflation (Guzelian & Mulligan 2015). There is strong empirical support for the FIH (Mulligan 2014b), but this also supports ABC theory. Data for certain industrial sectors provide stronger support for ABC theory and the FIH than others (Mulligan 2013a), which suggests the importance of Cantillon effects, where the creation of new money causes some industries to expand at the expense of others, as ABC theory predicts. Real business cycle (RBC) theory and the FIH are special cases of ABC theory (Mulligan 2013b). Fractal analysis of U.S. data strongly disconfirms real business cycle theory (Mulligan 2010), but supports a monetary origin for unsustainable expansions. Empirical data suggest that more activist monetary policy is less effective than rules based, non-discretionary policy (Mulligan 2011b), however, this result may simply reflect the fact that higher inflation or unemployment will frequently bring about a more activist policy response. It certainly can be expected to bring about stronger and more frequent calls for an activist policy.

9.7 The Financial Instability Hypothesis & Austrian Business Cycle Theory

In spite of the FIH's Keynesian origins, the FIH and ABC theory are not necessarily mutually exclusive. Expansionary monetary policy, hypothesized by the Austrians as the cause of the unsustainable expansion which leads to a recession (Mises 1912, 1949, Hayek 1931, 1933, 1935, 1939, 1941), may also contribute to the progressive abandonment of prudent borrowing and lending practices. Perhaps the only difference between ABC theory and the FIH is that Minsky sees the acceptance of greater risk, leverage, and lower returns as a natural and inevitable byproduct of prosperity, which to the Austrians, can only result from an expansionary monetary policy.

According to ABC theory, the lower market interest rate brought about by an expansionary monetary policy systematically biases household consumption-saving decisions in favor of immediate consumption. Malinvestment occurs whenever monetary expansion induces entrepreneurial planners to systematically overinvest in new production plans which are lower-yielding due to the lower interest rate (Horwitz 2000: 49). Under the influence of monetary expansion and the lower interest rate, all the higher yielding projects will still be financed, but now some of the newly created money will be used to finance lower yielding projects. This lowers overall productivity while enabling the economy to grow and unemployment to fall. In terms of the FIH, increases in the money supply create malinvestment by converting hedge finance units into riskier speculative finance units, and speculative finance units into even riskier Ponzi finance units, while simultaneously making financial intermediaries able and willing to lend in larger amounts while charging lower interest rates than before. This makes more leveraged firms—the speculative and Ponzi firms— seem more profitable, and thus better credit risks, and also increases appraisals of these firms' asset values and collateral, especially during a period of apparent prosperity. This apparent prosperity is always perceived as sustainable, whether it is or not.

A lower interest rate rewards consumers less for saving. The lower the interest rate falls below the original, pre-monetary-expansion rate which expressed people's actual time preference, the less consumers save and the more they spend on consumption, aka "overconsumption," an essential element of ABC theory (Mises 1949: 556, 564, Garrison

2001: 68-73). Without increasing the money supply there is no way to increase investment spending without increasing saving; thus there is no way to simultaneously increase both investment and consumption. Put another way, the expansionary monetary policy provides the additional funds required for the simultaneous—though unsustainable—increases in both investment and consumption. Because expansion of the money supply lowers the interest rate, it makes borrowing cheaper at the same time it encourages firms to borrow more, even in the absence of additional saving by consumers. The lower interest rate also biases consumers' consumption-saving decisions toward present consumption; at the same time it biases producers' decisions toward more investment. An unsustainable boom results because both consumption and investment rise simultaneously, as the amount of saving available to finance consumption and investment in any sustainable manner decreases (Carilli & Dempster 2001, Calandro 2004).

Minsky's FIH describes a similar process, where entrepreneurial planners become more optimistic about future business conditions the longer the expansion phase of the business cycle lasts. This over-optimism leads firms to borrow more and overleverage themselves to the point where the economy becomes increasingly fragile, and increasingly dominated by speculative and Ponzi finance units. Firms' risk-adjusted yields fall as lending and borrowing expand further and the unperceived actual risk increases over time. Once unrealistic entrepreneurial plans started during business cycle expansion start proving impossible to complete and keep in mutual coordination with the plans of others, entrepreneurial planners, finally stung by their over-optimism, respond by becoming unrealistically over-pessimistic. This causes a dramatic and sudden decrease in the demand for borrowed investment funds. Minsky's description of debt deflation seems to better capture the onset of recession and financial crisis than the more general description offered by Mises and Hayek. At this point in both ABC theory and the FIH, entrepreneurial planners attempt to reallocate their installed clay capital to next-best uses. This reallocation process is necessary to liquidate the malinvestments which were built up during the unsustainable expansion.

The resulting combination of malinvestment, overconsumption, and forced saving, creating bloated and unsustainable early and late stages of production and starved intermediate stages, eventually becomes obvious to entrepreneurial planners, not as an episode of blessed prosperity, but an era of deranged and unfulfillable expectations (Hülsmann 2001), dominated by Minsky's Ponzi finance units. As entrepreneurs realize their production plans cannot be kept in mutual coordination, and thus all brought successfully to completion, the exaggerated over-optimism of the boom transforms into an equally exaggerated over-pessimism of the bust.

In terms of the FIH, as speculative and Ponzi finance units impose greater risk on the banks and financial intermediaries they borrow from, and indirectly on their depositors,[43] it becomes more and more difficult for entrepreneurial planners to borrow the amounts of credit they need to keep their entrepreneurial plans, which constitute the economy's production structure, in mutual coordination. Eventually the firms' growing risk overwhelms the entrepreneurial planners' ability to continue to coordinate production. The unsustainable production structure finally collapses, lowering output and employment. When the economy reaches the stage of debt deflation and malinvestment

---

43 In addition to involuntarily saddling depositors with this undesired additional risk, most of it is actually borne by the Federal Reserve, the FDIC, and ultimately, the taxpayer.

liquidation, entrepreneurs face the cost of discarding and reallocating old installed, physical clay capital, human capital, and goods-in-process embodied in the old, unsustainable production plans and production structure.

According to the FIH, an unsustainable expansion happens naturally without any expansionary monetary policy. Since Ponzi finance units are forced to sell off assets to service their existing interest payments, once the market is sufficiently dominated by Ponzi finance units, this creates an oversupply of these assets being offered for sale, and the resulting debt deflation causes a financial crisis and a severe shortage of liquidity. It appears this crisis state can be brought about by a deceptively low critical mass of Ponzi and speculative finance units. Stock market prices for U.S. publicly traded stocks provide dramatic support for the FIH, as it can hardly be surprising that stock values fall dramatically at the onset of a recession. It becomes clear that this process is amplified and exacerbated by expansion of the money supply (Mulligan, Lirely, & Coffee 2014).

Davidson's (2008) evaluation of the 2007 financial crisis is that it did not unfold according to the FIH. He sees it as originating in the persistent and chronic dependency of mortgage underwriters on the continuing and unlimited securitization of traditionally illiquid mortgages, and their inability to maintain and keep growing that liquidity. Mortgage lenders traditionally held the mortgages they originated. Later, banks sold individual mortgages or large packages of them to other financial institutions, either to raise immediate cash or shield themselves from the uncertainty associated with future cash flows. Finally, mortgage portfolios were packaged as bonds, so-called mortgage-backed securities, with as many bad-risk loans included to ensure the AAA or Aaa rating which would guarantee the securities could still be sold as purportedly high quality debt. However, the unsuccessful selloff of securitized assets and derivatives which occurred in November 2008 was clearly driven by the sellers' need to raise cash.

Minsky initially framed the FIH in terms of conventional bank lending expanding without sufficient due diligence leading to over-leverage. The fact that exotic new financial instruments have proliferated to facilitate the same process is no real criticism of the FIH—instead it makes Minsky appear nearly clairvoyant. It is also difficult to argue that leading up to the 2007-2009 recession that the financial and housing sectors could have contributed to any sizable speculative bubble in the absence of an expansionary monetary policy, which accommodated ever increasing volumes of mortgage lending on increasingly favorable terms. The emergence of various tradable derivatives and securities which allowed for massive growth in these sectors seems to have both depended on and fueled the progressive over-optimism the FIH describes.

Substantial debate still needs to take place between Austrians and post-Keynesians over whether business cycles are the automatic and inevitable consequence of prosperity, as suggested by Minsky, or arise solely due to an expansionary monetary policy. The policy implications are profound. Consider the implications of inflation for the FIH. A stable macroeconomy is dominated by hedge-financed firms whose sustainable cash flows are sufficient to pay the interest and pay down the principal on the firms' borrowing. In Minsky's view, the longer the economy operates in a stable regime of hedge finance, the greater the likelihood of a natural increase in business optimism, leading eventually to the next stage, that of speculative finance, where firms borrow and take on additional debt in anticipation of future growth. If firms are able to continue for any substantial period as speculative finance units, increasing numbers of these hedge finance units will imitate them in search of the apparently effortless, but unsustainable, profits these firms realize in the short run. This shifts the balance of the economy toward higher risk activities and investments, as entrepreneurial planners forget the value of conservative safe risk management, and are seduced by the irresistible lure of greater leverage, without adequately appreciating the risk that always comes with it.

Finally, many firms begin to further over-leverage themselves through even more borrowing, and start to operate as Ponzi finance units, unable to service either interest or pay down their borrowed principal out of current cash flows. These firms must now sell off assets, or continually seek ever larger rollover loans. The cycle ends in crisis because at some point lenders have to stop lending to Ponzi finance units. When these firms have to sell off their assets to cover their operating cash flow requirements, this results in an oversupply of the assets they try to sell. These assets can be installed clay capital, which is generally less valuable to any alternative users or potential buyers, or financial assets such as loan portfolios or securitized debt. When too many of these assets have to be put up for sale because there are so many Ponzi and speculative firms trying to raise cash, this causes a collapse in their value.

In Minsky's view, each of the three stages leads naturally to the next; however, consider the impact of expansionary monetary policy, which rewards borrowers at the expense of lenders. To the extent that the progression from hedge finance, to speculative finance, to Ponzi finance occurs as a natural process, the process must be made worse by inflationary monetary policy. And if Minsky's FIH would not occur naturally without inflation to drive it, the expansionary monetary policy which drives the ABC would tend to promote such a process.

CHAPTER 10

Keynesian Stabilization Policy: Cause or Cure?

Keynesian stabilization policy is a philosophy and approach to macroeconomic policy which aims at preventing business cycle contractions and maintaining steady economic growth and low unemployment, inspired by John Maynard Keynes's (1883-1946) *General Theory of Employment, Interest, and Money* (1936). Keynesian stabilization policy seeks to alleviate the business cycle through government deficit spending during a recession. The corollary, that the government should run a surplus at all other times, has been largely forgotten and seemed to have fallen largely on deaf ears. Since what has been proposed by Keynesian economists since the 1930s, and what has been actually implemented by the U.S. government differ in minor details, the economic literature has been replete with rhetorical apologetics attempting to clarify what Keynes actually meant, what policies are actually Keynesian, and what the government should actually do to prevent recessions and the business cycle.

Keynes was already the author of *The Economic Consequences of the Peace* (1919), a penetrating and exceptionally well done critique of the Treaty of Versailles, the *Treatise on Probability* (1921), a path-breaking, philosophical, and somewhat eccentric work on statistical theory which emphasized the role of personal subjectivity and belief,[44] and *A Treatise on Money* (1930), a massive, two-volume exposition of what was then orthodox monetary theory. Any one of these famous books would have made Keynes's reputation, but somewhat ironically, today his reputation rests mostly on his magnum opus, the *General Theory*. The *General Theory* was produced after the Hoover and Roosevelt administrations in the U.S. had already embarked on the unprecedented increases in government purchases and public works projects of the New Deal, and Keynes sought to provide a veneer of theoretical justification and respectability for government policies which had already been implemented. Recall that FDR had campaigned extensively against Hoover's deficit financing of unprecedented government spending, but then continued the same Hoover policies once he was in office. The unsound economic policies of the New Deal converted what would have been a routine recession into a decade-long ordeal (Rothbard 1963).

10.1 Stabilizing Aggregate Expenditure

The heyday of Keynesian stabilization policy was the 1960s, when the U.S. government was actually attempting to pursue it more-or-less

---

44 For discussions of Keynes's Treatise on Probability, see van den Hauwe (2011) and Mulligan (2013c).

faithfully, and it appeared to be working. In the 1970s, when the U.S. experienced simultaneous high unemployment, unprecedented government deficits, and high inflation, this experience discredited Keynesian stabilization policy once and for all. It is no longer taken seriously by the economics profession, and some economic theory which was developed subsequently is accurately labeled "post-Keynesian." Although Keynesian stabilization policy has been thoroughly discredited, it still needs to be studied, because it still accurately describes ninety percent or more of the U.S. government's policy responses to the business cycle (Mulligan 2014).

The basic rationale for Keynesian stabilization policy comes from considering that total income (Y) is equal to the sum of personal consumption (C), private investment spending (I), government purchases (G), and net exports (NX). We can write this relationship as the accounting identity

$$Y = C + I + G + NX.$$

Although Keynes recognized that investment (I) was the most volatile part of total expenditure, he was unable to formulate a policy prescription which would be able to work effectively through investment spending. Investment (I) is generally the one component of total income (Y) that falls the most during a recession. Keynes accurately characterized investment spending as depending on "animal spirits" which for example motivate stock market speculation. It might be more precise to observe that investment spending on new and replacement capital equipment and construction depends on forward-looking expectations about the future. Potential investors view investment projects through an unjustified over-optimistic perspective during the later stages of the unsustainable boom which precedes a recession, and through an equally unjustified over-pessimistic perspective during a recession, sometimes extending into the early stages of the recovery phase of the business cycle. Thus, one problem with building a simple model of investment behavior is that the behavior of consumers and entrepreneurial planners switches from one mode to another, over-optimistic to over-pessimistic, over the course of the business cycle. Keynes acknowledged that apart from "animal spirits," investment depends primarily on the interest rate (r), and also on the overall size of the economy, represented by total income, output, and expenditure (Y). This relationship is written as

$$I = I(r, Y),$$

where investment spending would have a negative relationship with the interest rate, because higher interest rates represent a higher cost of borrowing to finance investment spending, and a positive relationship with total income, because generally, the larger the economy, the higher the level of investment spending, if all other things are held equal. However, the relationship between I, Y, and r, is not a strong one, nor is it particularly deterministic, partly because of investors' behavioral switching between over-optimism and over-pessimism. A further source of this difficulty is because artificially low interest rates will eventually give rise to an unsustainable economic boom. This results in increasing not only investment (I), but also income (Y) and consumption (C). However, when demand for investment spending grows, such as it typically would during a boom, investor over-optimism often results in additional loan demand, variously described as additional demand for loanable funds or additional demand for investible resources. This would tend to drive up interest rates—and even if accommodative, expansionary monetary policy keeps interest rates artificially low, interest rates will generally be higher than they would have been otherwise, because late in the unsustainable economic boom, firms continue to borrow to finance investment spending, often regardless of how high interest rates go. This increase in loan demand from overly optimistic business firms that want to expand during the boom raises interest rates.

Low interest rates may have no direct effect on government purchases (G), but generally speaking, the faster Y grows, the faster tax revenues and government purchases generally grow. During the boom, net exports (NX) will probably fall as the increase in revenue is spent partially on imports, unless all the country's trading partners experience the same boom simultaneously and to the same extent, meaning they will also purchase more from us, increasing our exports to more-or-less offset the increase in imports.

Since the cause of the unsustainable boom and therefore the following recession was an artificially low interest rate (r) in the first place, in the face of the recession, it would not make too much sense to prescribe further lowering interest rates (r) to attempt to bring about an increase in investment spending (I). However, this is the basis for the accommodative monetary policy which the U.S. Federal Reserve System and most other central banks normally pursue to combat a recession. That might not be effective, because prior to a recession, the interest rate has been kept artificially low for some years, and a continued lower interest rate would not help coordinate unsustainable complementary entrepreneurial plans which low interest rates initially rendered unsustainable. At best, further lowering interest rates could only prolong the unsustainable boom and delay the onset of the recession, though at the cost of making the recession even more severe and painful.

Instead, what Keynes prescribed was to increase government purchases (G), the one part of expenditure over which the government can exercise absolute control to the last penny, at least in principle, and to finance this expanded government purchases by borrowing rather than raising taxes. When the economy goes into a recession, C, Y, and I all fall, and Keynes's solution was to substitute government purchases for the lowered consumption spending (C) and private investment (I). It was crucial in Keynes's scheme that any increase in government spending not be financed by tax increases, because raising taxes would lower households' disposable income and therefore lower their consumption spending (C). Keynes argued that raising government purchases (G) and financing it by issuing treasury bonds was the only way to maximize the impact of the added spending. If the government keeps its budget balanced by raising taxes, the higher taxes result in reduced disposable income and therefore in reduced consumption spending (C), largely offsetting the benefit of the increase in government spending (G).

Consumer spending (C) can be distinguished from investment spending (I) by distinguishing between consumer goods and producer goods. Consumer goods satisfy peoples' wants in the present or near future, and are purchased by the households whose wants they will be used to satisfy. Producer goods are capital equipment, tools, buildings, and inventories, which are purchased by firms to satisfy consumer wants in the future. In addition, producer goods or investment goods only satisfy future consumer wants potentially, because in the face of an unknown and uncertain future which is always unfolding before us, consumers may not buy the combination of consumer goods which are offered for sale, either at all or at the prices asked by the producers.

Producer goods are intended to be used in a particular way according to the purchaser's entrepreneurial plan to produce goods and services in the future over a period of time which may be precisely defined or may be quite indefinite, for sale to consumers over that time period, or for as long as it continues to be feasible. The entrepreneurial plan producer goods are designed to operate in typically requires numerous other inputs to be combined in a precisely specified way with certain proportions of the services provided by the producer goods as well as numerous other inputs. In other words, the entrepreneurial plan employing producer goods must be coordinated with numerous complementary entrepreneurial plans put in operation by other entrepreneurs. This is what is meant by mutual plan coordination. The aim is to produce and deliver a definite stream of consumer goods for sale, which the producers anticipate they will be able to sell at a certain price which will justify their engaging in the productive activity of the entrepreneurial plan in the first place.

Whenever market conditions change, some entrepreneurial plans are disrupted and must be adjusted or re-coordinated in accordance with the new and changing constellation of market prices which continually signals any changes in relative scarcity among available inputs. In extreme cases of market disruption, some entrepreneurial plans will be abandoned entirely. This is determined in turn by the evolving state of consumer buying behavior and any changes in the productive activities, with their attendant needs for input resources, on the part of other entrepreneurial planners. Routine market disruption occurs whenever entrepreneurial planners experimentally seek to define or explore new market opportunities. The only solution to market disruption is to allow other entrepreneurial planners the freedom to address and respond to this newly introduced discoordination by adapting their production plans already in progress, to substitute away from newly more expensive, newly scarcer inputs toward newly cheaper, less scarce ones—sometimes introducing new alternative inputs.

Because producer goods satisfy our wants in the future, delaying the immediate gratification to accumulate more producer goods at the expense of fewer consumer goods allows the economy to grow faster, allowing the production possibilities set to expand outward more rapidly, enabling greater economic growth to provide more of both producer and consumer goods in the future. This is because unlike consumer goods which satisfy our wants directly, producer goods (that is, investment goods or capital goods) are productive resources, and the more producer goods available in an economy, the more output it is capable of producing. This is why low rates of time preference— that is, a high level of patience and willingness to delay immediate gratification—are associated with faster economic growth. The more a society's preferences are balanced toward producer goods—investment spending—the faster the economy will grow. The more balanced toward consumer goods—consumer spending—the slower the economy will grow, although at least the impatient consumers will enjoy greater satisfaction in the near term. If an economy is too biased in favor of consumer goods and against producer goods, investment spending may be too low to replace productive capital equipment as fast as it wears out. Economies that find themselves in this situation shrink as their capital equipment depreciates or wears out faster than it is replaced, and the amount of productive capital equipment falls over time.

10.2 Fiscal Policy

Keynesian stabilization policy focuses on using public expenditure (G) to replace the downturns in private expenditure which occur during recessions. It is important that increases in government purchases (G) be purchases of real goods and services which must be produced and therefore contribute to real output (Y). For example, this would not include government transfer payments, which are not provided to pay for real output. Transfer payments to households typically enable the households receiving them to increase their consumption expenditure, and thus contribute to increasing consumption (C) which is already captured in the accounting identity. Transfer payments to businesses typically enable the businesses to increase their investment expenditure on producer goods or capital equipment, increasing investment (I) which is also already captured in the accounting identity. Government purchases are generally purchases of consumer or producer goods, but rather than counting them in (C) or (I), these are accounted for separately as part (G), which includes purchases of goods and services by all levels of government, federal, state, and local.

However, one obvious shortcoming of Keynesian stabilization policy is that government purchases are not subject to the same market tests of usefulness as private expenditure. We do not buy consumer goods which do not satisfy our wants as well as the available alternatives—we always seek the best outcome in terms of satisfying our wants, given the constraints of our budget or income. Entrepreneurial planners do not buy producer or investment goods for which they do not anticipate the highest return possible. In any case, entrepreneurs will never seek to borrow to finance an investment project for which they do not expect at least as high a return as would be necessary to enable them to pay back the interest and principal on any borrowed funds and thus justify the loan. Government purchases do not have to meet this market test.

Even beyond these considerations, government purchases can be relatively more or less productive than otherwise. A bridge or interstate highway, which once built, experiences high use and heavy traffic, is clearly satisfying consumer wants. It would be exceedingly difficult and perhaps a bit perverse to suggest that such a highly traveled, heavily used government road would not or should not have been provided by a private turnpike or autostrade company if it had not been provided by the government. Because non-toll roads are provided free to users, though their construction and maintenance may be financed out of general, use, and fuel taxes, they generally suffer from overuse and traffic congestion, because users do not pay directly for all the expenses of their use. This could be alleviated in principle by tolling and congestion pricing. Overuse of a resource suggests that more should be provided, but for free government roads, overuse is generally a given, because they are normally underpriced at zero to the actual users. If they were priced appropriately, users would face incentives to economize on them and use less of the services they provide. This contrasts sharply with underutilized roads-to-nowhere, which the government also finances, and which also provide part of the building programme of Keynesian stabilization policy. Part of the New Deal's government expenditures included Post Offices and other unproductive assets. Timing of government purchases is equally critical.

Because of the timing of the public works expenditure responding to a particular recession, a road may be built before market conditions indicate a clear need for it. In this case, the government is immune from the market discipline a private firm would face. Market profit and loss incentives would discipline the private firm not to build the road before paying customers need to use it in sufficient numbers to generate enough revenue to service the debt taken on in order to build it.[45] Given the logic of Keynesian stabilization policy, the government's motivation is ostensibly merely to replace private expenditure by increasing its own expenditure, generally on assets which the private sector would never have purchased in the first place, because they do not generally satisfy private wants.

Any significant additions to government borrowing contribute to raising the interest rate (r) above what it would be otherwise. This increase in r would be beneficial during a recession, because it would contribute to restoring the economy and financial sector to normalcy. However, during a recession governments frequently offset this increase in the interest rate through an accommodative and expansionary monetary policy—expanding the money supply to keep the interest rate artificially low. The low interest rate helps finance additional consumption and investment spending, as well as reducing the interest burden to the taxpayer on government borrowing. This can be seen in the abnormally low interest rates which the Federal Reserve System has maintained since the start of the 2007-2009 recession and well into the recovery phase of the business cycle. The artificially low interest rate also makes the next recession inevitable.

---

45 The Iridium satellite network provides an example of market incentives penalizing a private firm for bad timing. When initially introduced as a Motorola subsidiary in 1997, the first generation Iridium network went bankrupt because it could not capture sufficient market share given its high expenses and inappropriately high pricing strategy. The second generation IridiumNEXT network is now profitable, with both lower expenses benefiting from cost saving technological advances which occurred over the intervening years, and a lower pricing strategy which enables the firm to better compete with alternative services. See Chapter 5, section 5.9 for a more detailed discussion.

Socialism v. Market Process

Part Four discusses the shortcomings of socialism and central economic planning from the perspective of market process perspective. Socialists argue that economic activity, including the production and distribution of goods, needs to be scientifically planned. Socialist planning is supposed to offer benefits in terms of a more equitable distribution of wealth, and to ensure that more wealth will be generated by ensuring that production will necessarily be planned in a more efficient, less wasteful manner. The promise of socialism was to rid the free enterprise economy of inefficiencies by eliminating wasteful competition, duplication of effort, unnecessary product differentiation, etc. under the direction of a benign and beneficent central planner or other democratically chosen authority. This would substitute the enlightened guidance of a public spirited, class conscious central economic planner for the wastefully profit-motivated entrepreneurial planning of competitive capitalism. However, the central economic planner will always be remote from the preferences and aspirations of the actual consumers who provide entrepreneurial planners the market discipline of profit and loss, and central planners are equally remote from this market discipline which contributes to strengthening the efficiency of the market economy. Market competition, which provides winners and losers, is just a different side of the market coordination provided by free enterprise, which only provides winners. It is entirely mistaken to consider free competition as anything but a mutually beneficial process which delivers substantial and ever increasing benefits to all participants. Information theory also contributes to the critique of socialism, because socialism and central economic planning imposes a much higher information burden on the central planner than has to, or can be borne by any individual entrepreneurial planner in a market economy.

Chapter 11, Planning & Competition, contrasts the central economic planning of socialism with the decentralized and competing, but mutually coordinated entrepreneurial plans which direct production in a market economy. Entrepreneurial planners introduce innovations which disrupt the existing mutual coordination among the plans of others in the short run, but in the long run improve mutual plan coordination, as consumers and competing producers eventually learn to adapt to and exploit innovations which were originally disruptive to better satisfy their own wants, improve production at lowered costs, and earn higher profits.

Chapter 12, Preferences v. Central Planning, develops a further shortcoming of socialism, which is its disregard for consumer sovereignty. Central planning ignores consumer preferences and is, at best, far less responsive to changes in preferences. This is a major shortcoming since consumer preferences change all the time. Central planning assumes some static and idealized preferences as a given, and does not seek to address either the actual preferences of real consumers, or the way these evolve from moment to moment.

Chapter 13, Market Process & Information Theory, introduces some insights from information theory and applies them to problems of central economic planning. Chapter 14, Mathematics of Comparative Statics, serves to illustrate how limited possible extensions to the prevailing mainstream formalism can be. It is difficult to suggest that they can help approximate the tentatively welfare maximizing outcomes of market process, much less that they can infallibly arrive at final results which are global welfare maxima.

CHAPTER 11

Planning & Competition

One of the key features of a market economy is that entrepreneurial planning is decentralized. Producers implement and maintain entrepreneurial plans which guide their activities, but it is equally important to realize that entrepreneurial planners include all the buyers and sellers in a market economy. In one sense entrepreneurial plans are all separate and independent, but in a deeper sense they are interdependent, since each one depends on its success for the planner's ability to coordinate their plans with the plans of others. This network of interdependent entrepreneurial plans employs the local knowledge of everyone who participates in economic activity as either a buyer or seller. The mutual coordination of entrepreneurial plans is an essential feature of a market economy (Kirzner 1996: 39-41), and this level of mutual coordination and plan sophistication tends to increase over time, making possible an ever-increasing level of want satisfaction and human welfare.

Even when one entrepreneur introduces a disruptive innovation,

293

temporarily lowering the mutual coordination among some entrepreneurial plans in the short run, in the longer run, the entrepreneurs who are affected negatively by a disruptive innovation still have the opportunity to adjust their plans to take advantage of the disruptive innovation. In the long run, this brings about a higher level of mutual plan coordination and allows for a higher level of the satisfaction of wants for the individuals in society (Lewin 1997). In contrast, the central economic planning called for by socialism does not allow for the employment of this local knowledge, which central planners ignore. It does not allow for consumer choice, and ignores precisely the information used by entrepreneurial planners to coordinate their plans with one another and with consumers. Central economic planning also ignores consumer preferences, which are diverse and constantly changing, and does not subject producers to the profit-and-loss discipline of the market. Entrepreneurs in a market economy take risks and some fail all the time, at their own expense. The reward of profit, and the penalty of economic loss, is not permitted under central planning. Far from being an advantage of socialism, the removal of the profit-and-loss discipline of competitive markets, fatally cripples socialism and central planning, preventing it from benefiting consumers and workers.

11.1 Central Economic Planning

Gerald P. O'Driscoll (1977) and Kirzner (1984a, 1984b, 1997) have noted the enduring appeal of viewing economy-wide allocative efficiency as a static state of affairs. Ignoring the continuous dynamic of ever-changing market conditions is both an analytical convenience and a gross oversimplification. This superficial view enables the economy to be mistakenly understood as something amenable to being managed by a central planner, as opposed to something which arises from real world market processes. The static target of allocative efficiency is not a real thing, but only a theoretic ideal which can seemingly be achieved by socialism's less robust theory. The moving target which exists and evolves over time in the real world cannot be reached so easily. Nevertheless, Kirzner concludes "our ability to treat society as an entity for which coordination efficiency considerations are relevant, depends on the possibility of economic calculation in that society (Kirzner 1984b: 159)." No one individual has access to, or command of, the staggering amount of information which would be required to direct the economy to reach any of the ambitious and over-reaching goals of socialist central economic planning, such as to maximize social welfare (Leijonhufvud 1981: 279).

In order to implement a central economic plan, one especially vital component of the necessary information set would be the fully articulated and explicit set of personal preferences of each individual in society. If that does not seem too prohibitive an information burden for a central plan, consider that each individual's preference set is always subjective and unique to that individual. Consider further that these myriad, highly numerous preference sets evolve from second to second for each individual. And that they are largely unarticulated and inarticulable. Even survey data from an exhaustive and excruciatingly detailed questionnaire would be uninformative. Although we can observe objectively what choices an individual actually makes in the real world, we cannot observe anything more subtle than the binary choices of a particular individual's preferring good A over good B at specific points in time. What we can observe is only past behavior, which cannot provide information about the future, which has not yet come to pass. We cannot reliably extrapolate from these past observations, or assume that the individual's revealed preferences will remain unchanged, or that they have evolved or will continue to evolve over time in any predictable pattern.

The Austrian school had not made market process too explicit until the late 1930s—and the fact that market process was left largely implicit in Austrian economics writings as in more mainstream texts tended to handicap the Austrians in responding to socialist arguments for central economic planning. It was argued that economic activity needed to be organized according to scientific principles, both to insure efficiency in production and resource allocation, and to fulfill the goals of government policy. Among the most prominent arguments in favor of central economic planning included those of Abba Lerner (1903-1982) (Lerner 1934, 1936, 1937, 1938) and Oskar Lange (1904-1965) (Lange 1935, 1936, 1937, 1938). The outcome of the socialist calculation debate[46] might have been far more decisive if the Austrians had focused earlier on market process and information theory—the idea that prices should be understood as conduits which summarize and communicate sparse and efficient specialized information about relative scarcities and consumer preferences. This information can only be generated in a market economy where consumers are free to choose among alternatives, and cannot otherwise exist or be expressed. It is the transmission of this information through prices which allows the market to generate a spontaneous order which coordinates resource

---

46 Ludwig von Mises had argued that market prices were necessary for efficient resource allocation (Mises 1922). This led to the socialist calculation debate, an extended academic discussion and debate, which included Lerner, Lange, and numerous other scholars and intellectuals on both sides, through books and articles attempting to explain how resources could theoretically be allocated and production organized in a socialist society (Vaughn 1980, 1994, Lavoie 1985).

allocation and planned activities of production and distribution. Prices are what allow numerous and competing entrepreneurial planners to bring about the mutual coordination of their plans, and to restore mutual coordination in the face of disruptive innovations by other entrepreneurial planners (Kirzner 1996: 39-41).

Defining the problems and limitations of human knowledge in general, and specifically with regard to the knowledge contained in and communicated by market prices, and recognizing how markets work to overcome these various knowledge problems and limitations contributed to the Austrian school's distinctive, definitive, and devastating criticism of socialism. If one assumes the static-equilibrium model of perfect competition, it might appear, as it did to many at the time, at least superficially attractive to remove unnecessary and wasteful competition to improve efficiency. However, the standard static equilibrium model is not sufficiently realistic that it can support any such sweeping proposal to remake society and the economy. Market participants do not and cannot know the market general equilibrium in advance, with its purported knowledge of all input and output quantities, allocations, and prices. They cannot know this in advance because it only arises after the fact through market process, and only in the fullness of time as individuals engage in voluntary exchange which gradually reconciles the offer prices of potential buyers with the asking prices of potential sellers. Before the fact, the ultimate market solution is equally unknowable to a central planning authority (Popper 1962 I: 108-113).

11.2 Entrepreneurial Planning in Market Process

Entrepreneurial planners act in the face of risk and uncertainty about the future (Langlois 1994). They are not always successful, but the degree of their success in earning profits for themselves, as well as in consistently providing increasingly affordable goods and services to consumers of increasing quality and cheapness, has been fairly remarkable. It was always claimed and assumed that the omniscient and omnipotent central economic planners of socialism would create a radiant future for us which could be implemented without any deviation from the central plan. However it does not matter what resources the central planner has control over or how much data they collect and use for the basis of their plans. Market data can only be data of what has transpired in the past—it is inherently historical data which records past transactions which have already taken place. This historical data has no utility for or authority in describing or delimiting the future, which has yet to take place and only unfolds before us in the fullness of time. Market process provides outcomes which may approximate the efficiency and welfare requirements of a theoretical general equilibrium, but only by giving us a means to act on and exploit whatever decentralized and inarticulable information we can access and act on as individuals.

In a market economy we are permitted to act on our own preferences. In a socialist economy we are only offered the constrained and delimited choices selected for us in advance by the omniscient and purportedly public spirited central planner. Efficiency and welfare maximization will always be beyond the grasp of the central planning authority of a socialist command economy which takes the welfare-maximizing and information-generating decisions out of the hands of individual actors, where they always belong in reality. Only individuals can perform their own implicit economic calculations, and the entrepreneurial planning needed to direct their own enterprises. Entrepreneurial planning in a market economy is always based on the planners' individual preferences, expectations, and subjective information, and only succeeds to the extent that the planners' individual preferences, expectations, and subjective information are successfully coordinated with that of others, whether consumers or other producers.

Individuals' subjective information and beliefs can be signaled publicly through their choices like experimenting with different ask or offer prices, but cannot be explicitly articulated or otherwise shared outside the context of voluntary market transactions. Because the only way agent preferences are fulfilled and coordinated is through these myriad individual choices in a market economy, which are always voluntary and freely chosen, the information needed to arrive at the resource allocation decision or solution cannot be developed, arrived at, or simulated in any other way. Socialist planning imposes "choice" with absolute disregard for the actual preferences and local knowledge of the producers and consumers in their society—central planners seek to deliver, not their closest approximation or best guess about what consumers actually want, but their closest approximation to what they think agents should want. Implicitly, they are hoping that the diverse preferences of many individuals will "average out," but planners have made no attempt to measure the underlying data which goes into the average, because it is unobservable. Furthermore, central planners are probably subject to a general bias toward whatever choices they would identify as being more virtuous and public spirited, in preference over the actual choices and preferences of actual consumers. The closest thing we do in a market economy to observing consumer preferences is to observe consumer choice when a transaction occurs, but for this to happen, consumers must be offered a choice in the first place.

11.3 Socialist Planning v. Market Process

In sharp contrast to the entrepreneurs in a market economy, who bear the cost of any mistakes they make in experimental innovation, central planners do not face any such profit-and-loss discipline. Instead, it is consumers who bear the burden of the central planner's errors of judgement in a socialist planned economy. If the central planner makes a decision which oversupplies a relatively undesired output, consumers have to live with it. More often, however, the consumer lives without, as chronic shortages are widespread under central planning. Curiously, in spite of constant shortages of most goods, an equally prominent feature of central planning is the constant oversupply of certain other, relatively undesired goods, which meet no one's need especially well, and which arrive in overstocks, but then linger on the shelves. This demonstrates the disconnect between consumer preferences and the choices imposed by central planning. When these undesired products are purchased, it is largely because no other products are available. It is difficult to reconcile this reality with the promise of more efficient, scientifically managed central planning.

In a free market, entrepreneurs compete to observe price divergences where identical goods are offered for sale at two different prices, and through arbitrage, correct the discrepancies—this might be considered market process's routine housekeeping. Price divergences result whenever there is an initial failure to fully coordinate entrepreneurial plans, but entrepreneurial awareness is the only cure for these diverging prices, and entrepreneurial awareness is rewarded, at least temporarily, with arbitrage profits. Without competition, entrepreneurs cannot fulfill their essential role of removing market efficiencies and improving the coordination among the plans of numerous other market participants. There would be no incentive to improve mutual plan coordination or contribute to higher levels of social cooperation because there would be no reward for doing so.

In contrast, in an idealized centrally planned economy there can never be any divergence in the prices of a particular commodity. Prices are the same everywhere, because they are set by the central planner. Far from signaling market efficiency, the non-market prices chosen by the central planner do not contain or transmit any information regarding consumer preferences or relative scarcities of either products or resources. Prices under socialism merely reflect an arbitrary decision by the central planner relying on incomplete information. Choices made based on these centrally planned prices cannot contribute to improving efficiency in the same way as the prices which result from free consumer choice in a market economy. Under central planning, prices are meaningless. In general, because Marxist theory contributed nothing more sophisticated than the labor theory of value to inform price setting under socialist planning (Popper 1962 II: 170-179), a socialist economy normally copies prices from the nearest available market economy the central planners can observe. Socialist economies have to do without the value offered by price setting in free markets in terms of applying local knowledge.

In a market economy the frequently maligned profit motive performs the indispensable function of moving the market toward a higher state of coordination and productivity, enhancing wealth and increasing the value of the resources employed in the now-better coordinated entrepreneurial plans—including the value of labor. The profit motive also continues to act in the face of changing market conditions, which invariably introduce new coordination failures among pre-established production plans which have already been put into operation. The market may never arrive at the optimal outcome of the neoclassical model, and if this optimal outcome is ever reached, it may not persist long, but the market tendency is always to move closer to this ideal condition. Central planning, in contrast, cannot make this claim.

The socialist economy does not permit profit, which Marxists consider a morally reprehensible temptation of the corrupt capitalist society. Profit is the income earned by the providers of entrepreneurial planning. Entrepreneurs earn profits by innovating to improve the organization of productive activities in ever increasing complexity, efficacy, and efficiency. Profit is unnecessary if all planning is centralized under a government bureau which cranks out arbitrary five-year plans to direct the activities of the socialist economy's industrial plants. It does not take too much insight to perceive what a static state of affairs this describes. The actual economy in the Soviet Union was actually far more dynamic with an especially thriving and innovative aerospace industry.[47]

Market process relies on entrepreneurial alertness and competition to uncover previously unrealized opportunities and improve the

---

47 The Soviet aerospace industry was organized in design bureaus named for their chief designers, such as Tupolev, Ilyushin, Mikoyan-Gurevich (MiG), Antonov, etc. The industry produced military aircraft for the Soviet Armed Forces, civil aircraft for Aeroflot, and civil and military aircraft for export, primarily to other Communist bloc countries, but sometimes competing with free market suppliers. Although the government was virtually the sole customer for military aircraft, this situation was little different than for Western firms. After the fall of Communism, several of the design bureaus became publicly traded joint stock corporations.

allocation and use of productive resources. This competition allows entrepreneurs to make possible higher levels of social cooperation, better use of available resources, and greater mutual coordination among entrepreneurial plans. Only entrepreneurial awareness can make resources found in nature productive, by understanding how they can be used to create a good or service which can potentially satisfy the wants of consumers. Competition for profits rewards anyone who is able to improve on the allocation of input resources or of the combination of produced output, though because successful competitors who earn extraordinary profits will be imitated, that imitation and the resulting entrance of new competitors subsequently reduces continued profit opportunities created by any particular innovation. This drives entrepreneurs to innovate further, rather than rest on the laurels of any one successful innovation.

Entrepreneurs need not be capitalists in that they need not own any capital at all—they can also profit from buying undervalued goods and resources and selling them to others or using them where they can be more productive and valued more highly. They can profit from this arbitrage precisely because it guarantees goods will be utilized with higher efficiency, and where they can yield greater revenue to the seller and generate higher benefits for the buyer. Central planning would mistakenly prohibit this kind of arbitrage as wasteful, inefficient, and perhaps, immoral—because it would be contrary to, and therefore prohibited by, the central plan.

CHAPTER 12

Preferences v. Central Planning

Kirzner and Hayek observed that central planning authorities lack any first-hand knowledge at the level of individual consumers and producers. Even in a market economy, this knowledge is implicit and inarticulable; nevertheless we constantly act on individual knowledge which remains unspoken, and which is often not consciously realized. This can be seen both in our choices of the goods and services we buy as well as those we choose not to buy. At best, central planners have to rely on crude aggregates or summaries, which purport to average hypothesized individual measurements and proxy for subjective individual appraisals that can never be really be quantified or made explicit. The central planner does not face the same optimization problem as that faced by individual consumers or entrepreneurial planners,[48] but substitutes a simpler,

---

48 See Chapter 15, Some Mathematics of Conventional Modeling of Firm and Consumer Behavior, for a discussion of the optimization problems faced by firms and consumers. One of the shortcomings and limitations of the optimization approach to economic modeling is that it effectively ignores the reality of entrepreneurial innovation by assuming it has all been accomplished in advance.

macro-optimization problem—which, though it has the advantage that it is much simpler and can actually be solved analytically, it can never have any economic meaning.

From the neoclassical perspective of constrained optimization, the centrally planned outcome must be miss-specified for at least some consumers—if not for all. It would actually be an exceedingly rare and exceptional occurrence for a centrally planned optimization problem to be correctly specified for *any one individual* out of the many that it presumes to benefit. At best, central planners can only force the substitution of their misspecified aggregate optimization problem for the myriad actual optimizing choices of individual agents, whose knowledge is in constant flux, both expanding and becoming dated, who face direct financial and welfare incentives to economize effectively, and who optimize in terms of unique, subjective, and inarticulable preferences (Boettke 1998, 2000). Perhaps the most important difference between central planning and market process is that individuals exercise free choice in market exchange, and under central planning, choice is limited, if not eliminated entirely. The productive side of the economy is subject to rigid coercion under central planning. Consumers are not coerced so nakedly, but delimiting their available choices and subverting consumer sovereignty has the same effect.

12.1 Central Planning v. Entrepreneurial Planning

The social allocation of resources arrived at through market process, far from being amenable to improvement or further optimization through coercion and the imposition from above of purportedly scientific central planning, depends crucially for its validity on free choice at the individual level, where actual choice occurs and individual preferences reside (Hayek 1952: 169-178). Government intervention, including central planning, can only impair the allocative efficiency of the market. Although one promise of socialist planning is improved efficiency, to the extent improved engineering efficiency is achieved, it will not be in the service of producing those goods and services most urgently desired by consumers. The only way to approximate the combination of outputs which will generate the highest level of welfare is to allow markets to operate freely. Consumer preferences drive and reward entrepreneurial innovation and arbitrage, by allowing prices to change in accordance with consumer choices in the first instance, and letting the same preferences determine the prices of required input commodities at one remove. Market process results in resources being allocated in accordance with and producing that combination of goods and services which are most desired by consumers (Kirzner 1963: 44-46). At the same time, allocation can always be improved through successful entrepreneurial experimentation, but this is only permitted in a free market where the entrepreneur assumes all the risks of whatever innovations they decide to pursue. Recall that a consumer is behaving entrepreneurially whenever they decide—for or against—to try a new alternative product. It may satisfy their wants better than their old, familiar choice, or not, but they cannot find out which if they do not try it.

Entrepreneurial experimentation is only rewarded to the extent it is ratified by free choice at the level of individual consumers. Central planning avoids this familiar profit-and-loss discipline, and this is never to the consumer's advantage. Entrepreneurs face the market discipline of profit-and-loss, and they pay the price when their speculative experiments fail (Ikeda 1994). The economy progresses, as uncoordinated entrepreneurial failures are swamped by the more numerous successful experiments which the market rewards, and which predominate over time. Kirzner (1997) notes that individual level planning is essential in a market economy and goes on all around us, and that individual plans are always speculative, forward-looking, and seek to overcome the uncertainty of an unknown future which is yet to unfold before us. This is what makes the plans of individual producers and consumers entrepreneurial, and explains why they require constant revision in the face of changing conditions and the acquisition of new information. This continual plan revision and the accompanying need to remain alert to changing market conditions as they emerge might be characterized as routine "plan maintenance."

Individuals are free to make the critical choices of what plans to adopt or attempt, what information to seek or be alert to, and when and in what areas to revise their plans—as individuals, we bear the cost and responsibility of implementing our own plans, and benefit if our plans succeed as anticipated. An essential feature of entrepreneurial plans in a market economy is that they are constantly in flux as they are being adjusted to respond to and generate new information, including the information we uncover regarding the plans of others.

12.2 Socialism & its Critics

The socialist calculation debate contributed to the refinement of market process theory and enhanced our understanding of the role of entrepreneurship in maintaining competitive markets. How markets use and share information is as crucial to understanding market process as it is to appreciating the futility of directing similar activities on a command basis—the purported basis for supposedly scientific economic planning, which it was claimed would avoid the wastefulness of profit and competition. In fact, socialist-planned economies ignore the market information about consumer wants which should inform the choices of entrepreneurial planners in a market economy. Entrepreneurial planners compete with one another to best fulfil consumer wants, improve social cooperation, and improve mutual plan coordination. The most innovative entrepreneurs attempt to address latent wants so far left unaddressed by the market economy. In contrast, a central economic plan is devoid of information, almost a fantasy version or parody of a real economy. The fulfillment of consumer wants is not the end goal of a centrally planned economy. Central planners attempt to mimic or simulate superficial characteristics of a thriving market economy. Production goals are issued for agriculture and heavy industry, but these are just arbitrary numbers. Without the meaningful prices generated by market process, the allocation of resources or productive activity are not informed by and can have no relationship with consumer wants.

Don Lavoie's (1951-2001) doctoral dissertation critiqued the socialist program to implement central economic planning. Socialism, it was argued, would consequently improve allocative efficiency, eliminate wasteful competition, abolish exploitative profits, increase aggregate welfare, etc. Lavoie noted that the Marxian socialist application of these concepts was utterly divorced from actual consumer preferences or from consumer autonomy and choice (Lavoie 1985). Even if central planning could deliver anything which was efficiently produced in an engineering sense, the choice of what to produce could not be allocatively efficient in the absence of market prices and the profit motive to direct and reward production. Furthermore, without accurate market prices—which can only arise from and through market process—the choice of input combinations cannot be allocatively efficient either. Producers have to economize on the use of scarce resources to recognize consumer choice over which outputs are most desired, earning higher profits the better they succeed. Without economizing on more expensive resources and substituting cheaper ones, central planning cannot arrive at an efficient result.

James M. Buchanan (1919-2013) presented a critique of central planning based on its inability to offer some mechanism, hopefully more humane than brute force, to motivate individuals to seek preferences other than their own; namely, those of the central planning authority (Buchanan 1969). Buchanan's observation was that if central planning were to succeed, it would need to be able to assume control over not only the processes of allocation, production, and distribution, but also the actual preferences of consumers. If consumers did not want the output central planning delivered, what would central planning have accomplished in terms of improving social welfare? Buchanan argued that central planning of resource allocation, output production, and distribution would constitute only half the battle for a centrally planned economy. Socialist planners would either have to resort to brute coercion, or employ some kind of aggressive mass marketing propaganda or advertising to promote wider acceptance of the consumer preferences they assumed as the basis for their planning.

This countered a common socialist trope that advertising in capitalist economies is wasteful and manipulative, and serves no productive purpose. Consumers in a socialist society would need to be informed at a minimum of these preferences assumed for them by the central planning authority, and perhaps they could even be cajoled into changing their actual preferences to conform to those underlying the central plan. The nature of mass marketing in a socialist society would be focused more on propagandizing for class consciousness and obedience to the government's central planning authority. This contrasts with mass marketing in a capitalist society, which attempts to persuade consumers that the product will offer them some benefit (Geroski & Mazzucato 2003).[49]

In Buchanan's view, central planning could never be considered successful unless it could successfully align actual consumer preferences with those incorporated into the plan as underlying assumptions. Similarly, in a market economy, entrepreneurial planners do not succeed except to the extent the consumer wants they seek to fulfill are actually held by at least some consumers. Lavoie (1985) also argued that Mises' information argument against central planning was more fundamental, and thus trumped Buchanan's argument that for central planning to work, consumers would have to be persuaded to adopt the preferences and motivations that the central planners had originally assumed for them.

Buchanan also presented a closely related argument that because interpersonal welfare comparisons are both impossible and meaningless, there can be no meaningful social welfare function for central planners to maximize, and thus no formal optimum for a central economic planner to target. Welfare economics was built on the implicit assumption that the utility, satisfaction, or welfare of each individual in society is additive. Léon Walras (1834-1910) originally conceived of these utility concepts as having cardinal properties, like distance which can be measured with a yardstick. It ultimately turned out that these qualities were only ordinal rather than cardinal. In other words, a person's preferences can be expressed and observed to show that

---

49 See Kirzner (2018: 232-253) for a discussion on how advertising is essential for market process.

they value A over B and B over C, and that therefore they must also value A in preference to C, etc., but it cannot be meaningful to assert that an individual, say, values A twice as much as B. An early and now-abandoned argument in favor of the redistribution of wealth started with the general observation that, for each individual, diminishing marginal utility, the notion that increasing one's consumption of A by x percent improves one's well-being by some amount less than x percent, applies generally to all consumption goods. Therefore it also applies to the wealth or income which funds all consumption spending. The argument was made that if everyone's utility functions were the same, or the analysis adopted a generic utility function featuring diminishing marginal returns to wealth, taking wealth or income away from the rich would only reduce their utility a relatively small amount, and redistributing that amount to the poor would increase their utility by a comparatively larger amount. Thus, wealth and income redistribution were mistakenly presented as welfare improving and efficiency enhancing public policies. This argument fails because the ordinal utility of one individual cannot be compared with anyone else's.

It may seem fair or just to take from the rich and give to the poor, but there is no scientific basis to claim that the person who loses wealth or income through redistribution is having their welfare reduced by a smaller "amount" of welfare—something which can only be measured ordinally—than the "amount" of welfare gained by the poor person who receives the redistributed wealth or income. This view that wealth redistribution could be welfare enhancing was held by many economists (Cannan 1888, 1932, Harrod 1938), but was definitively debunked by Lionel Robbins (1898-1984) (1932) and Hayek (1978a), and has been shown to violate the Arrow (1950) impossibility theorem (Mulligan 2009).

Hayek argued that the single market price, arrived at through the cooperation and interaction of everyone who participates in market exchange—or voluntarily refrains from participating—is the freely and spontaneously attained goal of central planning—the "correct" price. This is equally true for the whole constellation of market prices, and for the resulting marketwide allocation of resources. The real benefit of market exchange is that it is always voluntary. Thus, whenever a consumer buys a product, the voluntary nature of the exchange suffices to demonstrate that the consumer's expected benefit from consuming or possessing the product exceeds the value to the consumer of the money price they voluntarily give up, or any other product the consumer might have spent those funds on, but voluntarily has chosen not to. Similarly, the voluntary sale by the producer-seller also suffices to demonstrate that the seller values the money they receive for the product greater than the product itself.

Since both parties to a voluntary exchange always benefit, the market economy allows these benefits to accrue with every exchange. Market exchange is not a zero sum game, and competition and the possibility of entrepreneurial innovation contribute to each subsequent exchange providing even greater benefits over time, as new and better products are introduced and offered for exchange on the market, at lower prices, as time passes and more entrepreneurial innovation is attempted and succeeds.

CHAPTER 13

Market Process &
Information Theory

One of Hayek's greatest contributions to the socialist calculation debate was his work on the knowledge limitations facing central planners. Central planners set prices as arbitrary assertions of relative value uninformed by market process. Unlike prices in a market economy, prices under socialism are not tentative experimental forays seeking to tease out further information about the beliefs and preferences of other market participants. Socialist planners intend the prices they set to be definitive and final statements regarding this now-fulfilled aspect of the plan. Not only does central planning need to make use of a greater volume of information than any one individual can possess, but the nature of that information is fundamentally different from what is generated through market process. The information of market process is decentralized and spread throughout the economy, residing in each individual who participates in exchange. The most important characteristic of market process's information set is that it is dispersed, but by being dispersed over every individual, the amount of information is much greater than can be processed by a socialist central planner.

13.1 How Market Process Increases & Spreads Information

Market exchange both spreads dispersed knowledge more widely (Boettke 2012: 222) and generates new knowledge of market conditions which did not exist before a voluntary and mutually beneficial exchange takes place. In the Austrian view, successful entrepreneurship depends on a property called epistemic heterogeneity (Tarko 2013), in much the same way that market exchange depends on the division of labor. Epistemic heterogeneity refers to a diversity of perceptions about the underlying reality. This can come from different people having reached different stages of the same course of perceptual development, from people's experimental development of different tentative, internal theories of the underlying reality, or from each person's unique and subjectively different course of experience. Even though the underlying reality is the same for everyone, each of us only experiences a unique fraction of that reality, and though these experiences may overlap, our interpretation is subjective and generally will always differ in certain respects. Because perception results from unique trajectories of individual experience, the perceptions of different individuals differ, not only because each individual experiences different unique, concrete subjects of perception. We can describe perceptual differences regarding the same underlying reality as a matter of differing perspectives. Furthermore, each individual's perceptual apparatus is unique because it derives from and is conditioned by a unique experience and memory, though perhaps many of these differences are generally unremarkable. Each individual's unique historical trajectory through a common underlying reality delivers or generates fundamentally different experiences, even after broad commonality of experience and social norming impose some degree of convergence.

Everyone has unique preferences and knowledge, but mass-media advertising helps cluster and normalize preferences to some extent (Geroski & Mazzucato 2003). Is this due to the ability of predatory advertising techniques to manipulate consumer behavior in a predictable and deterministic manner, or does it result from mass-media's ability to reach broad swathes of consumers who exhibit consistent, relatively stable patterns of mass media consumption, thus identifying and taking advantage of the latent clustering of consumer preferences? It would not have been as easy to reach the same broad target demographics before the emergence of mass media. Search engine optimization (SEO) attempts to make use of browser history or other observed consumer behavior to more precisely target advertising at desired demographics.

Entrepreneurs perceive a subjective, Bayesian prior information set,[50] from which they derive their subjective business opportunity set. Only that part of the whole information set which an individual entrepreneur can make use of at any point in time can be eligible to be identified for attention and further exploration. The entrepreneur may also be able to identify gaps in their relevant knowledge, about which

---

50 A Bayesian prior is an individual's subjective belief of the probability of an event prior to observing any evidence which would enable the formation of a more informed estimate of the probability. As more evidence is collected and more experience obtained, the Bayesian prior is updated, presumably becoming more accurate and informative over time.

it might be helpful for them to learn more, given the entrepreneurial plans they have in mind for further development and implementation. This is how an entrepreneur will guide their alertness, and direct the collection and discovery of additional knowledge to expand their subjective business opportunity set, or better understand the specific hard limits beyond which their business opportunities cannot presently be expanded in particular directions. This is also how alert entrepreneurs identify potentially more fruitful areas for attention and further exploration.

13.2 The Business Opportunity Set

The business opportunity set for each entrepreneurial planner is a unique, subjective, and *idiosyncratic* view of a social reality which captures their expectations about objective physical conditions, and subjective perceptions of the probable behavior and preferences of others, and an assessment of the most probable future trajectories of those factors. The subjective state of knowledge on which entrepreneurs rely describes the relation of the individual's state of knowledge to the objective physical environment and the subjectively perceived social environment. All probabilities are conditional, and none are ontologically final or definite (Phillips 1970). Quantitatively, risk is unambiguously greater than the uncertainty of a particular event x, but the two quantities converge as the information set expands approaching full information. However, the two quantities may diverge initially at low information levels until we better discover how limited our information really is. Risk is a probability assessment of the likelihood of a specific state of affairs (x) which is conditional on a specific underlying knowledge of the world (X),

$$risk(x) = p(x \mid X)$$

where the vertical slash indicates conditionality, thus $p(x \mid X)$ is read as the probability of event x occurring, conditional on a certain state of the world described by information set X. Uncertainty also has to factor in the possibility that the hypothesized information set may be incorrect or incomplete in the sense that it may omit relevant information, recognizing that there may exist a range of different underlying possible states of the world $(X_1, X_2, ...)$,

$$uncertainty(x) = \{p(x \mid X_1), p(x \mid X_2), ...\}$$

where each $p(x \mid Xi)$ is always strictly less than 1, however,

$$uncertainty (x \mid B) = \textstyle\sum_i p(x \mid X_i, B) p(X_i \, B).$$

Entrepreneurial planners face risk where the outcome is not known but is governed by a known probability distribution (Knight 1921). Uncertainty is fundamentally different because the underlying probability distribution is not known, and in many cases is fundamentally unknowable (Langlois 1994). Provided the underlying distribution can actually be known, sufficient information can convert a situation of fundamentally unquantifiable uncertainty to one of more precisely quantifiable risk. Entrepreneurial planners act on their subjective appraisals of both risk and uncertainty when they are not able to precisely compute risk, or when the information burden of doing so is too high (Mulligan 2013c).

Tarko (2013: 334) has noted the similarity between this formulation and the approach of O'Driscoll and Rizzo (1985: 37-38) where the Xis represent differing potential frameworks and the overall background or meta-hypothesis B. Entrepreneurial planners reduce the impact of uncertainty over time through (a) the act of gaining experience in implementing their plan, including experience they gain in marketing the product to potential buyers (a practical form of Bayesian updating), and (b) intentional awareness and research, which can include both scientific and market research.

13.3 How the Business Opportunity Set Evolves Over Time

Itti and Baldi (2005, 2006) propose a theory of information surprise where "wows"—their unit of surprise—are associated with the arrival of additional information I, and are measured as the difference between the before and after information states. Information is always subject to a cardinal measure, unlike utility. Surprise s is measured as

$$s = \log_2 p(x \mid I, X) - \log_2 p(x \mid X)$$

where the expression $\log_2 p(x \mid I, X)$ represents the quantity of the expanded information set after the arrival of the new information I, and $\log_2 p(x \mid X)$ is the cardinal measure of the original information set as it was before the arrival of the new information I. The unit of a wow occurs when the arrival or discovery of new information I is sufficient to double the information content.

Austrian or radical surprise occurs when it is discovered that some part of the previously accepted underlying information set X is significantly wrong or that X was merely incomplete and then must be replaced with a new underlying set of assumptions or hypothesized information set Y. Note the original information set X may or may not be a proper subset of the new and more complete or more correct information set Y. Then the difference in wows of surprise becomes

$$s = \log_2 p(x \mid I, Y) - \log_2 p(x \mid X).$$

In this last formulation the entrepreneur must estimate the extent other participants, including competitors, suppliers, and customers, accurately perceive or misperceive the state of the new business opportunity set. The entrepreneur must subjectively estimate the extent of their miscalculations, given the forthcoming innovation which the entrepreneur is about to introduce. These subjective estimates may rely on hard calculation, imitative or repetitive heuristics, a sense of aesthetic intuition, or any combination.

There is no assumption that all participants share a common information set (Tarko 2013: 335), thus in this context insider trading would serve the desirable end of dispersing and further disseminating the most relevant, most valuable market information.

Surprise weighted by its probability becomes the Shannon-Weaver negentropy measure of information (Brillouin 1956). Note that these weightings are always strictly less than one, so surprise always exceeds the information content numerically. Multiplying by the probabilities gives

$$I = ps = p \log_2 p(x \mid I, Y) - p \log_2 p(x \mid I, X) =$$
$$p [\log_2 p(x \mid I, Y) - \log_2 p(x \mid I, X)]$$

where ps is the probability p multiplied by the surprise s, and then overall surprise is

$$I = ps = p \log_2 p(x \mid I, Y) - p \log_2 p(x \mid X) =$$
$$p [\log_2 p(x \mid I, Y) - \log_2 p(x \mid X)]$$

The second expressions on the right of the equations are only operable if the different information sets Y and X do not affect the subjective appraisal of the probability of x occurring.

Tarko (2013: 336) proposes the following sequence of entrepreneurial decisions:

1. Estimate the future market demand for a contemplated new product or service x.
2. Determine or estimate the firm's *technical* or engineering efficiency in producing x.
3. Determine the quantity of output x required to produce Q_x, based on the appraisal in step 2, and jointly the price P_x to offer x for sale at, based on the estimate of market demand in step 1, as well as (a) expectations (internal to the firm) about how easily (that is, after how long) competitors will be able to copy x, and (b) the firm's future discount rate.

The firm will initially sell a new good x for a monopoly price which exceeds the marginal cost, $P_x > MC_x$, but their doing so will attract competitors. The additional supply of good X from the competing new entrants will lower the price, eventually wiping out profits so the firm attempts to maximize the stream of future monopoly profits,

$$\pi(Q_x(t), P_x(t)) = Q_x(t)[P_x(t) - MC_x(t)].$$

Clearly, the passage of time allows the entrepreneurial planner's information set to grow but also allows some information to age out of relevance, and for the general spread of knowledge throughout the market to lessen the innovating firm's initial advantage. Some innovations are obviously easier for potential competitive entrants to observe and subsequently imitate than others. The passage of time also allows the relevant and potentially unexplored information set to expand. The unexplored or unknown part of the information set may be hypothesized to be finite but not bounded, and it expands over time, if only because new states of the world come into being with each passing moment, expanding the purely historical record of what has been.

13.4 Listability, Convergence, & Social Norming

In terms of Brillouin's (1956) negentropy measure of information content,

$$I = -\sum_i p_i \log p_i,$$

unlistability can be captured by hypothesizing that the number of possible outcomes i may approach infinity, but the subjective, perceived i must be finite and relatively much smaller than any actual, objectively realizable i. Unlistability is just another way of saying we can never know everything, and must have very limited practical implications (Tarko 2013: 338). What has real implications for the behavior of entrepreneurial managers is "the fact that different people conceive of different (listable) sets of possibilities (Tarko 2013: 337)." Numeric assessments of all probability distributions depend on subjective individual assumptions, so in general,

$$p(x \mid A) \neq p(x \mid B),$$

or in other words, different observers with different background information (information sets A and B), will assess the probability of a particular outcome x differently. Convergence to common beliefs, in which the hypothesis spaces for different individuals are progressively reconciled through social norming (Vosniadou & Ortony 1989, Samuelson 2004: 278, Clarke & Primo 2012, Tarko 2013: 341), enables the entrepreneurial plans of many competing producers and consumers to be mutually coordinated. In fact, the process of improving mutual plan coordination among entrepreneurial planners and consumers is part of the more general process of convergence to common beliefs through social norming. Social norming starts with the hypothesized, subjective theories of the world of a variety of individuals. We compare and reconcile these theories through discussion and observing the behavior they give rise to.

13.5 Epistemic Heterogeneity v. Social Norming

If we consider these subjective theories without reference to the possibility or desirability of interaction among individual agents, we will notice that they are always necessarily constructed with reference to each individual's unique trajectory of experience through both objective space-time as well as through the social environment. We would represent these experiential trajectories as a series of mostly parallel arrows through the representation of space (Butos & Koppl 2006). These need not be parallel, but unless two lines intersect at certain points, meaning two individuals encounter one another, or the trajectory of one is markedly different from others, though they need not be straight, these lines will be more-or-less nearly parallel, and more-or-less unremarkably so. Individuals with uniquely divergent experience may be represented by regions where the trajectories of their experience arrows veer off sharply from those of the others.

If epistemic heterogeneity is viewed as a continuum of subjective variation, innovative entrepreneurs will be the most extreme outliers, but successful entrepreneurs will be imitated and drive the future evolution of the realized distribution of understanding. Their experience lines will initially veer off from the mass of others, but if they subsequently meet with success, imitative competitors will enter the market, and their lines will veer off to follow that of the successful innovator who drives the future direction of the herd.

There seems to be an inverse correlation between perceptual horizon and market concentration, or in other words

short perceptual horizon = high time preference = strong social conformity/low epistemic heterogeneity = low market concentration = many nearly identical competitors

long perceptual horizon = low time preference = low social conformity/high epistemic heterogeneity = high market concentration = pure monopoly

Intermediate cases of monopolistic competition and oligopoly can be determined by the extent to which the innovator's perceptual horizon and time preference are unique. For innovators with uniquely long time horizons and low time preferences, the short time horizons and high time preference of potential imitators become a persistent barrier against their entry onto the market, preserving the original innovator's monopoly power, profits, and rents. When innovators and potential imitators both share long time horizons and low time preference, imitation will result in competing firms having similar objectives, expectations, and risk tolerance. As firms react to each other, the market becomes oligopolistic. If the innovator has a longer time horizon and lower time preference than potential imitators, the market will be a monopolistically competitive one, where products are marketed to opportunistically defined market niches and target demographics which may be transient, and products can be differentiated through branding, advertising, etc., to exploit temporary monopoly situations.

CHAPTER 14

Appendix on the Conventional Mathematics of Comparative Statics

Cost minimization and profit maximization exercises have become central to modern neoclassical economics but they virtually ignore entrepreneurial action. Entrepreneurial planners select and design production plans in the first place, and rely on their experience in carrying out a production plan and being alert to further opportunities to adjust and modify the production process to create additional economies. Entrepreneurs are constantly looking for ways to produce more output from each input or more output from the same level of inputs, trying to exploit and improve on the currently existing technology.

Even this account, which is far more expansive and flexible than the standard neoclassical theory of the firm, fails utterly to address or capture the market process of how the original technology emerged or came to be implemented. In addition, entrepreneurial planners will also be alert to opportunities to switch input resources or combine new inputs with those already used to produce more or cheaper output. Alert entrepreneurs will also look for opportunities to formulate new strategies to sell their output or some part of it for a higher price. They will exercise entrepreneurial awareness to look for potential opportunities to attract new buyers and devise new uses for the firm's output. Entrepreneurs will also be alert to opportunities to negotiate lower costs of the inputs they use, or find alternative sources, and find substitute inputs to replace more expensive ones.

In the standard comparative statics model of firm behavior, the entrepreneurial planners who manage firms and make the firms' decisions select the values of the choice variables in the firm's algebraic cost or profit functions to minimize the cost of producing a certain level of output, or maximize the profit earned by the firm. These two optimization conditions—cost minimization and profit maximization—are equivalent, and the two algebraic forms of expressing these equivalent economizing problems facing the firm are referred to as duals. Summing the quantities produced by many firms at different prices for each good provides the market supply curve for that good, which illustrates the collective behavior of the firms in response to changes in the price.

In the theory of the consumer, the conventional optimization exercise ignores any entrepreneurial innovations which imply changes in the number of the consumer's utility function arguments; that is, the number of different goods and services the consumer purchases to achieve utility from. However, it is very easy to see that in the real world entrepreneurial consumers are always trying out new products to see if they can improve on their current levels of utility or want satisfaction. Consumers can also condition or habituate themselves to get more enjoyment from particular goods or services, and would gain an advantage in terms of satisfying their wants if they can successfully cultivate or acquire a new taste for a good which is particularly cheap. This implies changing the algebraic form of the consumer's utility function. To some extent, the consumer can take at least limited control of changing their own preferences, purposely increasing their preferences for cheaper goods to improve their overall level of satisfaction.

Consumer income is the constraint in the consumer's utility maximization problem, and alert consumers will search for any opportunity to earn or negotiate additional income. Equivalently, alert entrepreneurial consumers will also search for lower priced consumer goods. Their search for lower prices provides the competitive pressure that contributes to lowering the prices of goods, and consumers may also attempt to negotiate lower prices for the goods they buy. Entrepreneurial consumers also search for goods and services of higher quality which provide added satisfaction, and will pay a premium for these superior goods and services. The way economists model consumer behavior generally ignores entrepreneurial consumers' alertness to all these opportunities and strategies to costlessly improve the satisfaction of their wants.

Without reference to market process, consumers are modeled as merely selecting the quantities and combinations of the different consumer goods and services which maximize their utility, and the solution to the utility maximization problem is always fully determined by the original statement of the problem. Summing the quantities of a particular good or service purchased by each consumer at different prices provides the market demand curve which illustrates the collective behavior of all the consumers in a certain market, in terms of how they respond to changes in the price of the good in question. It is hard to imagine anything more different from real world market process than an algebraic optimization exercise.

14.1 Introduction

Neoclassical microeconomics largely models economic behavior as a series of optimization problems. The assumption is that these calculus problems accurately mimic the behavior of optimizing real world decision makers—even if relatively few of those individuals know calculus at all, and the ones that do, do not actually use it to make these decisions. Market participants are thought of as knowingly optimizing algebraic objective functions which are always known in advance and subject to known cost or technical constraints. All the market information captured in the algebraic objective and constraint functions is assumed to be known fully and in advance of the entrepreneurial planner's decision of how much output to produce or how much to buy. Firms simultaneously and equivalently minimize their cost of producing output, maximize the quantity of output they produce for a certain total fixed cost, or maximize the profit they earn on the output they produce. Consumers choose the combination of goods and services which maximizes their utility from consuming the combinations of different products they purchase from the firms.

An optimization exercise is always subject to explicit constraints which are analytically expressed as algebraic functions which are also always known in advance to the firms or consumers doing the choosing (Robbins 1932). However, these algebraic objective and constraint functions can never be more than imperfect and oversimplified approximations of the actual, real world processes of producing output or obtaining satisfaction through consumption.[51]

In a sense, considered as mathematical models offering simplified versions of reality, cost, profit, and utility functions do not purport to be anything more than crude oversimplifications. The fundamental assumptions which underlie the modeling of firm and consumer choice as optimization problems to be solved under conditions of perfect information makes it impossible to accommodate the possibility of entrepreneurial innovation—there is assumed to be no additional information to uncover or be alert for.

Because innovation is always experimental, sometimes disruptive, and aims at uncovering new information which could not have been known or applied before the fact to better inform or support firm or consumer choice, entrepreneurship cannot be accommodated within an optimization model (Mulligan 2005). The uncertainty entrepreneurs overcome and exploit to earn entrepreneurial profits is taken out of an optimization problem by assumption, because the optimization exercise always assumes that the algebraic functions governing the behavior of economic agents are always known to the entrepreneurial planner in advance and can always be expressed algebraically.

The resulting comparative statics analyses economists use to illustrate the interaction between market supply and demand are usually presented in graphical form at the undergraduate level, while graduate courses are typically more formalized and feature mathematics which

---

51 It might be suggested that the true objective function is an unknowable and more complicated transcendental function which theorists crudely attempt to mimic with algebraic functions which are much simpler. Even when the objective function of an optimization exercise is rendered as a transcendental function, the underlying reality cannot ever be represented with such perfect accuracy. The underlying reality is, at best, some other, unknown transcendental function, if it can be expressed that way at all.

are both more sophisticated and explicit (Samuleson 1947, Debreu 1959, Silberberg 1978, Henderson & Quandt 1980, Chiang 1984, Varian 1984, Takayama 1985). The messy innovation and unpredictability introduced by the entrepreneur is assumed away and all the data of the market are treated as being perfectly known in advance, as well as necessarily being capable of being expressed completely in elegant and concise algebraic functions. These algebraic functions are usually chosen more for their mathematical tractability than for any resemblance to the underlying reality. This approach offers a great deal in simplifying complex phenomena so that certain aspects can be isolated and examined, but at the same time it fundamentally misrepresents the nature of market process and market competition.

The Austrian school of economics has always been profoundly skeptical about mathematical formalism: "In the imaginary construction of an evenly rotating system nobody is an entrepreneur and speculator. In any real and living economy every actor is always an entrepreneur and speculator (Mises 1949: 252)." Recall that entrepreneurial action sometimes improves mutual plan coordination and moves the market closer to a hypothetical equilibrium, but sometimes disrupts the plans of others and reduces the level of mutual plan coordination, at least in the short run, moving the market further away from the originally presumed target of the hypothetical, idealized equilibrium (Lewin 1997). Thus entrepreneurship cannot be captured or defined exclusively in terms of its relation to either equilibria or coordination among economic planners. Entrepreneurs are alert to opportunities for profit, which ultimately come from their successfully contributing to better satisfying consumer wants.

14.2 The Entrepreneurial Producer I: Cost Minimization

The neoclassical theory of the firm is developed in terms of the dual and equivalent cost minimization and profit maximization problems which form the basis for the upward sloping market supply curve. The firm's decision making managers are seen as using a fixed and unchanging production technology which is taken for granted,[52] as well as a given and static vector of resource and output prices, which are predetermined and assumed to be known in advance. The firm is assumed to be a price taker with no market power to influence the prices of either the inputs that they buy or the output that they produce. The reality is that prices emerge from market process in the first place, and market process governs their variation and evolution over time. Under the supervision of the firm's managers, the firm transforms a given set of inputs into a given output.

Furthermore, the type of market organization, that is, whether the product market is perfectly competitive, monopolistically competitive, oligopolistic, or monopolistic, is also assumed to be given, when in fact market organization is an outcome of market process which results from the action of entrepreneurial innovators and the strategic interaction and feedback among them.[53] The firm's cost minimization

---

52 It is recognized that technology improves over time, but the optimization problem is static in principle, always being constructed to take a certain unchanging production technology for granted. The fact that entrepreneurial planners experimentally implement technological advances to take advantage of the cost saving or other innovative opportunities they might provide is ignored. The economics literature has always recognized that this approach is unrealistic, but it is still followed in order to simplify matters and isolate the remaining variables.

53 See Chapter 7 for a discussion of how the choices and behavior of entrepreneurial planners determine market organization.

problem is constructed without recognizing that alert entrepreneurs might attempt to (a) improve the production process to extract more output from each input or more output from the same level of inputs, (b) substitute among different inputs or combine new inputs with those already being used, to produce either a greater quantity of output, lower the cost of production, or both, (c) devise and implement new marketing strategies to sell their output or some part of it for a higher price, (d) attract new buyers and devise new uses for the output to reach new market niches, or (e) reduce the costs of their inputs.

The theory of monopolistic-competitive markets emphasizes market segmentation and product differentiation which make the output produced by competing firms less perfect substitutes than they would be under perfect competition. It might be argued that the concepts of market segmentation and product differentiation allow for item (c) above, but this is only possible if the market is structured in a way that prevents firms from facing perfectly elastic demand for their products. In optimization theory, market structure is always predetermined by assumption; in reality it emerges through market process as a result from the behavior of entrepreneurial planners and the interaction among them. In reformulating Walras's (1874) theory of perfect competition, Makowski and Ostroy recognize "(1) prices are not exogenously given, they arise from bargaining," and also that "(2) the set of active markets is not exogenously given, it results from innovation (Makowski & Ostroy 2001: 480)." In other words, market prices emerge from market process directed by the experimental actions of innovative entrepreneurial planners. Thus, prices result from the behavior and interaction of market participants, buyers and sellers who bargain to determine the final price by reconciling their experimental ask and offer prices, working within the process of the market (endogenous determination of prices). The price of a market exchange is not predetermined by outside factors (exogenous determination) prior to the bargaining of the buyer and seller for each transaction. Since the conventional view is that entrepreneurs work primarily through firms, the inability of the neoclassical theory of the firm to accommodate entrepreneurial action is a major shortcoming.

14.2.1 The Standard Cost Minimization Problem

One way to formulate the conventional optimization problem facing the firm is to maximize the quantity of output produced by the firm subject to a fixed cost constraint. Here the firm is assumed to be a price taker and faces fixed prices for its output and inputs, which are all predetermined in perfectly competitive input and output markets. The objective function for optimization is the production function relating the quantities x_1 and x_2 of two inputs X_1 and X_2 to the quantity of the firm's output q, given as

$$q = f(x_1, x_2).$$

Unlike the consumer's utility function, the production function always has a cardinally-measurable physical or value output. As an example, the most commonly encountered production function is the two-input Cobb-Douglas production function

$$q = f(x_1, x_2) = Cx_1^a x_2^b.$$

Put in logarithms, this can also be expressed as

$$\ln q = \ln C + a \ln x_1 + b \ln x_2.$$

The input quantities x_1 and x_2 are the choice variables which, through the production function, jointly determine the amount of output q the firm will produce. Nevertheless, it remains highly questionable whether the real world process of production can ever be meaningfully captured by an algebraic function purporting to be, at best, an approximation. The possibility of using additional or substitute inputs X_3 through X_n is ignored—there is an implicit assumption that any substitution which may take place among inputs has already been carried out in an optimal and final manner by the entrepreneurial planner—the entrepreneur is eliminated by assuming they have already completed their contribution *before* any decision has taken place. In stark contrast, the work of the entrepreneurial planner is never completed in the real world. There is always room for further innovation. The key Austrian insight that production occurs over time (Menger 1871: 152,[54] Hayek 1931, 1933, 1935, 1939, 1941) is also ignored, as the passage of time would imply changes to the conditions underlying cost minimization and profit maximization.

The constraint function in the cost minimization problem is the producer's cost constraint, which is conventionally given as

$$C^0 = r_1 x_1 + r_2 x_2 + b$$

---

54 "The transformation of goods of higher order into goods of lower order takes place, as does every other process of change, in time (Menger 1871: 152)."

where r_1 and r_2 are the resource prices of input resources X_1 and X_2, x_1 and x_2 are the input quantities, b is the cost of fixed inputs, and C^0 is the fixed total cost. Again, the cost constraint and the input prices r_1 and r_2 are assumed to be given and known in advance. Prices are not determined by bargaining in real time, they are predetermined, that is, they are given in advance. No scope for entrepreneurial discovery or innovation is permitted (Kirzner 1984b: 154). Mises notes

> in the imaginary construction of the evenly rotating economy there is no room left for entrepreneurial activity, because this construction eliminates any change of data that could affect prices. As soon as one abandons this assumption of rigidity of data, one finds that action must need be affected by every change in the data. As action necessarily is directed toward influencing a future state of affairs, even if sometimes only the immediate future of the next instant, it is affected by every incorrectly anticipated change in the data occurring in the period of time between its beginning and the end of the period for which it aimed to provide (period of provision). Thus the outcome of action is always uncertain. Action is always speculation (Mises 1949: 252).

The contrasting view of neoclassical microeconomics is that action is always some form of optimization, and that the "correct" outcome is always predetermined by the unalterable public data of the market which is shared equally by everyone. There is no recognition that there is any undiscovered information for entrepreneurial planners to be alert for because all relevant information is publicly available and known to everyone. The firm's cost minimization problem fails to recognize the

scope for the real world uncertainty, ignorance, and risk which entrepreneurial planners have to try to overcome, or that entrepreneurs can
gain decisive competitive advantages when they successfully overcome
their own ignorance. The algebraic cost constraint in the cost minimization problem also suffers from leaving out the same alternative
substitute inputs X_3 through X_n as the production function, as well as
their prices r_3 through r_n. One way for entrepreneurial planners to
exercise alertness would be in searching for and negotiating lower input
prices[55] r_1 and r_2, or r1 through r_n, or in experimenting with combinations of different inputs that further minimize total cost (Schumpeter
1934: 133-135). Entrepreneurial alertness might also be exercised in
seeking to find ways to reduce the so called "fixed" cost b. Since b is
only fixed by construction, entrepreneurs should seek and be alert to
any potential opportunities to reduce fixed costs whenever possible.
The producer, having initially chosen the total cost of production C^0 or
had it imposed externally, is modeled as seeking to produce as much
output q as possible.

The constrained output maximization problem is set up as
maximizing

---

55 Makowski and Ostroy (2001: 483) criticize the standard treatment of perfectly
competitive firms as price-takers in the highly influential models of perfect
competition of Walras (1874) and Marshall (1890). These became the standard
accounts which have strongly influenced modern microeconomics and price
theory. As Makowski and Ostroy note, prices are specific to each transaction and
only converge toward a prevailing marketwide price through the competition of
market process. If a single market price ultimately emerges through competition, it may or may not be an equilibrium price. It can be extremely misleading
to model prices as having been predetermined before any competition occurs.
Such formal accounts of market process outcomes practically guarantee that
essential elements and principles will be overlooked or misconstrued.

$$V = f(x_1, x_2) + \mu(C^0 - r_1x_1 - r_2x_2 - b)$$

where $\mu \neq 0$ is an undetermined Lagrange multiplier. Finding the first partial derivatives of this function V with respect to the choice variables x_1, x_2, and μ, and setting them equal to zero provides the set of three first-order conditions for a maximum:

$$\frac{\partial V}{\partial x_1} = f_1 - \mu\, r_1 = 0$$

$$\frac{\partial V}{\partial x_2} = f_2 - \mu\, r_2 = 0$$

$$\frac{\partial V}{\partial \mu} = C^0 - r_1x_1 - r_2x_2 - b = 0$$

Algebraic manipulation yields the familiar relation

$$\frac{f_1}{f_2} = \frac{r_1}{r_2}$$

which states that, at a cost minimum, f_1/f_2, the ratio of the marginal products of the two resource inputs X_1 and X_2, must be equal to the ratio between their prices, r_1/r_2. These ratios between the marginal products and the resource prices define the rate of technical substitution (RTS) between X_1 and X_2. However, the minimum cost found through solving the optimization problem is subject to the implicit constraint that in setting up the cost problem, the quantities of any other potential or substitute inputs X_3 through X_n were arbitrarily set at zero. The first-order conditions can also be written as

$$\mu = \frac{f_1}{r_1} = \frac{f_2}{r_2}$$

indicating the contribution to output of the last dollar spent on each input f_i/r_i, must equal the Lagrange multiplier μ, which is thus the first derivative of output with respect to cost C, assuming the input prices r_1 and r_2 are held constant and the quantities of inputs used x_1 and x_2 are allowed to vary.

The second-order condition for a cost minimum is that the bordered Hessian matrix of second derivatives be positive:

$$\begin{vmatrix} f_{11} & f_{12} & -r_1 \\ f_{21} & f_{22} & -r_2 \\ -r_1 & -r_2 & 0 \end{vmatrix} > 0$$

The cost minimization problem can be made more realistic by allowing total cost to vary. When C is allowed to vary, the differential of the cost equation is

$$dC = r_1 dx_1 + r_2 dx_2$$

The fixed cost b drops out because it is assumed to be a constant which thus has a differential equal to zero, though if entrepreneurial search aims at lowering b, and does successfully lower it, it would then vary and not drop out of the first-order conditions.

The cost minimization problem facing the firm may also be formulated as minimizing a *variable* cost function subject to the constraint that a certain fixed and predetermined quantity of output must be produced with the given technology fully described by the algebraic production function. This constrained cost minimization problem is expressed as minimizing

$$Z = r_1 x_1 + r_2 x_2 + b + \lambda [q^0 - f(x_1, x_2)]$$

where $\lambda = 1/\mu \neq 0$ is also an undetermined Lagrange multiplier, which in this case is the reciprocal of the μ in the equivalent output maximization problem. The partial derivatives of this cost function Z are set equal to zero to find the first order conditions:

$$\frac{\partial Z}{\partial x_1} = r_1 - \lambda f_1 = 0$$

$$\frac{\partial Z}{\partial x_2} = r_2 - \lambda f_2 = 0$$

$$\frac{\partial Z}{\partial \lambda} = q^0 - f(x_1, x_2) = 0$$

The first-order conditions allow us to solve for the following relations,

$$\frac{f_1}{f_2} = \frac{r_1}{r_2} \quad \text{or} \quad \frac{1}{\lambda} = \frac{f_1}{r_1} = \frac{f_2}{r_2} \quad \text{or} \quad RTS = \frac{r_1}{r_2}$$

The Lagrange multipliers λ from the variable cost problem and μ from the fixed cost problem are related as reciprocals of one another. λ gives the first derivative of cost with respect to output; that is, the marginal cost of output. Because this is a minimum, the second-order condition requires that the bordered Hessian matrix of second derivatives be negative:

$$\begin{vmatrix} -\lambda f_{11} & -\lambda f_{12} & -f_1 \\ -\lambda f_{21} & -\lambda f_{22} & -f_2 \\ -f_1 & -f_2 & 0 \end{vmatrix} < 0$$

Manipulation of this condition demonstrates it is equivalent to the second-order condition for constrained output maximization.

14.2.2 Limitations of Standard Cost Minimization

The optimization problem is based on the principle of intentionally optimizing a known objective function subject to known constraints, removing much of the uncertainty faced and overcome by real world entrepreneurial planners. Because in reality these things are not generally known in advance, and generally will not be known even after the fact in sufficient detail to allow an entrepreneurial planner to set up a meaningful cost minimization problem for their firm or production process, the information these exercises provide about how markets work is strictly limited. The standard model of perfect competition imposes extreme, and extremely unrealistic, information requirements (Makowski & Ostroy 2001: 480). Furthermore, algebraic functions can never be more than crude approximations of the ever-changing real world processes of producing output or obtaining satisfaction through consumption. Limitations of the applicability of optimization problems should be recognized in that the true objective function may not ever be known with certainty to market participants, and may not even be capable of being expressed as an algebraic function, even if "known" (Kirzner 1984b: 154). This may be an example of Hayek's (1945) inarticulable knowledge.

An alert entrepreneur would always seek to discover ways to adjust the production process by adopting improved technology to produce more output from each input, or equivalently, extract the same level of output with fewer inputs (Schumpeter 1934: 129-133). Instead, the optimization problem assumes a technology which is static, unchanging, and given in advance, rather than one which emerges through market process as competing entrepreneurial planners introduce new innovations, experiment with technological adjustments, experimentally substitute inputs with greater or less success, etc. The optimization problem is necessarily untenable unless the technology has been optimized in advance. In reality, production technology *results* from the creative process of human action and entrepreneurial discovery. Technology is created, not given,[56] and because it is continually improved on, there is never any final optimum to reach, only old optima to be improved on with the use of better technologies.

---

56 More precisely, technology is created by innovators and given to imitators. Imitation of technological improvements is an important mode of entrepreneurial behavior. This is discussed in Chapter 5 as a distinction between first-order (primary) innovation and second-order (imitative) innovation.

14.2.3 Static Input Set

Entrepreneurial alertness might also be applied in discovering new inputs X_3 and X_4 to either substitute or complement X_1 and X_2 in producing a particular output. Because the optimization problem arbitrarily excludes any additional potential inputs X_3 through X_n, a more realistic cost minimum would be defined by

$$\mu = \frac{f_1}{r_1} = \frac{f_2}{r_2} = \ ... \ = \frac{f_n}{n}$$

This more global optimum still assumes a pre-determined and static technology, and can never be fully realized, as the scope for entrepreneurial alertness in discovering new inputs is inexhaustible. The optimum implies a definitive final outcome which can both never actually be reached, and never be exceeded. In neoclassical microeconomics the optimization problem is constrained by arbitrarily setting the quantities of these potential additional inputs X_3 through X_n equal to zero. Even in the context of the optimization problem, imposing this indefinite number of arbitrary constraints, though analytically necessary to arrive at a manageable solution, is also necessarily unrealistic. Furthermore, even as modified, this optimization exercise still ignores the possibility that the entrepreneurial planner should be alert to any potential choice of different outputs (Schumpeter 1934: 134).

Entrepreneurial planners may also switch inputs, use new inputs, or both to produce cheaper output. These choices are experimental efforts to create and uncover new information, not an optimization process. If the production technology A which is assumed uses inputs a and b, and a different production technology B uses inputs c and d, and can produce the same output at a lower unit cost, obviously technology B should be used, but the optimization problem assumes this is known in advance. Such underlying facts can only be discovered through entrepreneurial experimentation, experience, trial-and-error, entrepreneurial alertness, discovery, etc. These less cut and dried examples of entrepreneurial innovation cannot be modeled as optimization processes because they cannot meaningfully be represented as having predetermined outcomes which are always wholly contained in the statement of the problem. From the perspective of realism, entrepreneurship is necessary, but from the perspective of theory building, entrepreneurship is too messy, complicated, and imposes uncertainty and indeterminate outcomes.

A prior commitment to an established but more expensive, less efficient, technology A may prevent or discourage the eventual discovery of the greater benefits potentially offered by a less expensive, more productive, technology B. There are always better, as opposed to relatively worse, ways to combine inputs, but never a final best way, the global optimum, which forever precludes any potential future discovery of an improved technology. This holds even when the input set is assumed to be fixed, because real world technology is never fixed and always improves eventually.[57]

---

57 Technological change will always occur and eventually everyone in society will benefit from each advance and new discovery. Entrepreneurial planners can rather effortlessly surf this rising tide of seemingly automatic technological improvement. Because entrepreneurs compete with one another, they gain additional advantages through alertness to the most relevant technological advances which they can exploit and take advantage of. Some degree of scientific progress might occur automatically anyway, but it is important to realize that the profit and loss incentive structure of market process helps motivate and reward the discoverers of new technologies and new scientific knowledge (Ikeda 1994: 23-24). If market process offered no material reward for scientific discoveries, civilization would probably not have advanced as far or as rapidly as it has.

14.2.4 Information Constraints

One fault of the optimization problem is that it assumes as given in advance both the objective function being minimized or maximized, and the constraint functions. In the context of an optimization problem, the information expressed by these algebraic functions is held fixed, though in reality it changes frequently due to entrepreneurial innovation and market process. Provided the information in the objective and constraint functions is attainable, in the real world it can only be uncovered through extensive search and entrepreneurial alertness. Perhaps the most severe criticism against viewing economic decision-making as the outcome of solving an optimization problem is that real world decisions always rests on fallible expectations, many of which never come to pass as expected, and which are always subject to revision. An entrepreneurial planner could theoretically solve an otherwise valid optimization problem based on their unique, subjective, and fallible expectations of prices at which the inputs can be bought, and output sold (Kirzner 1990: 167). If the entrepreneur's expectations are not later realized, the producer may lose money in spite of having optimized, because market participants often fail to optimize with respect to what turns out to be their true circumstances. True circumstances can only be known after the fact and can only be discovered through experience. The true circumstances emerge and become accessible to us only in the fullness of time, but by then it is too late. This is an example of Kirzner's Knowledge Problem A, which causes planned exchanges to be impossible to fulfill. Kirzner notes that these kinds of problems are self-correcting (Kirzner 1990: 169-171), as market participants either learn to adjust their plans to recognize the realities of the market which are actually less favorable than they had hoped or anticipated, or they withdraw from the market.

It is also possible for the optimization exercise to lead to the erroneous conclusions that inputs cannot be obtained at sufficiently low prices, or output sold at sufficiently high prices, or that production technology, input quality, or consumer demand for the output are actually better than entrepreneurial planners had anticipated (Kirzner 1990: 168-9). These cases are examples of Kirzner's Knowledge Problem B, in which exchanges that are theoretically feasible and would have been beneficial were never planned or undertaken, because no entrepreneurial planner was aware of the feasibility or benefits of the potential exchanges. Entrepreneurs always seek to discover such opportunities, but many must always remain undiscovered. These instances of Kirzner's Knowledge Problem B are not self-correcting, and await entrepreneurial discovery before anyone can be aware of them. Alert entrepreneurs can profit by uncovering and remedying instances of Knowledge Problem B.

These objections to optimization modelling based on Kirzner's two knowledge problems can also be expressed, drawing mainly from Hayek (1949) and Kirzner (1984a, 1984b, 1990) by saying that the information set assumed by and which underlies the standard optimization problems does not exist in reality. It is clear that no person possesses the necessary information set in its totality, but the optimization problem assumes perfect and complete information is mutually shared by all market participants. In reality, it is more accurate to suggest that each market participant may possess some relevant information, much of which is purely subjective, such as individual preferences, which individuals act on but cannot articulate. They can communicate their preferences through their buying and selling behavior. Much of this information is held exclusively by certain individuals; for example, each individual's own subjective preferences, their plans for future consumption and production, etc. Individuals also differ in their alertness, both in terms of intensity and application (Kirzner 1979: 170). Entrepreneurs overcome the social problem of communication whenever they generate flows of information that stimulate revision of others' previously uncoordinated decisions and entrepreneurial plans toward greater mutual coordination (Kirzner 1984a: 147), moving the market toward a never-realized state of final equilibrium. The very concept of market equilibrium is merely an analytical convenience with little practical relevance (Nelson & Winter 1982, Makowski & Ostroy 2001).

Market prices summarize relevant information which would otherwise be useless to market participants in satisfying their wants, but the inadequacies in market prices—such as when the price of one product varies significantly in an inefficient market—also create the profit-and-loss incentives for alert entrepreneurial planners to experiment with price adjustments (Kirzner 1984a: 149). A price may summarize economic information regarding the supply and demand conditions in the relevant markets, without signaling whether the price represents an equilibrium or a dis-equilibrium. Entrepreneurs compete in adjusting prices in a "competitive process which *digs out* what is in fact discovered (Kirzner 1984a: 150)." The competitive process Hayek describes, where "competition is valuable only because, and so far as, its results are unpredictable and on the whole different from those which anyone has, or could have, deliberately aimed at (Hayek 1978b: 180)," is utterly incompatible with modeling entrepreneurial planning as an optimization problem. Market process always arrives at results of ever-improving quantity and quality without reliance on any explicit optimization solution.

Kirzner's (1963: 44-46, 1984b: 160) view is that dis-equilibrium prices offer pure profit opportunities for alert entrepreneurs who can discover them and then arbitrage among the different prices which temporarily prevail in different markets. This profit arbitrage incentive allows entrepreneurs to profit while they contribute to adjusting dis-equilibrium prices towards equilibrium. Although, by construction, an equilibrium is never necessarily reached, and if it were reached, is never persistent, the Kirznerian entrepreneur always acts to lessen the extent of the divergency among prices and dis-equilibrium. The equilibrium which is approached constitutes a spontaneous order, a level of coordination which results from human action but not from human design (Hayek 1967). In contrast, a Schumpeterian entrepreneur moves the market price vector away from equilibrium, by introducing new production technologies, marketing and distribution methods, and creating disruptive new entrepreneurial plans which increase the social dispersion of knowledge (Kerber 1994). This distinction is explored more fully in section 14.4. Both kinds of entrepreneurship are ignored and assumed away by viewing the work of the entrepreneurial planner as solving an optimization problem.

The cost-minimization problem also fails to recognize the mode of entrepreneurial action which occurs when a firm voluntarily chooses to take on added production or selling costs to make the product more desirable to the consumer (Kirzner 1973: 24), a familiar strategy for converting a perfectly competitive market into a monopolistically competitive one. Schumpeter (1934: 135) mentions a kind of entrepreneurship consisting of a search for new markets for an existing product. Increased consumer preference for the product can (a) justify increased production or selling costs, (b) enable the firm to increase product price, and (c) be engineered by improving product quality or enhanced marketing strategies, but these issues and potential opportunities are ignored in optimization problems. This category of entrepreneurial action includes both increased production costs incurred to improve the subjective quality of the product in consumers' eyes, and increased selling costs, for example, of marketing or advertising, which also aim at improving the buyer's subjective perception of the product's quality or desirability, and therefore their willingness to pay a higher price (Geroski & Mazzucato 2003).

14.2.5 Extensions of Standard Cost Minimization

The production function can be adapted to demonstrate entrepreneurial innovation, but only at the cost of excessively limiting the choices faced by entrepreneurial planners.

14.2.5.1 Additional Inputs

Within the cost minimization exercises, additional choice variables can be introduced to capture some, though not all, potential for entrepreneurial action. At least three inputs must be included, each of which can be considered a composite commodity: X_1, the bundle of inputs already used in producing output Q; X_2, the bundle of inputs subject to entrepreneurial discovery being modeled in this specific instance; and X_3, the bundle of inputs still remaining undiscovered. The constrained cost minimization problem is then

$$Z = r_1x_1 + r_2x_2 + r_3x_3 + b + \lambda[q^0 - f(x_1, x_2, x_3)]$$

and the partial derivatives of Z are set equal to zero to find the first-order conditions. The entrepreneur introduces the innovation of violating the previously assumed linear constraint that $x_2 = 0$, but the constraint remains that $x_3 = 0$ by assumption. Before entrepreneurial action, the first order conditions are:

$$\frac{\partial Z}{\partial x_1} = r_1 - \lambda f_1 = 0$$

$$\frac{\partial Z}{\partial \lambda} = q^0 - f(x_1, x_2, x_3) = 0$$

After entrepreneurial innovation, the first order conditions become:

$$\frac{\partial Z}{\partial x_1} = r_1 - \lambda f_1 = 0$$

$$\frac{\partial Z}{\partial x_2} = r_2 - \lambda f_2 = 0$$

$$\frac{\partial Z}{\partial \lambda} = q^0 - f(x_1, x_2, x_3) = 0$$

Because a linear restriction has been removed, the minimum cost after entrepreneurial discovery must always be lower than the before-entrepreneurship minimum, provided the constraint was initially binding. Although this optimization exercise, constructed to show the optimum before and after entrepreneurial innovation, does capture one highly delimited, highly stylized kind of entrepreneurial innovation, many other kinds are not amenable to this kind of deterministic analysis or representation in such a restrictive cost minimization or profit maximization problem. From a theoretical perspective, the kind of predefined innovation modeled here thus could not be particularly valuable. No one learns anything terribly profound about the process of entrepreneurial innovation from looking at such augmented optimization exercises.

14.2.5.2 Technological Improvement

Suppose the Cobb-Douglas production function $q = f(x_1, x_2) = Cx_1^a x_2^b$, represents the production technology understood by managers and engineers prior to an innovation. The prior, restricted production function has the logarithmic form

$$\ln q = \ln C + a \ln x_1 + b \ln x_2.$$

This production function is nested in the more general transcendental-logarithmic (translog)[58] form

---

58 Before taking logarithms, the translog is

$$q = f(x_1, x_2) = Cx_1^a x_2^b (x_1^2)^c (x_1 x_2)^d (x_2^2)^e.$$

The Cobb-Douglas form imposes the constraints that the second-order terms are all zero, and it is convenient, though not necessarily realistic, to assume that innovative entrepreneurs' discovery or implementation of a more efficient production technology is equivalent to removing the zero constraints on the second-order terms. The second-order translog form can be thought of as nested within third or higher-order, but as yet unknown, forms. Thus entrepreneurial discovery can be modeled as an indefinitely ongoing process. Nevertheless, potential improvements which entrepreneurial planners could realize by adopting other new technologies, which are unknown before the fact, are explicitly excluded.

$$\ln q = \ln C + a \ln x_1 + b \ln x_2 + c \ln x_1^2 + d \ln x_1 x_2 + e \ln x_2^2.$$

Suppose a particular entrepreneurial discovery consists of learning how to make use of the additional second order combinations of inputs in the translog function, which are the last three terms, $c \ln x_1^2 + d \ln x_1 x_2 + e \ln x_2^2$. The resulting, more flexible, cost minimization problem will enable the firm to achieve lower costs and higher profits, because implicit restrictions which were initially imposed on the second order terms in the production function have now been lifted.[59]

The difficulty faced by the approach of modeling entrepreneurship as nothing more than the removal of certain constraints which are known and specified in advance is that if the less restrictive, more productive technology were actually known to the entrepreneurial planner in advance, they would have made full use of it in the first place. This construction can only be set up in an environment where the before and after optima are both fully predetermined and contained in the statement of the optimization problem, and only the entrepreneur is ignorant of the difference. This is a particularly sterile, artificial, and unrewarding way of modeling entrepreneurial innovation, because it constrains the entrepreneur exclusively to realizing artificial productivity gains only as defined in advance by economists, who are

---

59 This model can be made even more general and open-ended by realizing that the second-order translog is nested in third and higher order functions. However, the additional precision offered by higher-order terms rapidly becomes negligible (Todd 1963). Thus this approach to modeling open-ended technological progress rapidly becomes analytically futile as well as computationally cumbersome. In most cases, the benefits of technological change are more likely to increase exponentially. Treating technological advances as removing constraints on increasingly higher-order translog terms would mistakenly model technological advances as *decreasing* exponentially!

not generally practicing entrepreneurs.[60] Real world entrepreneurs recognize no such constraints. Thus one way of expressing the limitations of the optimization approach to modeling entrepreneurial planning is that it reduces entrepreneurial discovery to an Easter egg hunt, where the only prizes entrepreneurs can uncover must always be defined in advance and planted by omniscient and omnipotent economists. This is a stronger argument against than in favor of viewing economic behavior as mere optimization. The real state of affairs is that entrepreneurs often uncover advances undreamed of by anyone else, or even by themselves prior to the discovery (Horwitz 2000: 29-30).

14.3 The Entrepreneurial Producer II: Profit Maximization

The firm's cost minimization problem is often represented by its dual optimization problem, the problem selecting the amount of output to produce to maximize the firm's profit.

14.3.1 Standard Profit Maximization

The prices of the firm's output and the inputs it uses are fixed and predetermined. Since more inputs are required to produce more output, the entrepreneur is free to vary cost along with output, and the unconstrained profit maximization problem is written as

---

60 Cantillon, Turgot, and Say would be the most notable exceptions. See Chapter 3 for a discussion.

$$\pi = pq - C$$

where p is the output price, assumed to be given, as the firm is assumed to be a price taker in a perfectly competitive market. Substituting in the production function for q and the cost function for C, the profit function is conventionally written as

$$\pi = p f(x_1, x_2) - r_1 x_1 - r_2 x_2 - b$$

which is maximized with respect to the choice variables x_1 and x_2, which are the quantities of the input resources X_1 and X_2 the firm uses to make its product with the production technology represented by the production function $q = f(x_1, x_2)$. The constraint on maximizing profit is the production technology, which enters directly into the profit function, so there is no need to introduce a Lagrange multiplier. Again, limitations imposed by the assumptions of a technology which is predetermined in advance, static, and unchanging, and the limited choice of inputs invalidate the exercise in so far as it would apply to real world entrepreneurial choice. The first-order conditions are

$$\frac{\partial \pi}{\partial x_1} = pf_1 - r_1 = 0$$

$$\frac{\partial \pi}{\partial x_2} = pf_2 - r_2 = 0$$

which can be written as

$$pf_1 = r_1 \text{ and } pf_2 = r_2$$

The partial derivatives of the production function with respect to the inputs are the marginal physical products f_i for each input. Multiplied by price, they provide the marginal revenue products, which are set equal to the input prices r_1 and r_2 at the profit maximum. This is the familiar condition that an input is used as long as its marginal revenue product exceeds or equals its cost to the producer, that is, the input price for each resource, r_i. However, the constraints that the quantities of additional potential inputs X_3 through X_n are still fixed at zero, guarantee this is a constrained optimum—because some potential entrepreneurial discovery has been assumed not to have occurred yet. The true or global optimum is inherently unknowable and can never be completely determined. Furthermore, the optimum changes whenever the technology changes the production function.

Second-order conditions for profit maximization require that the principal minors of the unbordered hessian matrix of second derivatives alternate in sign:

$$\begin{vmatrix} \dfrac{\partial^2 \pi}{\partial x_1^2} & \dfrac{\partial^2 \pi}{\partial x_1 \partial x_2} \\[2ex] \dfrac{\partial^2 \pi}{\partial x_2 \partial x_1} & \dfrac{\partial^2 \pi}{\partial x_2^2} \end{vmatrix} = p^2 \begin{vmatrix} f_{11} & f_{12} \\ f_{21} & f_{22} \end{vmatrix} > 0$$

and

$$\frac{\partial^2 \pi}{\partial x_1^2} = pf_{11} < 0 \quad \text{and} \quad \frac{\partial^2 \pi}{\partial x_2^2} = pf_{22} < 0$$

The full-rank conditions ensure that profit will always be decreasing with respect to further applications of both inputs simultaneously, while the second set of conditions ensure that profit will always be decreasing if the firm uses more of either input.

14.3.2 Limitations of Standard Profit Maximization

Because entrepreneurial search activity is ignored, important features of economizing action are disregarded and assumed away (Kirzner 1984b: 156). For example, one area for entrepreneurial action is to seek monopoly ownership of a resource. This broad category of human action includes both cornering the market for a particular input, and the creation of any form of intellectual property such as patents, trademarks, branding, or trade secrets. Schumpeter (1934: 152) discusses how temporary monopoly profits always accrue to innovators. Entrepreneurial planners follow such strategies all the time. Because maximization and minimization exercises always assume that input and output prices are fixed and given in advance, this kind of entrepreneurial strategy is necessarily ignored. Entrepreneurs should always desire to be monopolist resource owners because that allows them to charge a higher price for their output than non-monopolists can (Kirzner 1973: 21). Entrepreneurs also seek to increase the price of their output through becoming monopoly suppliers of the output, or monopolistic-competitive suppliers, for example, through creating intellectual property in their output, or through advertising, branding, and differentiating their output from competitiors' (Geroski & Mazzucato 2003). Recognizing that market structure is determined by the competitive process of the market is part of Makowski and Ostroy's (2001) reformulation of the Walrasian general equilibrium model of perfect competition (Walras 1874).

The selling price of output is always assumed to be given, thus the vector of prices is not permitted to adjust to allow a more efficient allocation of production. Producers are not permitted to experiment with adjusting the type of output they produce, which is also assumed to be given in advance. One obvious area for real world entrepreneurial innovation is offering different kinds of output for sale to consumers (Schumpeter 1934: 134-135). The role flexible prices and their experimental adjustments by entrepreneurial planners play in overcoming Hayek's (1949) problem of dispersed knowledge and coordinating the plans of producers and consumers is similarly ignored (Kirzner 1984a: 139-140). Kirzner notes that equilibrium prices, if they could persist, would signal market participants' plans to each other, and thus guide future planning. In contrast, dis-equilibrium prices signal to alert market participants how newly revised entrepreneurial plans may benefit market participants in the future (Kirzner 1963: 271). In Kirzner's view, dis-equilibrium prices predominate, thus entrepreneurial opportunities are everywhere. Entrepreneurial consumers and producers who take advantage of these dis-equilibrium prices move the market toward dynamic equilibria which generally can never be reached, and if they are reached, are not persistent.

14.3.3 An Expanded Profit Maximization Exercise

The profit maximization exercise could be expanded to realize a more global optimum, which would be represented by the n conditions

$$pf_1 = r_1, pf_2 = r_2, \dots , pf_n = r_n$$

but it should be emphasized that this optimum can never be reached in the real world. In reality, most of the n conditions for a global profit maximum are necessarily invalid. It is the ignorance of economic agents which always sets all but a few of the indefinite number of x_is equal to zero. We can never know all the potential inputs or technologies which could be used to produce a given output. Thus the realized profit maximum is always constrained, and thus can always be improved on by alert entrepreneurs. The optimal solution also assumes a fixed output price p and fixed input prices r_i, and the assumption of static production technology ensures the first and second derivatives (f_is and f_{ij}s) of the production function are also constant. None of these conditions is realistic, and they are only assumed to keep the profit maximization problem relatively simple. Some of the most trivial entrepreneurial activity can be described algebraically as removing the constraints on p, and the x_is, r_is, f_is, and f_{ij}s; however, this still fails to capture all potential entrepreneurial action, as entrepreneurial planners also seek through choice, awareness, and discovery to produce those outputs which will yield the highest profits.

14.4 The Entrepreneurial Consumer

We do not generally think of entrepreneurship as taking place outside firms or outside of the supply side of the economy. However, given Mises' definition, "acting man exclusively seen from the aspect of the uncertainty inherent in every action (Mises 1949: 253)," it is clear the consumer can be an entrepreneur in the act of consumption. In the neoclassical theory of the consumer, consumers maximize an unknown and unobservable algebraic utility function, which must be specified in a finite number of arguments, subject to a budget constraint. In a formal sense, an entrepreneurial consumer would always be (a) experimentally trying out new consumer goods and services, which become new arguments in the utility function, as well as (b) trying out new ways of extracting additional utility from the old arguments representing the goods and services the consumer already uses. For example, entrepreneurial consumers would experiment with new preference functions in an effort to shift their indifference curves inward. The neoclassical conception ignores both kinds of entrepreneurial consumption, by assuming they have been carried out in advance. The algebraic functions used in setting up the utility maximization problem result from market process and the entrepreneurial planning of the consumer, which is assumed to be final, complete, and unchangeable before the consumer makes any choices of what goods or quantities to buy.

To account for the possibility of entrepreneurial consumption, the number of arguments in the utility function and budget constraint must also be made indefinite, as with the cost and profit functions. In addition, the entrepreneurial consumer would always be trying to increase their income, as well as searching for lower prices and for new and higher quality goods and services to buy and consume. Entrepreneurial consumers are alert to improving (a) the number of utility function arguments, (b) the algebraic form of the utility function, (c) consumer income, (d) the prices of consumed goods, and (e) the quality of consumed goods. More fundamentally, the utility maximization problem ignores entrepreneurial consumers' alertness to these opportunities to costlessly improve the satisfaction of their wants.

14.4.1 Conventional Utility Maximization

Kirzner (1973: 18) notes the convention of treating consumers as merely passive price-takers is only an analytical convenience. The consumer's optimization problem is usually defined as maximizing a preference or utility function subject to a budget constraint. In the two-good case the budget constraint is

$$y^0 = p_1 q_1 + p_2 q_2$$

where y^0 is the consumer's income, which is assumed to be fixed in advance, and p_1 and p_2 are the prices of the two consumer products Q_1 and Q_2 respectively. Thus unreality is introduced by arbitrarily setting the quantities of any potential other consumer goods or services Q_3 through Q_n at zero. Entrepreneurial alertness which consumers might exercise through discovering additional products is assumed away and ignored. The vector of prices facing the entrepreneurial consumer is also assumed to be given. Thus any entrepreneurial activity, bargaining, or negotiation which aims at improving the vector of prices from the consumer's perspective is also ignored. The consumer seeks to maximize the subjective, unobservable, ordinal utility function[61]

---

61 Jevons (1871) originated the utility function as a cardinal measure, but it is now understood that utility can only be ordinally. That is, we recognize that we prefer good A to B and B to C, and thus must prefer A to C—an ordinal measure, but it is not meaningful to claim that a person prefers good A 20% more than good B, and prefers B 30% more than C, etc. These imply a cardinal utility measure, but it turns out to be unworkable. People's preferences just do not work like that.

$$U = f(q_1, q_2)^{62}$$

where q_1 and q_2 are the quantities of the two consumer goods Q_1 and Q_2 the consumer consumes, subject to the budget constraint (Debreu 1959: 55-58, Silberberg 1978: 214-233, Henderson & Quandt 1980: 8-18, Chiang 1984: 400, Varian 1984: 113-115, Takayama 1985: 179-183.)

Because the utility function is assumed to be fixed, no scope is allowed for the entrepreneurial consumer to extract additional utility or well-being from equal amounts of the same consumption goods. However, imagine a household budgeting for a fixed amount of consumption goods with prices which are fixed over a period of time. A household which experimented with new food recipes could enjoy higher well-being by discovering they prefer certain recipes, or even by discovering recipes they dislike and avoiding them. This new knowledge would shift the utility function closer to the origin. The optimization problem ignores this possibility of entrepreneurship in consumption, by assuming it has occurred in advance and that the utility function we assume has resulted from a process of optimizing discovery which has been carried out to its final solution. Entrepreneurial consumers would also seek to negotiate lower prices for consumer goods, and higher household incomes (Rothbard 1962: 183-200). This entrepreneurial behavior is all ignored by convention. Conventionally, the Lagrangian function to be maximized is

---

62 One of the most commonly used functional forms is the Cobb-Douglas utility function, $Ut = Aq_{1t}{}^a \, q_{2t}{}^b$. Varian (1984: 128-130) discusses some alternatives functional forms, including constant-elasticity-of-substitution utility. Because the utility function is an ordinal rather than a cardinal function, it is often modeled without specifying any explicit algebraic function.

$$V = f(q_1, q_2) + \lambda(y^0 - p_1q_1 - p_2q_2)$$

where λ is the as yet undetermined Lagrange multiplier. First-order conditions for an optimum are obtained by setting the first partial derivatives with respect to q_1, q_2, and λ equal to zero:

$$\frac{\partial V}{\partial q_1} = f_1 - \lambda p_1 = 0$$

$$\frac{\partial V}{\partial q_2} = f_2 - \lambda p_2 = 0$$

$$\frac{\partial V}{\partial \lambda} = y^0 - p_1q_1 - p_2q_2 = 0$$

Transposing the second terms in the first two equations and dividing yields the condition that the marginal utilities of the two consumption goods must be equal to the ratio of their prices to maximize utility,

$$\frac{f_1}{f_2} = \frac{p_1}{p_2}$$

The ratio of the first partial derivatives of the utility function, f_1/f_2 is the rate of commodity substitution or marginal rate of substitution between consumption goods Q_1 and Q_2. The first-order condition for a maximum expresses the equality between the rate of commodity substitution and the price ratio. The first two equations can also be written as,

$$\frac{f_1}{p_1} = \frac{f_2}{p_2} = \lambda.$$

The first-order conditions are necessary but not sufficient for a maximum. The optimum must occur at a local convexity to be a maximum. The second order condition for a local maximum is that the bordered Hessian matrix of second derivatives must be positive definite:

$$\begin{vmatrix} f_{11} & f_{12} & -p_1 \\ f_{21} & f_{22} & -p_2 \\ -p_1 & -p_2 & 0 \end{vmatrix} > 0$$

The second-order condition for a maximum is satisfied by the assumption that the utility function is regular strict quasi-concave, which also guarantees a global maximum.

14.3.2 Limitations of Utility Maximization

Hayek notes the dispersal of knowledge as an economic problem, "a problem of the utilization of knowledge which is not given to anyone in its totality (Hayek 1945: 520)." Dispersed knowledge provides one opportunity for entrepreneurial innovation and arbitrage. Entrepreneurial planners seek out, or at least remain alert to, the dispersed character of this knowledge, hoping to profit through offering information to those who can benefit from it, but do not yet possess it. Thus, entrepreneurs act to further spread specialized knowledge. This kind of entrepreneurial activity overcomes dis-equilibria based on information asymmetries, by acting to move the market toward equilibrium and symmetric information. This equilibrium can never be fully and finally realized, furthermore, in the act of overcoming asymmetric information dis-equilibria, entrepreneurs may also upset some of the entrepreneurial plans of others. This prevents or lessens the coordination of individual plans at least in the short run, and ensures a new dis-equilibrium state even as it enables the market to move toward a better equilibrium in the longer run. This interpretation of the entrepreneurial innovation leaves room for both Schumpeter's and Kirzner's views of the entrepreneur. Entrepreneurs profit from removing information imbalances and bringing about a movement toward informational equilibrium, where everyone enjoys equal, and more complete, information (Kirzner 1963: 271, Kirzner 1973: 66-67, Horwitz 2000: 29).

14.5 Market Coordination & Equilibrium: Schumpeter's & Kirzner's Views

Kirzner and Schumpeter give competing views of the role of the entrepreneur. For Schumpeter the entrepreneur seeks to shift the production function and cost function (Triffin 1940: 168, Schumpeter 1962: 104-105, 132). For Kirzner the role of the entrepreneur consists of noticing that the cost and revenue functions have already shifted or are in the process of changing: "entrepreneurship for me is not so much the introduction of new products or of new techniques of production as the ability to *see* where new products have become unexpectedly valuable to consumers and where new methods of production have, unknown to others, become feasible (Kirzner 1973: 81)."

Kirzner and Schumpeter offer diametrically opposed views of the role of the entrepreneur in relation to market equilibria (Kerber 1994). Schumpeterian entrepreneurs destroy equilibria (Schumpeter 1934: 64), whereas Kirznerian entrepreneurs effect adjustment toward new equilibria (Kirzner 1973: 72-73). Although a new attempt at reconciling these competing views risks oversimplifying them, it seems hopeful to suggest the two views of the entrepreneurial function arise from differing concepts of the underlying reference equilibrium. In Schumpeter's scheme, the hypothesized equilibrium is associated with the ideal but unrealistic state of an evenly rotating economy. This hypothetical reference equilibrium is never reached in reality because innovative actions of entrepreneurial planners prevent the economy from ever settling in an evenly rotating state. Schumpeter defines entrepreneurial action with reference to a hypothetical pre-existing equilibrium which could never actually be reached or realized; the hypothesized equilibrium is presumed to be the starting point for the creative destruction of entrepreneurial innovation. It is this hypothetical non-existent prior equilibrium which entrepreneurs compete to improve on and which provides alert entrepreneurs with potential profit opportunities to exploit and capture.

Kirzner views entrepreneurship as moving the market toward a hypothesized equilibrium where entrepreneurial plans are more fully coordinated than before. This equilibrium is also never final but can be seen as the goal of the entrepreneurial action after the fact; Kirzner's equilibrium is moved toward the hypothetical equilibrium state after the entrepreneurial action. In Kirzner's view the purported "final" equilibrium is the goal of entrepreneurial action, but this is a goal that is never reached and never really final. Schumpeterian entrepreneurs create new information asymmetries. The actual dispersion of the asymmetric information created by Schumpeterian entrepreneurs lessens the level of mutual coordination among existing entrepreneurial plans which are already in the process of being carried out. Kirznerian entrepreneurs exercise alertness to discover already-existing information asymmetries. The Schumpeterian and Kirznerian entrepreneur may well be two different persons, but can equally well be the same person. Kirznerian entrepreneurs exploit information asymmetries to earn entrepreneurial profits.

Imagine an initial state of affairs, where information is dispersed, but market participants, ignorant of their own ignorance, are unaware of the asymmetric character of the information they possess. In this context, are market prices equilibrium prices? *Not in the Schumpeterian sense, but certainly in the Kirznerian sense.* A Kirznerian entrepreneur can exploit this opportunity by brokering information about resource and product prices, but only after they discover and become aware of the information asymmetries. For example, the entrepreneur would need to observe diverging prices before they could perceive the opportunity for arbitrage. Then the extent of the entrepreneur's success eliminates the information asymmetry, eventually eliminating the entrepreneurial profit opportunity.

In Kirzner's view, prices remain in a presumed equilibrium until entrepreneurial alertness discovers information dispersal and asymmetry, and an entrepreneurial planner acts to take advantage of the arbitrage opportunity presented by this discovery, which subsequently forces prices to adjust and removes the information asymmetry and the opportunity for further arbitrage (Kirzner 1963: 44-46). Price adjustments affected by Kirznerian entrepreneurs act to reestablish a new equilibrium where entrepreneurial plans will be better coordinated and consumer wants can be better satisfied (Kirzner 1984b: 160).[63] A Schumpeterian entrepreneur exploits the asymmetric information in such a way that they might benefit if they can extend or maintain the dispersal of knowledge. The Schumpeterian entrepreneur disturbs and destroys the old equilibrium; the Kirznerian entrepreneur moves the market toward a new one (Kerber 1994). Kirznerian entrepreneurs avoid risk and cost (Blaug 1998: 223) because they move the market toward a new equilibrium which could only exist hypothetically after the innovative entrepreneurial action. Schumpeterian entrepreneurs introduce disruptive innovations and move the market away from the pre-established, though equally hypothetical equilibrium which is destroyed, or at least left behind, by the innovative action of the alert entrepreneur. The Schumpeterian entrepreneur may succeed at moving the market out of equilibrium, or at least away from a hypothesized equilibrium state; the Kirznerian entrepreneur can never really succeed in establishing a new equilibrium.

---

63 Kirzner defines market equilibrium as a static condition which can only be arrived at by removal of all unexploited profit opportunities. Given this definition, market prices are never equilibrium prices because there are presumably always profit opportunities which are both unknown, unsuspected, and therefore unexploited. It is certainly an epistemological impossibility to assert that there can be no remaining unexploited profit opportunities, as no one would ever be in a position to make such a claim. In this discussion, the situation considered is the discovery and exploitation of a hypothetical and discrete item of information which would theoretically constitute an entrepreneurial opportunity for the first person to (a) discover it, and (b) decide to act on this newly discovered information which they are the first to possess. Kirzner might not agree with the formulation used here that the market is actually in equilibrium until some agent discovers the previously unknown information. He would agree that as agents exploit new profit opportunities, the market moves toward a new equilibrium which may never actually be reached.

14.6 Conclusion: Optimization v. Market Process

Entrepreneurship is not amenable to limits imposed by any rigid mathematical formalism. Entrepreneurial planners can always be counted on to break out of any rigid ideological blinders which seek to circumscribe the limits of their potential innovations. This is partly due to the facts that (a) the concept of entrepreneurship remains poorly understood, (b) several alternative concepts, for example, Schumpeterian as opposed to Kirznerian entrepreneurship, compete for dominance, (c) these differing concepts are often used interchangeably, and most importantly, (d) entrepreneurs are so innovative their behavior often defies simple categorization.

The neoclassical optimization problem used to model firm and consumer behavior, and which underlies equilibrium comparative static analysis largely ignores entrepreneurial activity. Thus it ignores much of what is most interesting about economic behavior. Although some kinds of innovative entrepreneurial behavior can be described within the context of an optimization problem, many cannot. For example, production technology, created through certain kinds of entrepreneurial discovery, and implemented through other kinds, is always taken as given by economics for analytical convenience. The nature of entrepreneurial planning is treated as being beyond the scope of the economics discipline because it does not result from maximization or minimization. Entrepreneurial discovery results from something other than optimization because entrepreneurs act to remove the constraints on formal optimization problems which are an essential part of how the structure and context of firm and consumer economizing behavior are framed. There is no global optimum to an entrepreneurial planner, only various binding constraints which eventually fall before the onslaught of the human action of inquisitive, profit-seeking entrepreneurs.

In the long run, successful entrepreneurial planners always move the market from a less optimal to a more optimal state of affairs by removing constraints imposed by ignorance and uncertainty.[64] However, in the optimization problem, agents are modeled as purposely optimizing with respect to objective and constraint functions which are unrealistically represented as being predetermined and known perfectly in advance. In reality, entrepreneurial planners' understanding of these algebraic functions may be imperfect or uncertain, resulting in imperfectly implemented human action on which Kirznerian entrepreneurs can always improve. Naturally entrepreneurs profit from providing this service and offering the benefits to others.

It may also happen that Schumpeterian entrepreneurs can enter the scene and change the objective and constraint functions. This particular kind of human action automatically creates new opportunities for further Kirznerian entrepreneurship, as the other entrepreneurial planners may not immediately be aware that their objective and constraint functions have changed. Human action which is initially imperfect is driven even further off the mark by changing the algebraic functions the entrepreneurial planners initially assumed when they made their production and consumption plans, or were analytically modeled as having assumed.

---

64 This is not a normative statement but merely asserts that when entrepreneurs are successful, they improve resource allocation and better satisfy previously unmet consumer wants. Improving allocation and satisfying unmet wants allows them to collect entrepreneurial profits in exchange for improving the welfare and utility of consumers. The benefits they provide to others must be greater than the share they are able to capture for themselves.

CHAPTER 15

Conclusion

Although market process was well established early on in the economics literature, significantly predating Adam Smith, over time the process of how markets work came to be increasingly overlooked, deemphasized, and ignored. As discussed in Part One, in many ways market process is implicit in the mainstream economics of the last quarter millennium—it has come to be taken for granted. Eventually this most fundamental economic theory of market exchange being driven and directed by entrepreneurial innovation came to be explicitly supplanted in the mainstream economics literature by more mundane and deterministic comparative statics and general equilibrium approaches.

As we have seen, the actions of the entrepreneur are central to market process, which is driven by entrepreneurial alertness, innovation, and experimentation. Entrepreneurial innovation is always forward-looking, always experimental, and always speculative—and has to be applied in the face of an unknown and uncertain future which unfolds before us in the fullness of time, and where any entrepreneurial innovation or decision is inherently risky and potentially subject to failure. However, entrepreneurs would not have too much to gain from merely examining past market conditions with a view to speculating on how they might have been better implemented, or otherwise have been more fully exploited. Such an analysis can inform entrepreneurs about how they can improve on past production decisions and better market the introduction of alternative and new goods and services. The more interesting and pressing problem facing entrepreneurial planners is to successfully introduce new products and techniques in the face of prevailing or emerging market conditions in order to improve on the satisfaction of consumer wants today and in the near future. Entrepreneurs can accomplish this, for example, through introducing new goods and services, suggesting new uses for old goods and services, or employing new ways of marketing or combining goods and services.

Entrepreneurial planning is central to the definition of market competition, going far beyond the conventional and familiar static equilibrium models of mainstream economics. Standard approaches to modeling and describing competitive markets emphasize a final market outcome which satisfies arbitrary formal requirements. In sharp contrast, market process economics focuses on the entrepreneurial management of business enterprises in the face of market dis-equilibria which change and evolve over time. The market process approach represents a major conceptual departure away from mainstream neoclassical formalism and toward greater realism. Perhaps the central feature of market competition which is often lost is that in a competitive market, entrepreneurs compete with one another to offer better ways to coordinate the forward-looking plans of consumers and other producers. Successful entrepreneurial innovations may create short run disruptions, but always lead to a higher level of cooperation among producers and consumers, and a greater degree of mutual coordination among the entrepreneurial plans of others.

This book has introduced the reader to market process, and applied market process theory to explaining how entrepreneurs contribute to and arrive at market outcomes, such as the prices goods and services are sold for, the quantities of output produced, and how market organization emerges. Markets are driven by competitive entrepreneurs to self-organize as perfectly-competitive, monopolistic-competitive, oligopoly, or monopoly markets, and it is the interaction and feedback among competing entrepreneurs which determines which kind of market develops. Market process theory has also been used to explain the progress of an economic expansion through the interdependent mutual coordination of entrepreneurial plans. As we have seen, the degree of complexity and mutual interdependency among these entrepreneurial plans can become unsustainable, which ultimately leads to recessions. Finally, market process theory has been used to illuminate various shortcomings of socialist economic planning.

This book has introduced the reader to market process economics and discussed how the expanding understanding of market process contributed to the progress of the history of economic thought. We examined the manner in which market process thinking and approaches came to be largely displaced and superseded by the general equilibrium and comparative statics models of a competitive market equilibrium which ultimately came to dominate mainstream economics. At the same time we developed numerous arguments in favor of the superior explanatory advantages of the market process approach to economic phenomena.

The book necessarily begins with a general introduction to what is meant by market process. This necessitated exploring some of the differences between viewing market interaction as a process and viewing it as an equilibrium outcome. We also explored some of the relevant history of economic thought and discussed how the formal equilibrium view came to dominate mainstream economics. We also developed some of the implications imposed by the inability of the economics profession to address market process phenomena, particularly entrepreneurial innovation. The role of the entrepreneurial planner comes to be seen as being central to driving markets to operate the way they do, and reach the favorable outcomes they are able to attain. We also speculated on some areas for needed future research on market process and suggested how market process concepts might eventually regain the primacy they once held in microeconomics and price theory. The role of entrepreneurs is central to market process and has been emphasized throughout the book. Through the prism of market process theory, we can understand entrepreneurship not so much as a mysterious activity undertaken by a special class of market innovators, as much as a routine and omnipresent process of innovation and risk taking.

We also employed market process theory as a framework to explain how different forms of market organization arise naturally through the interaction among different entrepreneurial planners. These forms of market organization are perfect competition, monopolistic competition, oligopoly, and monopoly. Market organization is thus something which emerges as the result of market process and the actions and interactions of entrepreneurial planners. In other words, market organization is determined by the feedback among entrepreneurial planners. The way entrepreneurs respond to the various dis-equilibrating and re-equilibrating innovations introduced by other entrepreneurs turns out to play a major role in determining which kind of market organization develops. Entrepreneurs compete with one another to organize higher and more sophisticated levels of coordination of production in society, and to make possible higher levels of mutual coordination among the plans of other entrepreneurs, including those of entrepreneurial consumers. Although some of the strategies employed by entrepreneurs are due to technological constraints, the interplay and interaction among their strategic responses results in the precise form of market organization which emerges—perfect competition, monopolistic competition, oligopoly, or monopoly.

Entrepreneurial planners innovate and design firms and other business enterprises. Entrepreneurial innovation may include the introduction of new products, technologies, or even whole new industries, but may also be as simple as only experimentally setting a higher or lower price for an existing product, or a minor modification to an existing product. In addition to introducing changes in competitive markets, entrepreneurial planners also have to respond to the innovations introduced by other entrepreneurs.

As entrepreneurs compete for profits and seek competitive advantages over other entrepreneurs, the introduction of many innovative products, practices, and techniques by entrepreneurial planners temporarily moves the market farther away from an idealized condition of mutual plan coordination. Nevertheless, the most important task and most socially valuable function of entrepreneurial planners is to make possible a higher level of mutual coordination among the planned consumption and production activities of all the other people in the economy. Although disruptive innovation can reduce the level of mutual plan coordination in the short run (Lewin 1997), this always results in higher long run welfare and greater coordination among the entrepreneurial plans of others. Entrepreneurs profit to the extent they contribute to improving this mutual, long run plan coordination (Kirzner 1996: 39-41).

We developed a market process account of the business cycle. This started by first examining how entrepreneurial planning and market process normally contribute to the sustainable coordination of the economy's complex arrays of flexible and interdependent entrepreneurial plans which coordinate productive activities over time to satisfy consumer wants while still accommodating entrepreneurial experimentation. Experimentation generally leads to improved plan coordination over time, higher levels of production, lower costs, and the introduction of new products. However, under expansionary government policy, entrepreneurs are driven to construct an expanded network of production plans which become increasingly fragile, resulting in numerous and widespread plan rigidities which then limit the sustainability of the market's ability to keep bringing plans into mutual coordination. This market process account of the business cycle provides Austrian business cycle theory with more explicit microeconomic foundations. We also demonstrated how the business cycle, which is often presented rhetorically as a fatal shortcoming of a free market economy, actually results from the socialization of money and credit media, financial risk, leverage, and public debt. As a result, the market process account of the business cycle offers more of a critique of socialism than of capitalism.

Entrepreneurial planners compete against each other to improve mutual plan coordination, but their ability to do so depends crucially on market-determined interest rates, which are necessary to coordinate saving and investment over time. Financial markets provide the financial capital necessary to fund business expansion and extend entrepreneurial plans, rationing these funds in accordance with the rate of interest. The interest rate needs to reflect the actual time preference of people in the economy for the entrepreneurial plans funded by borrowing to actually be sustainable and capable of being brought to completion and mutual coordination with the plans of others. Real people decide how much of their income to save and consume based on the relationship between the market interest rate and their own time preferences. Expansion of the money supply results in unsustainable investment and the parallel inability of entrepreneurial plans which are misaligned with the time preferences of people in the economy to either remain in mutual coordination, or even be brought to successful completion. When further economic expansion becomes unsustainable, the discoordination and mutual incompatibility of entrepreneurial plans formulated and entered into during the environment of artificially low interest rates triggers a recession. We also examined a critique of Keynesian stabilization policy and the most popular public policy responses to recession.

Finally, we presented a market process analysis of the shortcomings of socialism and central economic planning. Socialists have argued that economic activity, including the production and distribution of goods, should be centrally planned according to scientific principles. Socialist planning is supposed to offer benefits in terms of a more equitable distribution of wealth, and to ensure that more wealth will be generated by ensuring that production will necessarily be planned in a more efficient, less wasteful manner; for example, through dispensing with wasteful competition. The promise of socialism was to rid the free enterprise economy of inefficiencies by eliminating such wasteful features as duplication of effort by competing producers, unnecessary product differentiation, etc., under the direction of a benign and beneficent central planner or other democratically chosen authority. This would allow for the substitution of the enlightened guidance of a public-spirited, class conscious central economic planner for the wastefully profit-motivated entrepreneurial planning of competitive capitalism. However, the central economic planner will always be remote from the preferences and aspirations of the actual consumers who provide entrepreneurial planners the market discipline of profit and loss, and central planners are equally remote from this market discipline which contributes to strengthening the efficiency of the market economy. Market competition, which provides winners and losers, is just a different side of the market coordination provided by free enterprise, which only provides winners. It is entirely mistaken to consider free competition as anything but a mutually beneficial process which delivers substantial and ever increasing benefits to all participants. Information theory also contributes to the critique of socialism, because socialism and central economic planning imposes a much higher information burden on the central planner than market competition has to, or can be borne by any individual entrepreneurial planner in a market economy.

We contrasted the central economic planning of socialism with the decentralized and competing, but mutually coordinated entrepreneurial plans directing production in a market economy. Entrepreneurial planners introduce innovations which may disrupt the existing plan mutual coordination in the short run, but in the long run improve mutual plan coordination, as consumers and competing producers eventually learn to adapt to and exploit innovations which were originally disruptive. This enables them to permanently better satisfy their own wants, improve production at lowered costs, and earn higher profits. A further shortcoming of socialism is its utter disregard for consumer sovereignty. Central planning ignores consumer preferences and is, at best, far less responsive to changes in preferences as consumer tastes change and evolve over time. Clearly this is a major shortcoming and disadvantage since consumer preferences change all the time. Central economic planning assumes some static and idealized preferences as a given, and does not seek to address either the actual preferences of real consumers, or the way these evolve from moment to moment. We also introduced some insights from information theory and applied them to problems of central economic planning.

References

Anstis, Ralph (1997) *Man of Iron, Man of Steel: Lives of David and Robert Mushet.* London: Albion House.

Aquinas, St. Thomas (1947) *Summa Theologica.* 5 vols. New York: Benziger Brothers.

Armentano, Dominick T. (1990) *Antitrust and Monopoly.* 2nd ed. Oakland, California: Independent Institute.

Armentano, Dominick T. (2007) *Antitrust: the Case for Repeal.* 2nd ed. Auburn: Ludwig von Mises Institute.

Arrow, Kenneth J. (1950) A Difficulty in the Concept of Social Welfare. *Journal of Political Economy* 58(4): 328-346.

Arrow, Kenneth J. (1959) Toward a Theory of Price Adjustment. In: Abramowitz, Moses (ed.) *The Allocation of Economic Resources: Essays in Honor of Bernard Francis Haley.* Stanford: Stanford University Press.

Arrow, Kenneth J. (1994) Methodological Individualism and Social Knowledge. *American Economic Review* 84(2): Papers and Proceedings, 1-9.

Arrow, Kenneth J.; & Debreu, Gérard (1954) Existence of an Equilibrium for a Competitive Economy. *Econometrica* 22(3): 265-290.

Atkinson, R.J.; Winkworth, W.J.; & Norris. G.M. (1962) *Behaviour of Skin Fatigue Cracks at the Corners of Windows in a Comet I Fuselage.* London: UK Ministry of Aviation.

Bessemer, (Sir) Henry (1905) *Sir Henry Bessemer, F.R.S.: an Autobiography.* London: Engineering Ltd.

Binner, J.M.; Tino, P.; Tepper, J.; Anderson, R.; Jones, B.; & Kendall, G. (2010) Does Money Matter in Inflation Forecasting? *Physica A: Statistical Mechanics and its Applications* 389(21): 4793-4808.

Bischoff, Charles W. (1969) Hypothesis Testing and the Demand for Capital Goods. *Review of Economics & Statistics* 51(3): 354-368.

Blaug, Mark (1998) Entrepreneurship in the History of Economic Thought. *Advances in Austrian Economics* 5: 217-239. Stamford, Connecticut: JAI Press.

Boettke, Peter J. (1998) Economic Calculation: the Austrian Contribution to Political Economy. *Advances in Austrian Economics* 5: 131-158. Stamford, Connecticut: JAI Press.

Boettke, Peter J. (ed.) (2000) *Socialism and the Market: the Socialist Calculation Debate Revisited.* London: Routledge. 9 vols.

Boettke, Peter J. (2012) *Living Economics*. Oakland, California: Independent Institute & Francisco Marroquin University.

Bonsall, Thomas E. (2002) *Disaster in Dearborn: the Story of the Edsel*. Stanford: Stanford University Press.

Bordo, Michael David (1983) Some Aspects of the Monetary Economics of Richard Cantillon. *Journal of Monetary Economics* 12(2): 235-258.

Brillouin, Léon (1956) *Science and Information Theory*. New York: Academic Press.

Buchanan, James M. (1969) *Cost and Choice: an Inquiry in Economic Theory*. Chicago: Markham.

Buchanan, James M. (1986) Order Defined in the Process of its Emergence. In: *Liberty, Market and State: Political Economy in the 1980s* (pp. 73-74) New York: New York University Press.

Butos, William N.; & Koppl, Roger G. (2006) Does *The Sensory Order*. *Advances in Austrian Economics* 9: 19-50. London: Emerald.

Cannan, Edwin (1888) *Elementary Political Economy*. London: H. Frowde.

Cannan, Edwin (1932) Review of Robbins (1932). *Economic Journal* 42: 424-427.

Cantillon, Richard (1755) *An Essay on Economic Theory*. English translation of the *Essai sur la Nature du Commerce en Général*. Saucier, Chantal (trans.) Thornton, Mark (ed.) Auburn: Ludwig von Mises Institute, 2010.

Calandro, Joseph T. (2004) Reflexivity, Business Cycles and the New Economy. *Quarterly Journal of Austrian Economics* 7(3): 45-69.

Carilli, Anthony M.; & Dempster, Gregory M. (2001) Expectations in Austrian Business Cycle Theory: an Application of the Prisoner's Dilemma. *Review of Austrian Economics* 14(4): 319-330.

Casson, Mark (1982) *The Entrepreneur: an Economic Theory*. Oxford: Martin Robertson.

Casson, Mark (1987) *Entrepreneur. The New Palgrave: a Dictionary of Economics* 2: 151-153. London: Macmillan.

Casson, Mark (1995) *Entrepreneurship and Business Culture*. 2 vols. London: Edward Elgar.

Chamberlin, Edward H. (1933) *Theory of Monopolistic Competition*. Cambridge: Harvard University Press.

Chiang, Alpha C. (1984) *Fundamental Methods of Mathematical Economics* (3rd ed.) New York: McGraw-Hill.

Chiarella, C.; & Di Guilmi, Corrado (2011) The Financial Instability Hypothesis: a Stochastic Microfoundation Framework. *Journal of Economic Dynamics & Control* 35: 1151-1171.

Clark, John Bates (1899) *The Distribution of Wealth: a Theory of Wages, Interest and Profits.* New York: Macmillan.

Clark, John M. (1955) Competition: Static Models and Dynamic Aspects. *American Economic Review* 45(2): 450-462.

Clark, John M. (1960) *Competition as a Dynamic Process.* New York: Brookings Institution.

Clarke, Kevin A.; & Primo, David M. (2012) *A Model Discipline: Political Science and the Logic of Representations.* New York: Oxford University Press.

Coase, Ronald H. (1937) The Nature of the Firm. *Economica* 4(16): 386-405.

Cohen, Lionel Leonard, Baron Cohen (1955) *Report of the Court of Inquiry into the Accidents to the Comet Aircraft G-ALYP on 10 January 1954 and Comet G-ALYY on 8 April 1954* (The Cohen Report/Cohen Inquiry). London: UK Ministry of Transport and Civil Aviation.

Consumer Guide, Auto Editors of (1994) *Cars that Never Were.* Morton Grove, Illinois: Publications International Ltd.

Culbertson, J.M. (1957) The Term Structure of Interest Rates. *Quarterly Journal of Economics* 72: 489-504.

Daines, Robert (1994) *Edsel: the Motor Industry's Titanic.* London: Academy Books.

Davidson, P. (2008) Is the Current Financial Distress Caused by the Subprime Mortgage Crisis a Minsky Moment? Or is it the Result of Attempting to Securitize Illiquid Non-commercial Mortgage Loans? *Journal of Post-Keynesian Economics* 30(4): 669-676.

Debreu, Gérard (1959) *Theory of Value: an Axiomatic Analysis of Economic Equilibrium*. New Haven: Yale University Press.

Deutsch, Jan G. (1976) *Selling the People's Cadillac: the Edsel and Corporate Responsibility*. New Haven: Yale University Press.

Dicke, Tom (2010) The Edsel: Forty Years as a Symbol of Failure. *Journal of Popular Culture* 43(3): 486-502.

DiLorenzo, Thomas J. (1994) Industrial Organization and the Austrian School. In: Boettke, Peter J. (ed.) *The Elgar Companion to Austrian Economics* (pp. 382-388). Cheltenham UK: Edward Elgar.

Dos Santos, C.H. (2005) A Stock-flow Consistent General Framework for Formal Minskyan Analyses of Closed Economies. *Journal of Post-Keynesian Economics* 27(4): 11-35.

Dos Santos, C.H.; & Zezza, G. (2008) Simplified, 'Benchmark,' Stock-flow Consistent Post-Keynesian Growth Model. *Metroeconomica* 59(3): 441-478.

Edwards, Robert D.; Magee, John; & Bassetti, W.H.C. (1948 [2007]) *Technical Analysis of Stock Trends* (9th ed.) New York: American Management Association.

Fisher, Irving (1896) Appreciation and Interest. *Publications of the American Economic Association* (New York: Macmillan) 11: 23-29, 92-92.

Fisher, Lawrence (1959) Determinants of Risk Premiums on Corporate Bonds. *Journal of Political Economy* 78: 217-237.

Foss, Nicolai J. (1997) Austrian Insights and the Theory of the Firm. *Advances in Austrian Economics* 4: 175-198. Stamford, Connecticut: JAI Press.

Fossa, C. E.; Raines, R.A.; Gunsch, G.H.; & Temple, M.A. (1998). An Overview of the IRIDIUM Low Earth Orbit (LEO) Satellite System. *Proceedings of the IEEE 1998 National Aerospace and Electronics Conference.* NAECON 1998: 152-159.

Foster, Patrick (2008) *Studebaker: the Complete History.* Minneapolis: Motorbooks.

Friedman, Milton (1968) The Role of Monetary Policy. *American Economic Review* 58(1): 1-17.

Geroski, P.; & Mazzucato, Mariana (2003) Advertising and the Evolution of Market Structure in the US Car Industry. In: Waterson, M. (ed.) *Competition, Monopoly and Corporate Governance.* Northampton, Massachusetts: Edward Elgar.

Garrison, Roger W. (1985) Intertemporal Coordination and the Invisible Hand: an Austrian Perspective on the Keynesian Vision. *History of Political Economy* 17: 309-321.

Garrison, Roger W. (1989) The Austrian Theory of the Business Cycle in the Light of Modern Macroeconomics. *Review of Austrian Economics* 3: 3-29.

Garrison, Roger W. (2000) *Time and Money: the Macroeconomics of Capital Structure*. New York & London: Routledge.

Greaves, Percy L. (1974) *Mises Made Easier.* Dobbs Ferry, New York: Free Market Books.

Harper, David A. (1998) Institutional Conditions for Entrepreneurship. *Advances in Austrian Economics* 5: 241-275. Stamford, Connecticut: JAI Press.

Harrod, (Sir) Roy F. (1938) Scope and Method in Economics. *Economic Journal* 48: 383-412.

Hayek, Friedrich A. (1931) *Prices and Production.* (1st ed.)

Hayek, Friedrich A. (1933) *Monetary Theory and the Trade Cycle.* Reprinted (1966) New York: Augustus M. Kelley.

Hayek, Friedrich A. (1935) *Prices and Production.* (2nd ed.) Reprinted (1967) New York: Augustus M. Kelley.

Hayek, Friedrich A. (1937) Economics and Knowledge. *Economica* 4: 33-54

Hayek, Friedrich A. (1939) *Profits, Interest, and Investment, and Other Essays on the Theory of Industrial Fluctuations.* Reprinted (1969) New York: Augustus M. Kelley.

Hayek, Friedrich A. (1941) *The Pure Theory of Capital.* Chicago: University of Chicago Press.

Hayek, Friedrich A. (1945) The Use of Knowledge in Society. *American Economic Review* 35(4): 519-530.

Hayek, Friedrich A. (1946) The Meaning of Competition. In: *Individualism and Economic Order* (pp. 92-106). Chicago: University of Chicago Press.

Hayek, Friedrich A. (1952) *The Counter-revolution of Science: Studies on the Abuse of Reason.* Glencoe, Illinois: The Free Press. Reprinted (1979) Indianapolis: Liberty Press.

Hayek, Friedrich A. (1967) *Studies in Philosophy, Politics, and Economics.* Chicago: University of Chicago Press.

Hayek, Friedrich A. (1973) *Law, Legislation, and Liberty,* Volume 1, *Rules and Order.* Chicago: University of Chicago Press.

Hayek, Friedrich A. (1978a) *Law, Legislation, and Liberty,* Volume 2, *The Mirage of Social Justice.* Chicago: University of Chicago Press.

Hayek, Friedrich A. (1978b) *New Studies in Philosophy, Politics, Economics, and the History of Ideas*. Chicago: University of Chicago Press.

Henderson, James M.; & Quandt, Richard E. (1980) *Microeconomic Theory: a Mathematical Approach* (3rd ed.) New York: McGraw-Hill.

Hendry, Maurice M. (1972) Studebaker: One Can do a Lot of Remembering in South Bend. *Automobile Quarterly* 10(3): 228-275.

Herbener, Jeffrey M. (1992) The Fallacy of the Phillips Curve. In: Skousen, Mark A. (ed.) *Dissent on Keynes: a Critical Appraisal of Keynesian Economics* (pp. 51-71). New York: Praeger.

Herbener, Jeffrey M. (ed.) (2011) *The Pure Time-Preference Theory of Interest*. Auburn: Ludwig von Mises Institute.

Hicks, (Sir) John R. (1946) *Value and Capital* (2nd ed.) London: Oxford University Press.

Holcombe, Randall G. (1998) Entrepreneurship and Economic Growth. *Quarterly Journal of Austrian Economics* 1(2): 45-62.

Horwitz, Steven (2000) *Microfoundations and Macroeconomics: an Austrian Perspective*. London & New York: Routledge.

Hülsmann, J. Guido (2001) Garrisonian Macroeconomics. *Quarterly Journal of Austrian Economics* 4(3): 33-42.

Ikeda, Sanford (1998) Interventionism and the Progressive Disco-ordination of the Mixed Economy. *Advances in Austrian Economics* 5: 37-50. Stamford, Connecticut: JAI Press.

Ikeda, Sanford (1994) Market Process. In: Boettke, Peter J. (ed.) *The Elgar Companion to Austrian Economics* (pp. 23-29). Cheltenham UK: Edward Elgar.

Ionnides, Stavros (1992) *The Market, Competition and Democracy: a Critique of Neo-Austrian Economics*. London & New York: Routledge.

Jevons, William Stanley (1871) *The Theory of Political Economy*. Reprinted (5th ed.) New York: Augustus M. Kelly.

Kemper, Steve (2003) *Reinventing the Wheel: a Story of Genius, Innovation, and Grand Ambition*. New York: Harper Collins.

Keen, Steve (2001) Finance and Economic Breakdown: Modeling Minsky's Financial Instability Hypothesis. *Journal of Post-Keynesian Economics* 17(4): 607-635.

Keen, Steve (2013) A Monetary Minsky Model of the Great Moderation and the Great Recession. *Journal of Economic Behavior & Organization* 86: 221-235.

Kerber, Wolfgang (1994) German Market Process Theory. In: Boettke, Peter J. (ed.) *The Elgar Companion to Austrian Economics* (pp. 500-507). Cheltenham UK: Edward Elgar.

Keynes, John Maynard (1919) *Economic Consequences of the Peace*. London: Macmillan.

Keynes, John Maynard (1921) *Treatise on Probability*. London: Macmillan.

Keynes, John Maynard (1930) *Treatise on Money.* 2 vols. London: Macmillan.

Keynes, John Maynard (1936) *The General Theory of Employment, Interest, and Money.* London: Macmillan.

Kirzner, Israel M. (1963) *Market Theory and the Price System.* New York: Van Nostrand. Reprinted (2011) Indianapolis: Liberty Fund.

Kirzner, Israel M. (1973) *Competition and Entrepreneurship.* Chicago: University of Chicago Press.

Kirzner, Israel M. (1978) The Entrepreneurial Role in Menger's System. *Atlantic Economic Review* 6(4): 31-45. Reprinted (2015) in: Boettke, Peter J.; Sautet, Frédéric (eds.) *Austrian Subjectivism and the Emergence of Entrepreneurship Theory.* (pp. 151-174) Indianapolis: Liberty Fund.

Kirzner, Israel M. (1979) *Perception, Opportunity, and Profit.* Chicago: University of Chicago Press.

Kirzner, Israel M. (1984a) Prices, the Communication of Knowledge, and the Discovery Process. In: Leube, K.R.; & Zlabinger, A.H. (eds.)

The Political Economy of Freedom: Essays in Honor of F.A. Hayek. Amsterdam: Philosophia Verlag. Reprinted (1992) in: Kirzner, *The Meaning of Market Process.* (pp. 139-151) London: Routledge.

Kirzner, Israel M. (1984b) Economic Planning and the Knowledge Problem. *Cato Journal* 4(2). Reprinted (1992) in: Kirzner, *The Meaning of Market Process.* (pp. 152-162) London: Routledge.

Kirzner, Israel M. (1990) Knowledge Problems and Their Solutions: Some Relevant Distinctions. *Cultural Dynamics* 3(1): 32-48. Reprinted (2017) in: Boettke, Peter J.; Sautet, Frédéric (eds.) *Competition, Economic Planning, and the Knowledge Problem.* (pp. 87-105) Indianapolis: Liberty Fund.

Kirzner, Israel M. (1996) *Essays on Capital and Interest.* London: Edward Elgar. Reprinted (2010) Indianapolis: Liberty Fund.

Kirzner, Israel M. (1997) Entrepreneurial Discovery and the Competitive Market Process: an Austrian Approach. *Journal of Economic Literature* 35(1): 60-85. Reprinted (2017) in: Boettke, Peter J.; Sautet, Frédéric (eds.) *Competition, Economic Planning, and the Knowledge Problem.* (pp. 323-360) Indianapolis: Liberty Fund.

Kirzner, Israel M. (2017) *Competition, Economic Planning, and the Knowledge Problem.* Boettke, Peter J.; Sautet, Frédéric (eds.) Indianapolis: Liberty Fund.

Klein, Peter (1996) Economic Calculation and the Limits of Organization. *Review of Austrian Economics* 9(2): 3-28.

Knaack, Marcelle Size (1988) *Post-World War Two bombers, 1945-1973.* Washington: Office of Air Force History.

Knight, Frank H. (1921) *Risk, Uncertainty and Profit.* New York: Houghton Mifflin.

Lachmann, Ludwig M. (1947) Complementarity and Substitution in the Theory of Capital. *Economica* n.s. 14(54): 108-119.

Lachmann, Ludwig M. (1956) *Capital and Its Structure,* London: Bell & Sons. Reprinted (1978) Kansas City: Sheed Andrews & McMeel.

Lachmann, Ludwig M. (1986) *The Market as an Economic Process.* Oxford: Basil Blackwell.

Lange, Oscar (1935) Marxian Economics and Modern Theory. *Review of Economic Studies* 2(3): 189-201.

Lange, Oscar (1936) On the Economic Theory of Socialism I. *Review of Economic Studies* 4(1): 53-71.

Lange, Oscar (1937) On the Economic Theory of Socialism II. *Review of Economic Studies* 4(2): 123-142.

Lange, Oscar (1938) *On the Economic Theory of Socialism.* Minneapolis: University of Minnesota Press.

Langlois, Richard (1994) Risk and Uncertainty. In: Boettke, Peter J. (ed.) *The Elgar Companion to Austrian Economics* (pp. 118-122).

Cheltenham UK: Edward Elgar.

Lavoie, Don (1985) *Rivalry and Central Planning: the Socialist Calculation Debate Reconsidered.* Cambridge: Cambridge University Press.

Leibenstein, Harvey (1966) Allocative Efficiency vs. X-Efficiency. *American Economic Review* 56(3): 392-415.

Leijonhufvud, Axel (1981) *Information and Coordination: Essays in Macroeconomic Theory.* New York: Oxford University Press.

Lerner, Abba P. (1934) Economic Theory and Socialist Economy. *Review of Economic Studies* 2(1): 51-61.

Lerner, Abba P. (1936) A note on Socialist Economics. *Review of Economic Studies* 4(1): 72-76.

Lerner, Abba P. (1937) Statics and Dynamics in Socialist Economics. *Economic Journal* 47(186): 253-270.

Lerner, Abba P. (1938) Theory and Practice in Socialist Economics. *Review of Economic Studies* 6(1): 71-75.

Lewin, Peter (1997) Hayekian Equilibrium and Change. *Journal of Economic Methodology* 4(2): 245-266.

Lewis, Tom (1991) *Empire of the Air: the Men Who Made Radio.* New York: Harper Collins.

Lim, Jaejoo; Klein, Richard; & Thatcher, Jason (2005) Good Technology, Bad Management: a Case Study of the Satellite Phone Industry. *Journal of Information Technology Management* 16(2): 48-55.

Loewy, Raymond (1979) *Industrial Design.* Woodstock, New York: Overlook Press.

Lombardo, Gary A.; & Mulligan, Robert F. (2010) The Public Administrator: Regulating for Marine Transport Efficiency. *World Maritime University Journal of Maritime Affairs* 9(1): 29-44.

Lutz, F.A. (1940) The Structure of Interest Rates. *Quarterly Journal of Economics* 55: 36-63.

Makowski, Louis; & Ostroy, Joseph M. (2001) Perfect Competition and the Creativity of the Market. *Journal of Economic Literature* 39: 479-535.

Malthus, (Rev.) Thomas Robert (1798 [1914]) *An Essay on Population.* New York: E.P. Dutton.

Malthus, (Rev.) Thomas Robert (1820 [1836]) *Principles of Political Economy.* London: William Pickering.

Marshall, Alfred (1890) *Principles of Economics.* London: Macmillan, 1961.

Marx, Karl (1894) *Capital.* 4 vols. Engels, Frederick (ed.) New York: International Publishers, 2003.

Menger, Carl F. (1871) *Principles of Economics*. English translation of the *Grundesätze der Volkswirthschaftslehre*. New York: New York University Press, 1976.

Mill, John Stuart (1848) *Principles of Political Economy*. London: Longmans, Green.

Minsky, Hyman P. (1975) *John Maynard Keynes*. New York: McGraw-Hill.

Minsky, Hyman P. (1982) The Financial-Instability Hypothesis: Capitalist Processes and the Behaviour of the Economy. In: Kindleberger, C.P.; & Laffargue, J.P. (eds.) *Financial Crises*. (pp. 13-39) Cambridge: Cambridge University Press.

Minsky, Hyman P. (1986) *Stabilizing an Unstable Economy*. New Haven: Yale University Press.

Minsky, Hyman P. (1992) *The Financial Instability Hypothesis*. Jerome Levy Economics Institute Working Paper No. 74.

Mises, Ludwig H.E. von (1912) *The Theory of Money and Credit*. English translation of the *Theorie des Geldes und der Umlaufsmittel*. Munich: Duncker & Humblot. Reprinted (1980) Indianapolis: Liberty Classics.

Mises, Ludwig H.E. von (1922) *Socialism: an Economic and Sociological Analysis*. English translation of *Die Gemeinwirtschaft: Untersuchungen über den Sozialismus*. Jena: Gustav Fischer Verlag.

Reprinted (1981) Indianapolis: Liberty Classics.

Mises, Ludwig H.E. von (1949 [1998]) *Human Action* (5th ed.) Auburn: Ludwig von Mises Institute.

Mises, Ludwig H.E. von (1957) *Theory and History*. New Haven: Yale University Press.

Modigliani, Franco; & Sutch, Richard (1966) Innovations in Interest Rate Policy. *American Economic Review* 56: 178-197.

Moghaddam, M.; & Jenson, J. E. (2008) On the Death of the Resurrected Short-Run Phillips Curve: A Further Investigation. *Cato Journal* 28(1): 139-145.

Mulligan, Robert F. (2005) The Entrepreneurial Critique of the Optimization Paradigm. *Academy of Entrepreneurship Journal* 11(2): 47-69.

Mulligan, Robert F. (2009) Robbins as Innovator: the Contribution of *An Essay on the Nature and Significance of Economic Science. Quarterly Journal of Austrian Economics* 12(4): 81-88.

Mulligan, Robert F. (2011) An Austrian Rehabilitation of the Phillips Curve. *Cato Journal* 31(1): 87-98.

Mulligan, Robert F. (2013a) A Sectoral Analysis of the Financial Instability Hypothesis. *Quarterly Review of Economics and Finance* 53(4): 450-459.

Mulligan, Robert F. (2013b) New Evidence on the Structure of Production: Real and Austrian Business Cycle Theory in Light of Minsky's Financial Instability Hypothesis. *Journal of Economic Behavior and Organization* 89: 67-77.

Mulligan, Robert F. (2013c) The Enduring Allure of Objective Probability. *Review of Austrian Economics* 26(3): 311-327.

Mulligan, Robert F. (2014) The Central Fallacy of Keynesian Economics. *Quarterly Journal of Austrian Economics* 17(3): 338-364.

Mulligan, Robert F.; Lirely, Roger L.; & Coffee, David (2014) An Empirical Examination of Minsky's Financial Instability Hypothesis: from Market Process to the Austrian Business Cycle. *Journal des Économistes et des Études Humaines* 20(1): 1-17.

Mulligan, Robert F.; & Lombardo, Gary A. (2008) Entrepreneurial Planning in a Regulated Environment: the U.S. Federal Maritime Commission and the Maritime Industry. *Quarterly Journal of Austrian Economics* 11(2): 106-118.

Nelson, R.R.; & Winter, S.G. (1982) *An Evolutionary Theory of Economic Change.* Cambridge: Harvard University Press.

Niskanen, William A. (2002) On the Death of the Phillips Curve. *Cato Journal* 22(2): 193-198.

O'Driscoll, Gerald P. (1977) *Economics as a Coordination Problem.* Kansas City: Sheed Andrews & McMeel.

O'Driscoll, Gerald P.; & Rizzo, Mario J. (1985) *The Economics of Time and Ignorance.* Oxford: Basil Blackwell.

Parissien, Steven (2013) *The Life of the Automobile.* New York: St Martin's Press.

Phelps, Edmund S. (1967) Phillips Curves, Expectations of Inflation and Optimal Employment over Time. *Economica* n.s. 34(3): 254-281.

Phillips, A.W.H. (1958) The Relationship between Unemployment and the Rate of Change of Money Wages in the United Kingdom, 1861-1957. *Economica* n.s. 25(2): 283-929.

Phillips, Lawrence D. (1970) The 'True Probability' Problem. *Acta Psychologica* 34: 254-264.

Popper, (Sir) Karl R. (1962) *The Open Society and its Enemies.* 2 vols. Princeton: Princeton University Press.

Prychitko, David (2010) Competing Explanations of the Minsky Moment: the Financial Instability Hypothesis in Light of Austrian Theory. *Review of Austrian Economics* 23(3): 199-221.

Reichel, R. (2004) On the Death of the Phillips Curve: Further Evidence. *Cato Journal* 24(3): 341-348.

Ricardo, David (1817) *On the Principles of Political Economy and Taxation.* London: Murray.

Rickenbacker, Edward V. (1967) *Rickenbacker: an Autobiography.* New York: Prentice Hall.

Robbins, Lionel (1932 [1935]) *An Essay on the Nature and Significance of Economic Science* (2nd ed.) London: Macmillan.

Robinson, Joan V. (1933) *The Economics of Imperfect Competition.* London: Macmillan.

Rosenberg, Robert Leonard (1971) *The Ventures and Adventures of an Errant Entrepreneur: Milton (Ball-point) Reynolds (1892-).* PhD Thesis. University of Washington.

Rothbard Murray N. (1962 [2009]) *Man, State, and Economy.* Auburn: Ludwig von Mises Institute.

Rothbard, Murray N. (1963 [2000]) *America's Great Depression* (5th ed.) Auburn: Ludwig von Mises Institute.

Samuelson, Paul A. (1947 [1983]) *Foundations of Economic Analysis* (2nd ed.) Cambridge: Harvard University Press.

Samuelson, Larry (2004) Modeling Knowledge in Economic Analysis. *Journal of Economic Literature* 42(2): 367-403.

Say, Jean-Baptiste (1803) *Traité d'Économie Politique.* Philadelphia: Grigg & Elliott, 1834.

Schabackers, Richard W. (1930) *Stock Market Theory and Practice.* New York: B.C. Forbes.

Schumpeter, Joseph A. (1934) *The Theory of Economic Development.* Cambridge: Harvard University Press.

Schumpeter, Joseph A. (1954) *History of Economic Analysis.* New York: Oxford University Press.

Schumpeter, Joseph A. (1962) *Capitalism, Socialism, and Democracy.* New York: Harper & Row.

Sethi, R. (1992) Dynamics of Learning and the Financial Instability Hypothesis. *Journal of Economics/Zeitschrift für Nationalökonomie* 56(1): 39-70.

Silipo, D.B. (2011) It Happened Again: a Minskian Analysis of the Subprime Loan Crisis. *Journal of Economics and Business* 63: 441-455.

Silberberg, Eugene (1978) *The Structure of Economics: a Mathematical Analysis.* New York: McGraw-Hill.

Sklar, Robert (2002) *A World History of Film.* New York: Harry N. Abrams.

Smith, Adam (1776) *An Inquiry into the Nature and Causes of the Wealth of Nations.* 2 vols. Reprinted (1981) Indianapolis: Liberty Classics.

Solow, Robert M. (1956) A Contribution to the Theory of Economic Growth. *Quarterly Journal of Economics* 70(1): 65-94.

Sowell, Thomas (1963) The General Glut Controversy Reconsidered. *Oxford Economic Papers* n.s. 15(3): 193-203.

Takayama, Akira (1985) *Mathematical Economics* (2nd ed.) New York: Cambridge University Press.

Tarko, Vlad (2013) Can Probability Theory Deal with Entrepreneurship? *Review of Austrian Economics* 26(3): 329-345.

Thomas, Lloyd B. (1997) *Money, Banking, and Financial Markets.* New York: McGraw-Hill.

Todd, John (1963) *Introduction to the Constructive Theory of Functions.* New York: Academic Press.

Triffin, Robert (1940) *Monopolistic Competition and General Equilibrium Theory.* Cambridge: Harvard University Press.

Turgot, Anne Robert Jacques, Baron de l'Aulne (1766) *Reflections on the Formation and Distribution of Wealth.* Ashley, William J., trans. New York: Macmillan 1898. Reprinted (1971) New York: Augustus M. Kelley.

Turgot, Anne Robert Jacques, Baron de l'Aulne (2011) *The Turgot Collection.* Gordon, David (ed.) Auburn: Ludwig von Mises Institute.

van den Hauwe, Ludwig (2011) John Maynard Keynes and Ludwig von Mises on Probability. *Journal of Libertarian Studies* 22: 471-507.

Van Horne, James C. (1998) *Financial Market Rates and Flows* (5th ed.) Upper Saddle River, New Jersey: Prentice Hall.

Varian, Hal R. (1984) *Microeconomic Analysis* (2nd ed.) New York: W.W. Norton.

Vaughn, Karen I. (1980) Economic Calculation under Socialism: the Austrian Contribution. *Economic Inquiry* 18: 535-554.

Vaughn, Karen I. (1994) The Socialist Calculation Debate. In: Boettke, Peter J. (ed.) *The Elgar Companion to Austrian Economics* (pp. 478-484). Cheltenham UK: Edward Elgar.

Vosniadou, Stella; & Ortony, Andrew (1989) Similarity and Analogical Reasoning: a Synthesis. In: Vosniadou, Stella; & Ortony, Andrew (eds.) *Similarity and Analogical Reasoning*. New York: Cambridge University Press.

Walras, Léon (1874 [1954]) *Elements of Pure Economics*. New York: Irwin.

Wolff, Richard D.; & Resnick, Stephen A. (1987) *Economics: Marxian versus Neoclassical*. Baltimore: Johns Hopkins University Press.

About the Author

Robert F. Mulligan taught for two decades at Western Carolina University. His research interests include business cycle analysis, Constitutional Political Economy, Maritime economics, and fractal analysis of time series.

He earned a Bachelor of Science in Civil Engineering at the Illinois Institute of Technology in 1983, a Master of Arts in Economics at the State University of New York at Binghamton in 1990, a Doctor of Philosophy in Economics, State University of New York at Binghamton in 1993 and an Advanced Studies Certificate in International Economic Policy Research at the Institut für Weltwirtschaft Kiel in 1995.

About AIER

The American Institute for Economic Research in Great Barrington, Massachusetts, was founded in 1933 as the first independent voice for sound economics in the United States. Today it publishes ongoing research, hosts educational programs, publishes books, sponsors interns and scholars, and is home to the world-renowned Bastiat Society and the highly respected Sound Money Project. The American Institute for Economic Research is a 501c3 public charity.

INDEX

Made in the USA
Coppell, TX
01 March 2021